BARE RUINED CHOIRS

By Garry Wills

ROMAN CULTURE
THE SECOND CIVIL WAR
NIXON AGONISTES
BARE RUINED CHOIRS

BARE RUINED CHOIRS

Doubt, Prophecy, and Radical Religion

BY GARRY WILLS

DOUBLEDAY & COMPANY, INC.

Garden City, New York

1972

62711

ISBN: 0-385-08970-8
Library of Congress Catalog Card Number 75-175406
Copyright © 1971, 1972 by Garry Wills
All Rights Reserved
Printed in the United States of America
  First Edition

to my own two Johns

He took the plated armor in his tent
Left by his son behind, now fairly lent—
For Nestor's son, already in the field,
Went forward fighting under Nestor's shield.

—Iliad 14.9–11

CONTENTS

BARE RUINED CHOIRS

. . . those boughs which shake against the cold,
Bare ruined choirs, where late the sweet birds sang.
SHAKESPEARE, Sonnet 73

"The Catholic Seventies?"

It LOOKED AS THOUGH CATHOLICS, having ceased to be a People, just might become a power. Norman Podhoretz, with his interest in who is "making it," said so: "Just as the black assertion set the climate for the Sixties, I think you'll find a comparable Catholic, white-ethnic assertion in the Seventies." Pollsters were suddenly mumbling over their beads, telling off rosaries of votes—though Catholics had stopped saying the rosary. President Nixon was ingratiating himself with Knights of Columbus, and promised to aid parochial schools—just as those schools were closing, nuns leaving them, orthodox parents objecting to things taught in them. The Catholics' hour had come, though they did not seem to know it; had come, too late, just as their church was disintegrating.

The odd thing was the range of people angered by that church's crumbling. In some ways it was—what Lenny Bruce used to call it—"the only *the* church"; the extreme taken as a type, the least changeable part of our religious landscape, theological North Star. Through all shifts and alterations, men have said (or hoped), something remains. For many, it turns out, that something was Rome, or was symbolized by Rome. This church seemed to offer men some obscure pledge of the relevance of older things. What, then, is the world to make of Rome calling herself irrelevant? The North Star has not only dimmed, but wandered.

Malcolm Muggeridge, for one, thought it had no right to such frivolity. Just when he was rediscovering Christianity as a stick to beat the modern world with, he saw the most intransigent form of that faith rushing "to reproduce all the follies and fatuities of Protestantism." Rome might, after all, have had *him* but for this. True, Muggeridge recognizes he could not quite bring his dissenting self to recite any organization's creed. But he feels that dogma is good for all others, who should regularly attend the dogma of their choice. The content of the teaching is not what really matters, but its fixity. Anchors are meant to *hold*. As Dr. Johnson sensed, this church was to other churches as was faith itself to infidelity: "A man who is converted from Protestantism to Popery may be sincere: he parts with nothing; he is only superadding to what he had already had. But a convert from Popery to Protestantism gives up as much of what he had held as sacred as any thing that he retains: there is so much laceration of mind in such a conversion, that it can hardly be sincere and lasting." If Papistry itself should "convert," then Christianity's last redoubt would be fallen.

Other men did not ask for stability from Rome, but for some richness of tradition, continuity. Their regret was not political but aesthetic. The dramaturgy of the sung High Mass, the seasonal Latin prayers accumulated over centuries, the complex divine office chanted in monasteries—all these were things as tangible, for cherishing, as cathedrals or basilicas. Thus a cultured group in England, made up of people like Robert Graves and Nancy Mitford, wrote the Pope charging him with his cultural responsibility for this heritage, holding him accountable for its retention. One does not have to believe in Mayan gods to know Mayan treasure should not be squandered or lost. Whatever religious role is left them, curates should at least remain curators; and if the Pontifex Maximus could no longer be a "bridge builder," let him serve as custodian over his crumbling bridges. One signer of this letter to the Pope was Graham Greene, who spoke for "many of us (who) abandon Confession and Communion to join the Foreign Legion of the church and fight for a city of which we are no longer full citizens." Lapsed or lukewarm Catholics seemed angriest at changes in the liturgy—"I don't go to Mass myself, any more, but if ever I do, by God, I want to find the Latin Mass still there!" The Foreign Legion's lot is a hard one. While its members stayed true out of sentiment, men inside the gates were surrendering.

Others could forgo stability, or beauty, but thought of Rome as an avenue for escape—more Scarlet Woman than Pia Madre, the saucy old thing was still good for a flirtation. That is what the Catholic church had been to a rebellious young Boswell or Gibbon, a Beardsley or Firbank. Huysmans knew there could be no Black Mass without the Mass. Even in our day Tennessee Williams found some bawdy glamor left in the gal. Where else can one find robed priests like purple kings holding cups of silver and gold? There was profound lassitude and sadness in the thought that another exotic thing was dying off—that unresisting grayness, taking over everywhere, had engulfed one last horizon that was clearly marked.

Once again, this odd regret most swayed those who had been Catholics once. Elizabeth Cullinan has described an adolescent Catholic fantasy of going out "into the world" to find oneself, then returning at the end (with mellowed wise accommodations, of course) to childhood belief. All the fun of this daydream came from the fact that the church would always be there, and be the same—spice for your adventures while you wandered (What would Sister Nazianzen think of *this*?) and a haven when adventure time was over. You *can* go home—at least Catholics could.

The older Rome these different classes of men admired would not have thought much of their tributes. That church considered itself an entire ship, not merely an anchor; a home, not a museum; the norm, not an exotic or escapist abnormality. It is true that Chesterton makes King Alfred boast that Christianity takes better care of the world than could the world itself—"because it is only Christian men/Guard even heathen things." But this worldly advantage came as faith's afterthought or side effect. Faith coarsened down to mere political utility could not sustain itself. Believing may help some men do other things, from creating art to making money. But it cannot be called up just to serve this purpose, without poisoning its own springs—so that, as Eliot's Archbishop puts it, "Those who serve the greater cause/May make the cause serve them," in such a way that "Sin grows with doing good."

All this helps explain Rome's strength in the past: the Catholic church demanded faith, of an exigent fixed sort, for its own sake. And that is what makes the Catholics' current wavering strike an unexpected fear in others. Catholics were the last believers; dubiety among them is an omen. They kept one possibility open that seems now to be closing. Western culture itself resembles the character in Elizabeth Cullinan's story—gone out into the world and clearing wildernesses, grown worldly and adult, yet able to look back on the church of its mediaeval childhood as a center to rebel against; a rock to steer by, if only when steering around it; maybe even, for some, a place to come home to. There is a shudder at the news that "home" may not be there much longer, even if one had not intended to return. Some color and stability had gone out of life if even Rome could doubt. More than that: if this thing falls, then what can hope to stand? That is why Rome's crumbling can seem like the fall of a world—the cracking of an adamantine thing.

Even in this time of the church's uncertainty, others turn to Catholics for a stable politics of the middle; praise American Catholics as "ethnics" who vote regularly and oppose violence, who just may be the stuff for gluing our poor unstuck country together again. The shift of theological ground under their feet could lead Catholics to grasp at what seems least shaken in the realm of politics (though it might also make them panic, go on a rampage). In some ways, after all, a diminished church may be more exploitable, at first. Ivan Illich, not long before he suspended his own priestly activities, told a group of his fellows: "We have only a short time left when the Roman collar will open doors for us." The magic would not last long; he urged priests to use it while they could, and use it up. Writers, also, sense endangered magic, and do not want to lose it. Risk heightens awareness, deepens self-scrutiny; and may lead to that age-old condition of the literary life, defeat. Winners erect their own monuments, while losers ache with music. Thus a brilliant crew of novelists is rendering Catholic experience as never before. I have mentioned Elizabeth Cullinan—and could add Thomas Keneally, Wilfrid Sheed, and Walker Percy to the first rank, with other talents crowding them. There has been Catholic fiction in the past, but of a different kind. It spoke (in the French) from a burnt-out old-world faith, or (in the English) from a convert's late-arrived sensibility. By and large this fiction lacked a childhood; and that was important for two reasons. The child of a culture is that culture's victim; he sees it with a certain freshness (like the convert), yet from within, forced to take (or reject) it as a whole, not selectively. And the English-speaking world at large has had a childhood outside the Catholic culture of the European continent.

What we needed then, was a Catholic youth within a non-Catholic culture—and we seem to have got it just in time. Even those who leave no longer suppress their early church days (like F. Scott Fitzgerald), but use them—in William Gibson's case, to structure a whole book. And a convert like Walker Percy seems able to appropriate the whole Catholic subculture, to feel it as a dying thing "in the ruins." This new honesty is all shot through with nostalgia and the sense of loss—as in Keneally's description of a priest doomed to live painfully "between-gods," an alien in the rectory, at the altar, a Catholic who cannot go home, trapped in the seminary that trained him: "The cold fust of old books assailed him in the dark; devotional books, Dublin 1913, a good year for unalloyed faith. Why couldn't he have been alive and priested then? Saving up indulgences, averting tumours of the throat with a St. Blaise candle, uttering arcane litanies; going off to the holocaust the following year to be outraged at the intemperate use of the

Holy Name by the men in the trenches; dying in 1924 of dropsy, rosaries, and the certainty of Paradise."

This is the writing of men raised in an environment of churchiness—an atmosphere poisoned, as it were, by incense. I know a woman who says she thought as a child that holy water had a scent, so much were holy water and perfume mingled in the image of her mother's room, which was a place for saying rosaries. That was a closed world, now laid open to us in Miss Cullinan's *House of Gold*—the house that is less than a home because half a church: the priest-son who must become the "worldliest" member of the family, since all its social expectations are based on his career; the shame attached to unmarried children if they will not enter the priesthood or a convent; the girls separating into strong nuns exasperated with the weak kind, and weak nuns placidly demanding strength from those they exasperate; the mother who is too pious to be intimidated into mere goodness; the thousands of ways for the family that prays together to prey upon itself; how subtly good brings out evil, and faith despair.

The same pressures that afflict this Catholic home haunt the Catholic schools of Robert Marasco's *Child's Play*, Piers Paul Read's *Monk Dawson*, or Robert Byrne's *Memories of a Non-Jewish Childhood*. One of the more fascinating things about this literary development is the way books of the second rank (like Mr. Read's), or even of the third (like Mr. Byrne's), can fascinate when they draw on the subculture and its folkways. Byrne describes the fear of cumulative disasters that hounded altar boys who fell a step behind in the complex liturgical dance of the Mass:

I was on my way from the Gospel side to the Epistle side with the altar Bible [Missal, rather], which was not only heavy but was so big that I couldn't see where I was stepping. Genuflecting with such a weight sent burning pains through my thighs, but I had to pretend it was light as a feather. The small silver bell was kept on the bottom step when not in use—it was the altar boy's job to pick it up and give it a jingle several times during Mass when the people were supposed to fall on their knees or strike their breasts symbolically with their fists. . . . I was coming down the altar steps with the Bible, thinking about God only knows what, when I stepped right on the bell, sending it ringing across the floor. I lost my balance and had the sickening knowledge that the Bible was falling forward out of control. I took several wild steps to get under it, and I might have made it if I hadn't tripped over the hem of my cassock. When that happened I went down just as dramatically as if my feet had been knocked out from under me. With a stunning thud I landed full length on the floor. My face ended up inches from the bell, and for some crazy reason I got the idea that it was vital to get it back where it belonged, so I grabbed it and flipped it over to Hank as if it were a live grenade. He was taken by complete surprise. The bell hit him on the chest and he slapped at it down the front of his body trying to get hold of it. It was ringing furiously and people were kneeling down and striking their breasts all over the place. . . . Dear God, I prayed, forgive me, for I knew not what I did. . . . I had a notion to bolt from the church and hop a freight by Julian Dubuque's grave, but where would I go? How would I get in touch with other excommunicated people? What would life be like with defrocked priests, disgraced nuns, and perverted unbelievers? How far would I get in a cassock and surplice?

That passage suggests the real fear instilled by the awesomeness of the sanctuary, and the rather nagging way priests and nuns and parents had of impressing that awesomeness upon a child. With a similar touch, David Lodge (in *The British Museum Is Falling Down*) calls up the Catholic experience of courting as erotic brinkmanship, with summit meetings in the confessional to try out various forms of deterrence theory. Tom McHale, in *Principato*, draws bright caricatures—e.g., of the jock priest's preaching style: "It sounds to me like he ended up on God's team after all. As a booster. It takes money to keep God's boys in uniform, you know." Or the way Catholics shopped around for a lenient confessor: "Where the hell am I going to find another priest who'll listen to me over the telephone?"

To recover a world, you must recreate what childhood was like in that world—as the children do in *House of Gold*, struck by an almost sexual fear and unconfessable shame when they burst in upon a nun with her cropped hair uncovered. This Catholic version of the Actaeon myth catches the edgy self-importance of a churchy world—a proximity of consecratcd things and pcople, with accompanying peril that some unconsidered act might deconsecrate them. It was a place where nuns' habits were designed to hide all suggestion of the female breast; and therefore a world in which one might see a nun's breast (or its outline), breaking the tabu if only by accident, glimpsing denied realities. As Mr. Byrne writes: "For some reason it was fascinating to look at the toilets the nuns used. None of us could imagine a nun sitting on a toilet, certainly not Sister Raphael or Sister Conceptus."

Thus, though it was a world of faith, it was a world of deceptions too, and deliberate blindnesses; of things one should not see, and of consequent pretending not to see them. The attitudes, no matter how carefully inculcated, were strained—like the rapt composure one strove for on that mystic journey back from the communion rail, which always came off (and one knew it) as a taut and stumbling constrictedness—the postcommunion *rictus*. One had been trained to put a different face on, for the proprieties—which meant, in practice, for the sake of others. And in time the whole of one's own faith could be held for other people. Doubts were hidden for the sake of the children; or a priest's, for the sake of his flock; or the flock's doubts were minimized "in front of Father." Once this game began, there were always good reasons for keeping it up, until one was trapped by all the earlier moves, unable to leave without calling one's whole prior life a lie. The outcome was grisly—Catholics believing for the Muggeridges of the world, becoming live sacrifices to the desire that *some one* should believe in *something*. Catholics were the last believers—it was the thing they were supposed to be good at; and men always want an endangered species, of whatever order, to survive. Catholics might be a kind of spiritual Amish, with horse-and-buggy habits of the mind; but who would not regret the disappearance of Amish villages? Whole groups of people thus became the victims of type casting, of a role thrust on them in the cradle. It is the position of Bert Flax in Wilfrid Sheed's novel, *The Hack:* "Betty [Flax], and [her mother] Mrs. Forsythe, and Bert's friends, all wanted Bert to keep his faith for one reason or other. (We haven't got faith but Bert has.) It was a settled sort of thing. Bert without his faith would be unthinkable. . . . He wasn't even allowed to have doubts. Bert Flax's faith was a byword, a company image."

It was the company image that "church teaching does not change"; so debate about contraceptives had less to do with the intrinsic merits of the case than with that peripheral but inevitable question, "How do we explain the change without scandalizing people?"—i.e., without damaging the company image. Indeed, a weird new philosophy of "natural law" was invented almost wholly to put off change, or disguise it when it came, or deny it once it had been made—so freely had habits of falsehood grown up under cover of belief. The greatest enemy to belief is pretending to believe—especially when you are pretending out of deference to others. Believing "for the children's sake" was a way of trapping the children in lies, even though they were the lies of love—for the children would fear or resent (or, worst of all, accept) the task laid on them; believe, reciprocally, for their parents' sake, or pretend to do so, and breed their own children up in this pretense, closing the vicious circle of these sweet religious lies. Trying to believe for others is trying to will a faith into them that you do not have yourself—mother into child, Muggeridge into Catholics. One used to find the results of this in convent and rectory: priests and nuns hung on desperately to their training, not wanting to disappoint their parents, who had come to have a vocation to their children's "having a vocation." They felt called to their sons' "calling," and enjoyed a vicarious priesthood. Faith was a good thing one might not enjoy oneself, but had to keep passing around. A process had begun that could in time make all belief vicarious—no one had it, except to give.

Some could not account for the fact that Catholics, of all people, were great enthusiasts for the secularity and "death of God" fads in the Sixties. For many of them this came as a breath of release, a chance to stop pretending. There might be regret for lost belief, but not for that pretense. They almost reversed the gospel plea, and prayed: "Lord, I doubt; help thou my unbelief." Whatever harsh things can be said of the movement—and I shall be saying some later—there was this odd note of honesty in it. And it did have its religious side: if there *is* a God, one blasphemes against him by a feigned belief. When we say men act "in bad faith," we mean they ask us to judge them (usually favorably) out of a cognitive world they do not share; to think them better than they are, by not seeing the world as it is. They shift the whole horizon, to center it on them; they literally *make* believe, forcing reality, imposing trustfulness—make the Cause serve them, and sin with doing good. That betrayal was implicit in belief sustained just for guarding heathen things. Its ugliness was hidden by the fact that the pretense was always maintained "for others." This, it was hoped, would shift the guilt (if any) to those others, along with the faith. Men who did the pretending got nothing but credit for their orthodox velleities. Muggeridge is the final product of this process—a faithless Inquisitor, scourge of those deserting dogmas he does not believe in.

By escaping that chain of pretended beliefs, some Catholic writers have gained maneuvering room: a fictive belief collapses into believable fiction. One might have faith, or pretend to have it, as part of an endangered species; but one must *write* as part of the whole endangered genus, humankind. If Catholics are more "accepted" now, it is because they are becoming "like everyone else," can talk of their strange upbringing because they have (partially) escaped it. Both they and others may, in some respects, regret this homogenization; but it is good for everyone involved. Faith in another's faith won't do. Belief for the purpose of "guarding heathen things" is worthless; and it is baser to demand such sentry duty from others—a mutual hollowing out of each other's honesty. The world was willingly fooled into thinking Catholics believed. Catholics were fooled into believing for the unbelievers' sake. Neither would recognize the truth—that the one reputed virgin of credulity had, sometime in the night when no one watched, been deflowered by doubt. Even the church was just pretending. Belief may not have gone out of the world; but a class of "professional believers" is disappearing. And that is one slim source of comfort: the "crisis of belief" behind the world's crisis of authority has proved more than a crisis—it is a disaster—for pretense. It makes "cheap faith" less sustainable, and may brace men to shed, as well, bad faith, the faith it were a sin to hold to. (Help *this,* at least, our unbelief.)

There were more ironies than we first thought in the political analysts' prediction that the Seventies might be a decade of Catholic power. If they were right, Catholics are coming on strong as voters just when they are weakening as believers— and who would have thought that a Catholic decade would be one especially marked by doubt? Yet that is what Catholic power seems to promise now—power in weakness, a flaring up in one order as the consequence of "flame out" in another. Understanding this process should not only tell us much about Catholics and their troubles, but about our country and these times—since belief in all our large national myths is now endangered. For the first time, Americans as a whole feel somewhat uneasy singing their own national anthem: "Then conquer we must, For our cause it is just." In the wake of Vietnam, America, which has been very skilled in certitudes throughout its history, has become a new Rome capable of self-doubt. The development is astonishing, in a sense John Ruskin anticipated: "There are states of moral death no less amazing than physical resurrection; and a Church which permits its clergy to preach what they have ceased to believe, and its people to trust what they refuse to obey, is truly miraculous in impotence." That impotence is now apparent, and the miracle (or trick) cannot much longer be prolonged. The question is not, any more, whether our oldest institutions can crumble; but whether a purified faith can be reborn out of their ruins.

I · CHANGELESS

In an epoch of dissolution and transformation,
such as that on which we are now entered, habits,
ties, and associations are inevitably broken up,
the action of individuals becomes more distinct,
the shortcomings, errors, heats, disputes, which
necessarily attend individual action, are brought
into greater prominence. Who would not gladly keep
clear, from all these passings clouds, an august
institution which was there before they arose, and
which will be there when they have blown over?

—MATTHEW ARNOLD

ONE

Memories of a Catholic Boyhood

INTROIBO AD ALTARE DEI.

AD DEUM QUI LAETIFICAT JUVENTUTEM MEAM.

WE GREW UP DIFFERENT. There were some places we went, and others did not—into the confessional box, for instance. There were also places we never went, though others could—we were told, from youth, to stay out of non-Catholic churches. Attendance there would be sinful, a way of countenancing error. It was forbidden territory—though tasted by some *because* prohibition gave tang to the experience: we were assisting at evil rites. Even those who feel they long ago outgrew that tabu have residual feelings of wickedness, now and then, when attending non-Catholic services—like men who go with self-assuring mockery (mocks just a little too loud) into a dark house said to be haunted. We "born Catholics," even when we leave or lose our own church, rarely feel at home in any other. The habits of childhood are tenacious, and Catholicism was first experienced by us as a vast set of intermeshed childhood habits —prayers offered, heads ducked in unison, crossings, chants, christenings, grace at meals; beads, altar, incense, candles; nuns in the classroom alternately too sweet and too severe, priests garbed black on the street and brilliant at the altar; churches lit and darkened, clothed and stripped, to the rhythm of liturgical recurrences; the crib in winter, purple Februaries, and lilies in the spring; confession as intimidation and comfort (comfort, if nothing else, that the intimidation was survived), communion as revery and discomfort; faith as a creed, and the creed as catechism, Latin responses, salvation by rote, all things going to a rhythm, memorized, old things always returning, eternal in that sense, no matter how transitory.

Such rites have great authority; they hypnotize. Not least by their Latinity. It is not certain, philologists say, that "hocuspocus" is derived from *"Hoc est Corpus"* in the Mass; but the Latin phrases, often rhythmed, said in litanies and lists of saints' names, replicated, coming at us in antiphonies and triple cries (*Sanctus, Sanctus, Sanctus*), had a witchery in them, to hush or compel us as by incantation.

We spoke a different language from the rest of men—not only the actual Latin memorized when we learned to "serve Mass" as altar boys. We also had odd bits of Latinized English that were not part of other six-year-olds' vocabulary—words like "contrition" or "transubstantiation." Surely no teen-ager but a Catholic ever called an opinion "temerarious." The words often came imbedded in formulae ("imperfect contrition"), and the formulae were often paired in jingles (imperfect contrition and *perfect* contrition). Theology was a series of such distinctions: *ex opere operato* and *ex opere operantis,* homoousion and homoiousion, mortal sin and venial sin, matter of sin and intention of sin, parvity of matter and gravity of matter, baptism of water and baptism of desire, Mass of the Catechumens and Mass of the Communicants, the Church Teaching and the Church Taught, infallible and authoritative, valid and invalid, invalid by reason of the minister and invalid by reason of the material. Matter and form. *Materialiter et formaliter*. Black and white. The mode of theology was constant—a simultaneous linking and severing in the Scholastic *distinguo*. To know the terms was to know the thing, to solve the problem. So we learned, and used, a vast terminology.

That terminology haunts a Catholic's speech in ways he is often unaware of. One could tell, after a certain amount of talk with Senator Eugene McCarthy, that he was a Catholic, though theology had not formally been brought up or discussed. He uses casually such giveaway phrases as "occasion of sin," and "having scruples," and "particular friendship," and "rash judgment," and "special dispensation"—not terribly exotic expressions, but each with a special meaning for Catholics.

Even when we did not use different words, we pronounced them in a different way, a possessive way that took the words from others and made them, exclusively, ours. We said "doc-*trine*-al" because doctrine was ours. And "con-*temp*-late" because monks belonged to us. And "con-*sum*-mated" because what was con-*sum*-mated on the Cross was not the same as what is consum-*mate*-ed in the marriage bed. Though other Christians were devoted to our saints, they did not know how to pronounce their names. It was Saint Au-*gus*-tin, for instance, not *Aug*-us-teen. Or Saint *Jeh*-rom, not Je-*rome*. We did not pronounce them this way in order to approximate the Latin or mediaeval forms; in fact we were departing from both. We did it, ultimately, just to be different—to say *our* Augustine was not the same one claimed by Luther, the Augustine recruited into heresy.

The church judged things not out of a deeper antiquity, but from outside time altogether. That was borne in on us by an unanchored, anachronistic style (or mix of styles) in all things the church did. Going into a Catholic church of our day, one might think history was a rummage sale, and this place had been fitted out after visits to the sale. Here one century, there another, and all jumbled together. Here the soutane, there the crozier. In the drone of Latin, sudden gabbles of Greek. Ancient titles (*Pontifex Maximus*) and an ancient familiarity of address (*Paul* our Pope, and *Laurence* our Bishop). The humble pilgrim hat for cardinals, proud mitre for bishops, triple tiara for a Pope, and absurd biretta for priests (made absurder, with purple poofs, for monsignors

—yes, *monsignori,* for the patina of Italy was on all this mer-
chandise, like the fuzzy encrustations on a shipwrecked cargo).

It all spoke to us of the alien. The church was stranded
in America, out of place. And not only out of place here. It
belonged to no age or clime, but was above them all; it had a
"special dispensation" from history. History was a thing it did
not have to undergo. Thus the church could pick and choose
from any period, odd bits of all the ages clinging to her as she
swept along, but none of them catching her, holding her back;
she moved free of them all.

One lived, then, in contact with something outside time—
grace, sin, confession, communion, one's own little moral wheel
kept turning in the large wheel of seasons that moved endlessly, sameness in change and change in sameness, so was it
ever, so would it always be, a repetition like that frequent
"always"—*per omnia saecula saeculorum,* through all the ages'
roll of ages—punctuating our prayers. The form could be varied,
short or long, grand or simple: *per Christum Dominum nos-
trum Jesum Christum qui vivit et regnat per omnia saecula
saeculorum,* or just *qui vivis et regnas per omnia saecula saeculorum.* It could be said or sung by priest or people; or the
choir, after freer melodies (God! how free, then, and how
trivial), would chant it at the end, predictable end, return to
reality, to "always." The real was what *always* was; it was
eternal, unchangeable, like the church. Eternity, in those Latin
prayers, was ever nagging at us; never, in the flux of change
and seasons, letting us go.

We were, thus, a chosen people—though chosen, it seemed,
to be second-rate. Still, in that uncompetitive mediocrity we
found a certain rest denied to others, those who, choosing
themselves, achieving by themselves, were driven and badly in
need of being first-rate. Our mediocrity hid superior moral
tone, obvious to us, concealed from others, a secret excellence,
our last joke on the World (World, dignified by a capital letter, but dumb—Devil and Flesh knew what we were up to,
but not blundering, dim-witted World). We were distin-

guished by spiritual favors that made us just a bit—we had to admit it—odd.

A protective skein was thus woven all around us—not forming a time capsule, since it kept us at a far remove from time; an *un*time capsule, a fibry cocoon of rites and custom in which we were to lie, the chrysalis, till we broke through into promised Reality after death. It is no wonder that, for Catholics, the old childhood sequence of questions took on special promise, or menace:

"What are you?"
"What do you mean?"
"A Catholic, or a Lutheran, or what?"
"Oh, I'm nothing."
"How can you be a Nothing?"

For people brought up inside this total weave of Catholic life, it did seem that departure from one aspect of the faith meant forfeiting all one's connections with religion. A single authority ran through each aspect of one's upbringing. That authority stood behind every practice, endorsing them all. To doubt anywhere was to doubt everywhere. Since the authority was single, so should the acceptance be.

In such a context "losing one's faith" meant a loss of many good things, beginning with one's own past. It meant betrayal, not only a betrayal of grace, of God's gift, but of others—parents, children, all those woven up in the same cocoon. Tear the seamless weave for your own exit, you made a hole through which the world could seep in on dear ones, your friends still left there. Tension was thus established— on the one side, a very human urge to remain, at all cost, within this cradling, this gently nurturing, carefully tended pod, metaphysical womb. This was the home of reality, a seed that was ripening toward ultimate fulfillment. Its membranous covering let only truth's light come through, filtering evil and error out. To leave such a shelter was to fall forever in unchartable darkness.

On the other hand, since the acceptance asked for was total, there was an urge toward total rejection whenever ir-

ritants developed. At such a moment, an opposite totalism
came over Catholics like a spasm—belief that reality was just
outside, one must flail through to it with one blow. One sees
this oddly exhilarating *lack* of faith—a suspended-action continuing *loss* of faith—in some ex-Catholics (e.g., in that reverse
seminarian, Will Durant), their belief that wisdom lies in one's
great rejection, that outside the cocoon there is no further
goal to reach, one has taken the great final step.

In the past, D. H. Lawrence claimed, our civilization's
"dirty little secret" was sex. But the church's secret, hidden
away in official teaching, minimized when it could not be
ignored, was *change*. Other things came and went, captive to
history. But the gates of hell would not prevail against the
church, and the gates of hell often looked like history, or the
latest products of history—"modernism," science, rationalism.
We did not deal with such fads—what was sound in them the
church had always possessed, for what the church is, it always
was; what it could accept now, it could and did accept then
(that vague "then" not much explored). The church's past, so
far as it could be said to have one, was glimpsed in quick
raids made on history, meant to capture proof-texts showing
that our sacraments, our doctrines, were all there in the
Fathers (though not fully analyzed till St. Thomas Aquinas'
time). A book that young Catholics were steered toward, as
soon as they seemed bright enough to ingest it, was *The
Thirteenth, Greatest of Centuries* (1907, often reprinted) by
James J. Walsh. The church could pick one age or other as
"the best of times" inasmuch as that time lived up best to the
church's demands (which are the same in all times).

The experience of change came to Catholics as a form of
personal crisis. As a man grew, his views underwent some
alteration, enlargening—even his views of the church. If things
he had been taught seemed childish now, it was his own
earlier view that had been childish, not anything in the church
itself. He had to account for his own development in relation
to a fixed thing. When he could no longer do so, he had "lost
the faith"—outgrown that fixed thing. It failed him because it

did not change—the very fact that reassured and comforted those who stayed.

We have yet to learn all the good wrought by "Vatican Two," and all the damage. But the main point about the Council can be put quite simply: *it let out the dirty little secret.* It forced upon Catholics, in the most startling symbolic way, the fact that *the church changes.* No more endless roll of *saecula saeculorum.* No more neat ahistorical belief that what one did on Sunday morning looked (with minor adjustments) like what the church had always done, from the time of the catacombs. All that lying eternity and arranged air of time-lessness (as in Mae West's vestmented and massive pose) was shattered. The house with the arrested clocks, like Miss Havisham's Satis House ("The bride within the bridal dress had withered like the dress, and like the flowers") collapsed, by reverse dilapidation, out of death's security into uncertain life.

Some, of course, rejoiced at this entry of the incalculable into areas that had seemed too clearly-lit and solid, like endless marble corridors. They saw in this uncertainty a pledge of truthfulness—or, better, of adequacy. Nothing can be very deep unless troubled by mysteries, partaking of the mysterious, of dark things to be undergone, risks to be taken—intellectual risk, as well as moral.

But however bracing this experience of change has been to some, to the mass of Catholics it came as a shock, engendering disillusion. It threatened psychic ruin to them personally, as well as institutional jeopardy for the church. Such people recall the broken old woman in Mauriac's novel, *Maltaverne:*

She was stepping out firmly along the road, returning the greetings of those she met with nods and smiles proportionate to their importance, and yet what she chiefly suggested to me at this point in her life was that fly which a schoolfellow of mine, pretending to degrade Dreyfus, had gradually dismembered. Thus Mother was being stripped, day by day, of all her certainties. Nothing was true of all that she had believed, but the falsest thing of all was what she had mistaken for revealed truth.

Not only had such people conceived of their church as timeless; they tried to approximate that state themselves. The readjustment all men undergo when there is growth was, for them, reorientation back to one immutable thing.

Catholics inhibited change, so far as they were able, in themselves and in their world. Perfect faith and trust would quiet the soul in a peaceful attitude of rest. After all, if one possesses the Truth already, any change is liable to be a departure from that truth, diminution of one's treasure. "Mysteries" remained, but were well posted—things one does not solve (or even, therefore, think much about). It would be the sin of presumption to ask for understanding of them. In heaven it would all be clear. Man's poor mind cannot grasp the high and deep things. A peasant's or old woman's faith was the ideal for which one should strive. There is an element of truth in this "wise peasant" school of thought; but that element is exaggerated and perverted by non-peasants striving back toward intellectual rusticity. Jacques Maritain calling himself "the peasant of the Garonne" is a bit like Marie Antoinette playing shepherdess to imbibe arcadian virtue.

The church looked, on one side, like the last guardian of reason in a world of unfounded and shifting impressions. It held to a logical view of things, full of studied distinctions, its doctrine spelled out, endlessly examined in technical language. Yet its learning was formal, opposed to intellectual initiative or exploration. The reasons for this go far back, to Wittenberg, to Antioch—indeed, to Eden. But the form the obscurantism took in America is easily grasped by those who remember Bing Crosby's movie, *Going My Way.*

That movie was, under its cassocks and other disguises, the classic melodrama based on a mortgage foreclosure. But the mortgage there was not on an ancestral home; it was on the church, St. Dominic's. The old father (Barry Fitzgerald), debilitated by his own building program, was about to lose his parish. The heroine (Ingrid Bergman) would thus lose, not her Virtue, but her children—in the school. (No, come to think of it, she came into the Crosby series with *The Bells of*

St. Mary's—but the plot assumptions were the same, with a school to be built instead of a church to be saved.) The young romantic lead arrives ("Toora-loora-loora"), staves off ruin, gives his home back to old Father Fitzgibbon, gives her children back to the heroine, then "goes his way" to Rainbow's End.

It was, for all its shmaltz, surprisingly true to Catholic life, and to Catholic blindness about that life. The film celebrated all the church's faults as if they were virtues—right down to Father O'Malley's practiced golf game. There was a bit of hard truth at the film's soft core because the plot turned on the central fact of American parish life—the mortgage on St. Dominic's.

The later course of American Catholicism was largely settled in 1884 at the Third Plenary Council of Baltimore, where assembled bishops voted to require a Catholic education for every Catholic child. That one decision entailed many things. It meant a poor body of immigrants would have to make great sacrifices to build their own schools. It meant nuns would have to be recruited and trained in large numbers to staff the schools. It meant that these nuns would have at least as much formative influence on Catholics as priests did. It meant a populous convent next to a half-empty rectory. It meant that nuns would not be contemplatives in America, nor merely the teachers of young ladies from the upper class, but teachers of all Catholics, young and old, girl and boy. It meant Catholicism would be in large measure child-centered, its piety of a feminine sort—the church (with its rectory) would have to spend a great deal of its time and energy keeping open the school (with its convent). The course was set. As New York's Bishop Hughes used to say to all his pastors, "You must proceed upon the principle that, in this age and country, the school is before the church." The law was worked out, in parish after parish, when Sunday Mass was held in a barely completed auditorium or gymnasium, construction of the church itself still waiting on completion of the school.

The problem of building, equipping, and operating this

church-school complex formed a body of priests who advanced toward their monsignorate, their bishopric, by virtue of business skill. The most successful bishop was the one who had opened more schools than any other—Spellman was the champion on the East Coast, McIntyre on the West Coast. The priest must be good at account books, convincing to bankers, able to get along with businessmen; he found himself acquiring unexpected skills—like golf—to follow businessmen into their native haunts. Father O'Malley, the "with-it" priest of his day, even drags Father Fitzgibbon onto the links as part of the redeeming process at St. Dominic's. It was long a complaint of liberal Catholics that too much pulpit time was spent discussing money. But this reading of accounts was, for many Catholics, a tale of epic deeds accomplished. They had saved and labored to put up schools; they had put their children through those schools, dedicated their daughters to service in them as teachers; they wanted their efforts remembered, commemorated in the church for which they had made all these sacrifices. It was good to hear that the money was not being mismanaged, that one's pastor had a business head on his shoulders.

Burdened with the accounts of a large parish complex, then (if he succeeded) with all the schools in a diocese, the priest had little time for theology, or for study of any sort. He adopted the businessman's "no-nonsense" ways and practicality. He praised simple faith; he delivered a standard five-minute "ferverino" after the standard ten minutes of announcements and financial reporting on Sunday morning. His anti-intellectualism—defensive at first, and self-justifying—became in time self-gratulatory. "If you want theological niceties," he would say in effect, "go to the Jesuits. But if you want the basic truths of the faith, and experience out among the people, then come to the hardworking pastor, who knows—like his parishioners—what it is to pay bills every month." He even found a way to be proud of his jejune sermons. Catholics came to Mass to participate in the miracle of transubstantiation, to be mystically present at Calvary. The rite accomplished something of itself (*ex opere operato*), apart from the merits of the priest as singer or speaker. The Protestants, without a miracle to be performed, had nothing left to do but talk, and the service was good or bad according to the minister's skill as a talker. In other words, Catholics had the Mass; let Protestants have their lectures. Even so fine a prelate as Bishop Spalding faced the hard facts of the situation: "The ecclesiastical seminary is not a school of intellectual culture, either here in America or elsewhere, and to imagine that it can become the instrument of intellectual culture is to cherish a delusion."

If a young Jesuit, brought in to hear the extra hordes at confession before a feast day, got up at his allotted Mass the next morning and actually *said* something, the pastor would warn his congregation next Sunday that it is sinful to want one's ears tickled with novelty, or to come to Mass in pride as if it were a classroom where one argues or debates. "We come here to pray and be humble," he would say, to humble the "Jebbie." Seminaries seemed to have taught the ordinary priest only two passages from Thomas à Kempis, the famous ones that say "What doth it avail thee to discourse profoundly of the Trinity, if thou be void of humility, and consequently displeasing to the Trinity?" and "I had rather feel compunction than know its definition." These became, in the memory of many pastors, proof that humility would result from mere inability to discuss the Trinity, compunction from mere inability to define it.

The pastor had studied theology, of course—often, if he showed promise, in Rome. But such "intellectuals" as the church found in its midst did not want to compete at raising buildings. They were afraid of being stranded in some parish without books, without time to read, too busy even to teach in the parochial school—so such "intellectuals" remained laymen, or tried the seminaries and left them, or went to the teaching orders (Jesuit, Franciscan, Dominican, etc.).

The priests who would become bishops, young men "breaking their heads" over Latin formulae in Rome, were

open in their dislike of the ordeal, and charmingly rueful
about it in later years—like Cardinal Cushing, at the first
session of Vatican II, saying he could not follow any discussion
in Latin, and offering good American dollars to install an
instant-translation service modeled on the UN's.

Nonetheless, the priest *had* studied theology, in a formal
manner closed to nuns and laymen; so he was, in theory, the
prime teacher of religion for his parish. What this meant in
practice was that he stopped by the school, occasionally, to
test the kids in catechism recitation. He had no time to keep
up with developments in theology—more particularly, with
successive schools of biblical criticism. He had been taught to
distrust such techniques anyway. At the seminary, he learned
only the rudiments of New Testament Greek, and soon forgot
that little. (He was taught even less Old Testament Hebrew,
and forgot it faster.) These were mere gestures to an old ideal
of study, made obsolete (these priests felt) in a day of dynamic young construction-firm monsignors.

As the priest abdicated his teaching role with laymen and
adults, the only instruction left in the church was nuns' work
with children. Things were "leveling down." Priests, of course,
were supposed to guide the nuns entrusted to their care—from
the pulpit, in the confessional, and as the schools' "presidents."
The pastor approved the forms of study, exercised a censorship on books the school received or bought, and suggested
appropriate "spiritual reading" for each nun's special problems
or interests. His effectiveness in this area was crippled by the
fact that he did not do much reading himself (the breviary
took up what time he could give to the printed word). Thus
the books he recommended were those he had heard of in the
seminary, years ago.

The nuns lived minutely regulated lives, their waking
hours crammed with communal prayers, devotional exercises,
care of the convent and sacristy, a heavy teaching load, the
training of children for first communion (or May procession,
or confirmation), rehearsing of the choir and coaching of
altar boys. The "sisters" taught lower grades or higher without

much regard for comparative talents among them. They were not often allowed out of the convent—not even to visit libraries. Nonetheless, some of them read voraciously and became, against the good advice of increasingly uneasy pastors, more learned than the priests. Such nuns, with their intellectual interests kept alive against the odds, felt a special anguish at the sight of talent in young Catholics. They knew they could not feed that talent. Some of them waged a personal crusade to get bright students out of parochial schools. These children still had to go to Catholic schools—such was the curse laid on them by the Baltimore Council. But at least they could go to better schools—girls to those run by Madames of the Sacred Heart, boys to the Jesuits. Each of these, alas, cost money— so the nuns' crusading efforts were often futile. Just as well, perhaps. If they had succeeded, it would anger the pastor— young Catholics, brought up by nuns, often show "early signs of a vocation"; and if a girl is sent to the Madames, she may *become* a Madame, the boy become a Jesuit, just when "The bishop wants vocations out of this parish" to stock the schools with teachers, the rectories with school builders.

It was no wonder that, in this small world of rectory and convent, the intellectual level kept sinking. Nuns did the best they could, and taught some things very well, besides instilling a high level of discipline and piety. But it was, of necessity, a feminine piety, cloistered in its expression, deferential and unquestioning. The worst course taught in a Catholic school was invariably its theology course—more often (and more accurately) called "religion" or "catechism class." In college, it was often "Christian Apologetics." Nuns, though they taught Latin, were officially assumed not to know enough Latin to attend theology schools. Besides, where would they find such schools? The approved courses were offered only in seminaries, which were "off limits" to nuns, in fact, to all women. Cloister rules restricted women to visiting rooms and parts of the public garden. The education of priests and nuns was strictly segregated; so was the education of boys and girls, within the limits of economic necessity. When the diocese did not have separate high schools, one for girls and one for boys, there was a separation at all church and ceremonial occasions. (At first communion it was first the boys, in their white pants and shoes, then the girls in their doll-bride veils.)

Relations between priests and nuns remained formal after their respective courses of study. They did not meet for mere conversation or enjoyment of each other's company. The priest could visit the convent only on business, though with an over-lay of clerical good humor and the boisterous *bonhommie* that priests affected with nuns. The sisters, by contrast, never went into the rectory (that was cared for by a prudently selected laywoman of maximal years and minimal seductive-ness). Thus, between priest and nun—between the two who shared the educational mission on which the parish was fi-nancially based—a gap widened, each building up a stereotype of the other. As the priest became more bustling and efficient, nuns became more quietly prayerful and studious. The world-lier he, the less worldly she—he would condescend to "the good sister" as not "wise in the ways of this world" (he must shelter her from that). He would oversee her reading, protect her from contact with "the outside" that he was tough and realistic enough to handle. This attitude, incidentally, saved him from competition with the nuns. By "protecting" them from "dangerous" and "advanced" books, he perpetrated in them his own ignorance of fresh approaches to scripture, church history, or any Christian studies but the third-hand scraps he could dole out from his memory of seminary classrooms.

In this way the whole enterprise came to depend on shared ignorance. Escape from that ignorance was betrayal of a sort—nun betraying priest by departing from her expected role, betraying the priest to her students if she questioned any child's serene acceptance of the faith; curate betraying nun if he encouraged her to take a less submissive attitude to their pastor; people betraying pastor if they appealed to a bright young curate or nun for more intellectual nourishment than was contained in Sunday's mumbled five minutes of sermon. An unconscious conspiracy was entered into, each person secretly promising not to embarrass the next by knowing anything. We all took each other's hands and sat down together in the dark.

And there, in the dark, oddities of belief were bred. Theological metaphors, imprecisions, suggestions took on the aggressive life of superstitions, their inadequacy only partly disguised by a learned overgrowth of Latin phrases. Religious life was presented as a crude hydraulics of the soul. Mortal sin emptied the reservoir, instantly, of all grace (grace being a quantifiable store of fuel not burned in any known activity, just collected for its own sake, like stamps). Confession pumped grace back into the reservoir, but in lesser measure than before. Venial sins put leaks in the tank. Meritorious acts patched the leaks, added little jets and spurts of fuel. Manning the locks in this pipe system of the soul, one tabulated stores of grace, of merit, of indulgences, with prodigious feats of spiritual bookkeeping.

Actually, this picture of religious life was the sophisticated one, presented at later grades. First images were more rudimentary—the soul as a reverse blackboard, sin the chalk that "writes black" on it, confession the eraser to wipe out black spots. Communion as hygienic cannibalism—"Indian braves used to cut out the heart of their bravest leader and eat it," the nun would say (this led to her hissed injunction, as one came back from communion, "Don't chew the baby Jesus!"). The teaching of scripture degenerated into edifying anecdotage, with parabiblical myths brought in when one ran out of stories from the actual text ("The first drop of blood from Jesus fell on the centurion's heart"). The level of this prating sank lower and lower—yet who would criticize the good nun, the devoted pastor? Who would jeopardize a child's faith by laughing at what priests or nuns had told him? Question this or that silly story, one questioned the basic possibility of miracles, the ability of God to break his own rules, the reality of an imperious Providence above mechanical Nature. It *could* have happened. . . . So, with a thousand rationalizations, we clamped onto each other's hands, no one allowing anyone else to rise, to move out of the circle of men sitting in the dark.

Time could only make such a faith more vulnerable. The majesty of the priesthood dwindled as parishioners, awed in the sacristy, saw collarless priests deferring to bankers in the country club locker room. The dignity of theology dwindled to the level of the most mawkish story told one's children by a senile nun. Church history shrank to a series of background changes behind the same dreary parish church one knew—this church was *the* church as it had been, unchanging, down the ages. One took the mixed bag as a whole, or not at all.

So we lowered our threshold of credulity. In a sense, the more sophisticated one became, the quicker he could argue doubts away. Give an educated Catholic any miraculous absurdity anywhere, he could instantly reduce it to the abstract question of miracles *in se*—which, with Jesuitical skill, was further reducible to the difficulty of proving a negative. ("How can you be *infallibly* certain that miracles never occur?") Those performing such maneuvers did not, of course, see that the logical impasse posed had nothing, really, to do with the narrated pious inanity.

So everything came to depend on immediate, unquestioning, total acceptance. Anything said or done in one's neighborhood church was the belief and practice of Rome, of the Pope's church, of historical Catholicism, of "Peter." Any discontinuity between this church and *the* church would represent a breaking of the bond, dissolution of the circle, parting of hands. The urgency not to know increased, in quiet ways, as one came nearer to knowing—knowing not only about "the world," but about the church itself. Educated Catholics' ignorance of their own church's past history and teachings was amazing—it led to such things as belief that "the Pope" had "always" condemned contraception. The first papal mention of the subject came three decades into the church's nineteenth century of existence—that is, forty years ago, as recent as the Depression. To know such disquieting things might stir hard questions—difficulties pastors could not handle. So Catholics instinctively shied away from knowing them.

Indeed, all aspects of church teaching grew suspect once one looked at their history, discovered changes hidden in their past. I lectured, some years back, at one of the better Catholic colleges, and asked how many students had read a single work of a single Church Father—excluding, for the moment, St. Augustine's *Confessions* (which most would not have read in its entirety, but only the first ten books, if that). No hand went up. They were being taught a second-hand Thomism from the manuals. I asked if any student had read a single book of St. Thomas through. None had.

I later made a game of asking whether it would be heretical to say a Catholic could only go to confession once in his life—and every Catholic agreed that, yes, it *would* be heretical. Yet that once-in-a-life rule was the church's practice for a very long period of its life. St. Augustine never went to confession (though he would have gone if baptism had not been delayed until his thirty-third year). Confession was a sacrament one tried *not* to receive.

The church of other ages would have been unrecognizable to such Catholics. Few Catholics knew what language the Bible was written in, what languages the early church used; how Latin came into the liturgy as vernacular, then froze, excluding all later vernacular usage. Few knew the character and separate purpose of each Gospel. The Old Testament was an exotic book of stories blessed, for some reason, by tradition—a holier Arabian Nights (from parts of which nuns subtly diverted their students' attention).

The barest acquaintance with history would have destroyed most Catholics' image of the church—which was the reason (a suppressed one, unadmitted, even to oneself) why few Catholics learned any but the simplest outline of their own religion's past. One learned the list of Popes, without any idea of the difficulties involved in constructing that list. It was easier to pretend that the church *had* no past, only an eternal present. The church-then was just the same as the church-

now; and we already knew the church-now, so we had
nothing important to learn about the church-then. This Catholic ignorance of all other faiths *and of Catholicism* made the
entire field of history dangerous, a rich source of satire in the
Gibbon manner. And the wittier the satire, the more insistent
the church was on preventing Catholics from seeing it. Gibbon
and his like were all instantly put on the Index, perpetuating
Catholic ignorance. It was a strange situation. The church's
own attitude made it progressively more difficult to write
about the church in any but a critical way. One does not talk
to a man squatting in the corner, eyes shut, with his fingers
in his ears—one can only talk *about* him, with amusement, or
with pity more wounding than ridicule.

It is typical of Catholics that they knew very little about
what kept them knowing very little—knew little, for instance,
about the Index. For several reasons. It was published in
Latin (*Index Librorum Prohibitorum*). No one a Catholic
knew had ever looked at it—including the parish priest. No
one was ever likely to. The only "working rules" familiar to
confessors were the ban on non-Catholic translations of the
Bible and on non-Catholic works of theology (i.e., all religious books—all books dealing with the church, theology, or
the Bible—which did not have an *Imprimatur* on the opening
left-hand page), and the ban on "dirty books" as *ex natura*
on the Index. That last rule is a beautiful example of the
Catholic urge to codify reality and capture it in rules: evil
books were not rejected because they were evil (*if* they
were evil) but because, being evil, they were implicitly *legis-
lated against by the church*. Even a "liberal" Catholic of the
Forties or Fifties could say, as Thomas Merton did, that the
books he read as a schoolboy were "so inflammatory that
there would never be any special need for the Church to put
them on the Index, for they would all be damned *ipso
jure*."

Robbed of its past, the church existed in a present of
precarious immediacy. Faith bound one's whole life up in ties
of communal teaching, habits, discipline, authority, child-

hood assumptions, personal relationships. The church was enclosed, perfected in circular inner logic, strength distributed
through all its interlocking aspects; turned in on itself, giving
a good account of itself to itself—but so vulnerable, so fragile,
if one looked outward, away from it. It had a crystalline
ahistoricity; one touch of change or time could shatter it—and
did. No wonder we protected it as long as we could, with a
latent sense of its brittleness, and wept when it broke.

For though it was an enclosure, we lived there in most
pleasant captivity—unless memory, with softening Dickensian
touches, has romanticized our father's debtors prison. But, no,
it was more than that. Unlikely things, even then, surprised us
with meaning where we expected none. In fact, that which had
least to do with reason seemed the least irrational parts of our
lives. The liturgy, for instance. It did not, as it promised, take
us outside time; but to some degree it pitted us against our
own time, put us in an adversary posture toward the here-
and-now.

Since the sermon was so bad, the best Mass was the early
one on a weekday when there was no sermon, only the odd
mixed rites so familiar we could mumble proper responses in
our sleep. Much was written, in the Sixties, of "the underground
church," a strangely visible one (as if the catacombs had been
reconstructed in air, some streamlined new "El"). But eight
o'clock Mass on a Monday "in the old days" did have a feel
of the catacombs about it, of underground good rendered to a
world still bound in sleep. We came in winter, out of the dark
into vestibule semidark, where peeled-off galoshes spread a
slush across the floor. We took off gloves and scarves, hands
still too cold to dip them in the holy water font. Already the
children's lunches, left to steam on the bare radiator, ema-
nated smells of painted metal, of heated bananas, of bologna
and mayonnaise. Inside, we had an almost furtive air about
our cramped genuflection and inhibited first crossings of the
day—as if virtue were a secret we feared to confess even
here. The priest's words came to us disjointedly through a hiss
and protest of harshly awakened pipes. Girls without hats

hairpinned Kleenex to their heads—it fluttered as they strode to the communion rail, like a raffish dove ill-perched on these sharers in the mystery. At the rail, as one knelt on the hard marble step, there was first the priest's quick murmur over each communicant (*Corpus Domini Nostri Jesu Christi custodiat animam tuam in vitam aeternam*), then the touch of his thumb wetted down the line from tongue to pious tongue.

The whole thing clearly did not mesh with what we did afterward. It stood apart in shadow, as if we re-entered some oracular cave to puzzle meaning out of phrases both foreign to us and familiar. Isolated so, apart from the world, we could almost believe this was our own "last supper"—or, in John Donne's phrase, "the world's last night." But then the scuffling resumed; all the coughs and sniffs held in during consecration and communion formed a firecracker series of soft percussions. Back into the vestibule. And when, galoshes resumed, we came out, day had broken after all. The world was saved again.

To remember such mornings is to start one pigeon of a muffledly screeching flock. Memories throng back, each of them stirring others:

Altar-boy assignments at odd hours, when God was a morning woozily begun under candles, a sweaty afternoon of games ended in the incense-tessitura of preprandial Benediction—the crusty and unwieldy monstrance, spangled cope, and *Tantum Ergo*.

Or midnight Mass—the first time one has been out so late, and farewell to Santa Claus—a pompous affair served with twenty or so other altar boys: endless high candles to light (the long lighting-tree makes young arms ache), biretta of the celebrant to dispose of (it drops on the marble step with a cardboardy pop), as the organ undulates "When flowers blossomed in the snow . . ." The crib is dimmed-blue, suggesting Christmas night, and banked evergreen trees give off a rare outdoors odor inside the church as one extinguishes candle after high candle. The three kings will come in pine-needled silence (Epiphany is not a holy day of obligation), hooves of their camels unheard—already they inch over the sanctuary; they must arrive punctually by Twelfth-night.

A lenten procession, cross carried in front (swathed in purple), no organ to support the *a cappella* groan of "Pange lingua." The purple cloth is folded back, exposing the feet on the crucifix for people to kiss (priest making quick passes with a clean handkerchief, wiping the feet between each kiss).

An oddly jazzy lilt to *Flectamus genua,* sung over and over on Holy Saturday. All our food-chiseling during Lent (*ne potus noceat*) will end in a Saturday afternoon orgy of candy and stored-up sweets.

May procession in the warm night air of summer, "Hail Holy Queen enthroned above," as a girl in her prom "formal" teeters up a ladder with flowers to crown the plaster brow.

It was a world of quaint legalisms. Looking up a movie in the Legion of Decency list (if one had to look, it was probably "Condemned"). Wild surmise on the contents of a Friday soup—did it have gravy or meat products in it? Long debate, as midnight approached on Saturday, over using Mountain Standard Time to begin the precommunion fast. Priests groping their way to the Pullman lounge, for light to finish the breviary. *Dies Irae* on All Souls' Day as J. P. Morgans of the soul accumulate indulgences in purgatorial vaults by ducking in and out of church all day.

The bigger churches, with windows of a richly muddied color—fine gloom up behind the altar, busy commerce near the front doors. Unobtrusive boxes to be shriven in; baptismal font close to the pamphlet racks—a bigger holy water font; side-altar statues, stations of the cross, candled shrines where one could priest it over private liturgies.

Bells at the consecration—one was taught by the nuns to look up, murmur "My Lord and my God," and look down again. Heads buried in hands after communion (grade-schoolers peeking through their fingers). Breasts thumped quietly three times at the Confiteor ("through my fault, through my fault, through my most grievous fault"); one could tell a good deal about a person by his thumping style

—lordly sweep of hand, favored by priests and more prominent laymen (a sinner here, but an important one); sneaky soft beats (one would not guess what the rustle was all about, but for prior knowledge); the slow-motion laying of hands on one-self much favored by women, or Tarzan strokes done in Victor McLaughlin seizures of contrition, producing audible chest echoes. Genuflections were just as revealing—from the skip, the fluid mere *nod* of the body (sacristans were expert at this, because of frequent passage by the tabernacle) to the crum-pled abasement of total inner surrender (would she *ever* get up?).

Baptism in the spittle of repeated *Exorcizo*'s. Car blessings, name-saint days, letters dated by the church feast. Plastic holy water dips at bedroom doors, the Sacred Heart dark and Hispanic in a heavy frame. Scapulars like big postage stamps glued here and there on kids in swimming pools. "JMJ" at the top of schoolwork. The sign of the cross before a foul shot. Fishing pennies and dimes out of pockets pebbled with the fifty-nine beads and assorted medallions of a rosary. One's white first-communion suit, worn again and again on summer Sundays till winter darkened the year and one's clothes (and by next spring it would not fit). Awkward preadolescent girls in the first-communion line, all dumpiness made partly deli-cate with veils. Nuns who moved in their long habits with stately calm, like statues rocking. The deferential "-ster" pinned to all sentences ("Yester" for "Yes, Sister").

Holy cards of saints with eyes so strenuously upturned as to be almost all white. The Infant of Prague bulkily packaged in "real" clothes. The sight, in darkened churches, of a shad-owy Virgin with hands held palm-out at the level of her hips, plaster cape flowing down from those hands toward blue vo-tive lights unsteady under her like troubled water. Sand under the votive candles for putting out tapers; and a box of kitchen matches, for lighting tapers, stuck into the sand. The momen-tary waxen strangle of St. Blaise day, as crossed candles bless one's throat.

Certain feelings are not communicable. One cannot explain to others, or even to oneself, how burnt stuff rubbed on the forehead could be balm for the mind. The squeak of ash crumbled into ash marked the body down for death, yet made this promise of the grave somehow comforting ("Rest, rest, perturbed spirit").

There were moments when the weirdest things made a new and deep sense beyond sense—when Confession did not mean cleaning up oneself (the blackboard erased again) but cleansing a whole world, the first glimpse of sky or grass as one came out of church. When communion was not cannibalism but its reverse, body taken up in Spirit. Being inwardly shaken by unsummoned prayers, as by muffled explosions. Moments of purity remembered, when the world seemed fresh out of its maker's hands, trees washed by some rain sweeter than the world's own.

All these things were shared, part of community life, not a rare isolated joy, like reading poems. These moments belonged to a *people*, not to oneself. It was a ghetto, undeniably. But not a bad ghetto to grow up in.

· TWO ·

Fifties Catholicism:
Gregorian Chant and Encyclicals

LAVABO, INTER INNOCENTES, MANUS MEAS.

WHEN LIBERALS OF THE FORTIES AND FIFTIES spoke of a Catholic ghetto, they did not mean the racial or economic kind (though some of their immigrant forefathers had lived in such enclaves, apart from respectable American life). It was the ghetto mentality they referred to, an isolation from the intellectual currents of this country, from the "right" schools and fashionable journals. Breaking out of such a ghetto was the task of intellectuals, and no project had higher priority with liberals of that era than the formation of a body of intellectuals. Would-be sophisticates called out wistfully for one another. Mutual exhortations to "be sophisticated" were urgently, often naively, issued—young collegians encouraging each other (in effect) to read a dirty book for God.

But becoming an intellectual was only half the problem— and not even the more difficult half, once one had slipped by the parish priest into a "secular" university. The hard time came when, after some period of Masses at "the Newman Club," one returned to the parish. The place was likely to hit a bright sophomore, back from college for Christmas holidays and off to church with his family, as it did the novelist Wilfrid

Sheed: "more like a bus-station than a church; I had never felt half so isolated in a theatre or a ballpark . . . most sermons were worse than unbright; they were downright repulsive . . . I was trying to worship in some kind of great transportation center or super-market." There was the real task: not how to become an intellectual, but how to entertain that ambition and remain a Catholic, subject to stultifying sermons, superstition, and fear of the intellect; subjecting oneself and one's children to convent, rectory, and chancery.

It was a dilemma with some secular parallels. The Fifties liberal in America felt he had to escape Eisenhower's Mid-Cultist and McCarthyite country without becoming un-American, a "loyalty risk." He responded by working out the style of a "higher patriotism," that of *Encounter*, the Americans for Democratic Action, the Congress for Cultural Freedom. He invented "the non-communist Left," with all its ways of taking implicit loyalty oaths with minimal embarrassment. The Catholic liberal's task was not so different from this. The two could even become a single problem: opposition to Joe McCarthy might bring down on a Catholic the accusation of being un-American *and* a renegade to his faith.

How escape the parish while remaining a loyal son of Mother Church? The Catholic liberal responded with a theological equivalent of the higher patriotism: a higher churchiness, the style of a believing critic. He would be the *true* churchman of doctrine and liturgy—just as liberals throughout the country were the true patriots, fighting McCarthy's caricature love of country and "superpatriotism." The Catholic liberal would be more in love with incense than any altar boy; yet he would intellectualize his incense in a congenial setting. He made ceremony less vulgar by making it even more exotic. It was not Rome he disliked in his churches; it was Peoria.

The liberal became more an "old world" Catholic than his parish priest, going back to a romantic past in order to escape the cloddish present, to forge a possible future for educated Catholics. This kind of liberal liked to slip off on weekends to some monastery—to Tom Merton's Gethsemani, where he could rise in the middle of the night and listen to Trappists (silent at other times) chanting their "hours"; or to St. John's Abbey in Minnesota, where he might run into Gene McCarthy or his wife, Abigail (who reviewed books for the house liturgical journal, *Worship*); or to a retreat house, where he could observe monastic silence. In all this, he was obedient to Merton's injunctions, sent regularly out of Gethsemani to people "in the world," urging them to create their own spiritual cell in the bustle of life:

You should be able to untether yourself from the world and set yourself free, loosing all the fine strings and strands of tension that bind you, by sight, by sound, by thought, to the presence of other men. . . . Do not read their newspapers, if you can help it. Be glad if you can keep beyond the reach of their radios. . . . Do not complicate your life by looking at the pictures in their magazines.

It was the voice of a theological Dwight Macdonald, at war with spiritual Mid-Cult.

The liberal, in response to such directives, became quite a liturgist, and very proper. He said "acolytes," not "altar boys." And "the Eucharist" rather than "Holy Communion." Not "confession" or "EX-treme unction," but "penance" and "ex-TREME unction." He knew his Mass Book, the Missal, backward and forward, Latin and English—it fell open automatically to "the prayers at the foot of the altar," and he flipped ribbons expertly to pick, out of this complex book of limp leather and gilt-edge pages, just the right combination of variable prayers for the season, feast, and saint's day of the particular Mass he was "assisting at" (never just "attending").

He was a more frequent communicant than the ordinary Catholic, and he went often to conf—oops, to "penance." Indeed, he cultivated an exquisite sense of guilt, one largely borrowed from French literature, from Léon Bloy and Georges Bernanos, François Mauriac and Paul Claudel.* A tradition tracing back to Huysmans and the decadents, surfacing in English as the plight of Graham Green's Scobie, made him

---

*More detail is supplied on this and other facets of Catholic liberalism in the appendix to Chapter Two.

savor his own wickedness as proof of his own sanctity. In all this, again, the Catholic was moving with the general liberal trend. The postwar years were Auden's age of *Angst*, of fashionable alienation. Arthur Schlesinger, Jr. wrote that "anxiety is the official emotion of our time," and tried to temper the French weariness with "tough-minded" pragmatism.

The Catholic could argue, paradoxically, that his French tastes were meant to Americanize the church. He felt that Catholic intellectual life had fallen under the spell of those breezy debaters spawned in England by Chesterton and Belloc —e.g., Theodore Maynard, Arnold Lunn, C. C. Martindale, Christopher Hollis. At the institutional level, the American church looked to him like a mass of Irish pastors truckling to Italian cardinals. The American church, therefore, was *not* American. It was Ireland subject to Rome, with England providing diversionary camouflage. Only the French church seemed free to the liberal, and a study of it would teach Americans both the human condition in general, and (more particularly) how to forge an independent church. Postwar French Catholics were adventurous; the *maquis* and *le Général* had taught them to admire risk and apocalyptic rhetoric. They launched experiments like the Worker Priest movement. Their philosophers—a Gide or Maritain—were engaged in the existentialist boom. Their theologians—Jesuits Danielou and De Lubac, Dominicans Congar and Chenu—were to the Fifties what Dutch Catholics would become in the Sixties, restive and suspect, attacked with encyclical and anathema. Pius XII tried to silence the French with the encyclical *Humani Generis* just as Paul VI would try to silence the Dutch with *Mysterium Fidei*.

But the liberal was not really fighting Rome. He opposed the American church because it was all too American. Its bishops had been shaped more by the ethos of the local chamber of commerce than by the American Academy in Rome. The pastor was obnoxious, not for his theology or his transnational ties, but for his lack of theology and parochialism. He was Babbitt in a biretta—as (conversely) Billy Graham was Fulton

Sheen in a business suit. The liberal found it hard to talk with his priest, not in the sacristy, but on the golf course. While Paul Blanshard said that priests were foreign agents, the liberal sensed the more horrible truth, that they were aspiring nativists —heirs of their former persecutors, the Know-Nothings (about whom, with typical lack of historical perspective, Catholics knew nothing). The everyday church was narrowly American, its spirit more easily aroused by a Father Coughlin or Senator Joe McCarthy than by papal encyclicals.

Faced with this phenomenon, the liberal outchurched his own parish church, which he thought of as a fund-raising operation, school board, and eucharist-dispensary. The liberal became a lay priest (he was often an ex-seminarian). He bought a priest's breviary, and learned to recite the divine office. He often found like-minded people to recite the "hours" with him. The mood was heavily monastic. In 1950, when Robert Hoyt and some friends founded a Catholic daily, the *Sun Herald* (code for Morning Star, a title of the Blessed Virgin), the staff attempted communal life and said the breviary together. (The paper, presumably for other reasons, did not last long—Mr. Hoyt's hour would not come until, over a decade later, he founded the *National Catholic Reporter*.) One of the moving spirits behind that first attempt of Hoyt's was Carol Jackson, the editor of *Integrity*. She was full of ideas for "Catholicizing" everyday life. She even proposed a Catholic restaurant—to serve a natural and "spiritual" diet (what would later be called "macrobiotic")—and, significantly, wanted to give it a monastic name: "The Refectory." The home, too, was to be a place for communal song and prayer. As monks in their house made up a spiritual "family," so the family would become a prayer enclave in the world, with Papa as the prior, presiding over liturgical dramas at the dinner table, Mama meanwhile doing all the work of "lay brothers" in a monastery (cooking, cleaning, preparing the sanctuary).

Obscure rites and signs were unearthed from Dom Prosper Guéranger's fifteen-volume *Liturgical Year*, and pilgrimages were made—e.g., to Monsignor Hellriegel's church in St. Louis

—to see what *real* ceremonies looked like. Each of these trips made the return to one's parish more enervating—the Latin mumbled unintelligibly, the choir's performance exactly suited to its syrupy repertoire, the statues meretricious, the stations of the cross both lugubrious and laughable. The liberal squirmed in his pew, and yearned for Gregorian chant—performed, of course, in Latin; a desire for the vernacular developed later. The emphasis on the Missal and on chant made the Fifties liberal fond of Latin—without a knowledge of Latin, he could not read the "real" breviary of the priest, just some leaden translation.

If the liberal could not get his Gregorian properly intoned, he would go even farther away from the parish, seeking exotic things. The Ikon Guild would send him Eastern Orthodox chants or the African "Missa Luba," with tom-toms to invigorate the Latin *Gloria*. The liberal admired France's great cathedrals (Claudel, after all, had been converted by the splendor of High Mass in the cavernous recessive *théatre* of Notre Dame). But Ralph Adams Cram had convinced him that St. Patrick's in New York is sham Gothic, and a true "voice of the people" was to be preferred—which sent the liberal off in search of steel-and-glass fish-shaped churches, and driftwood-swirl Madonnas, and wrought-iron abstract tracery for the stations of the cross (artily photographed in *Jubilee*). This was the higher mediaevalism of "native craftsmen," and as such had the blessing of Eric Gill. (Yet the liturgist stayed with Gothic for his church vestments—priestly gowns were to be "conical" in form, chasubles long and flowing, not the skimpy U-shaped affair used at most parish Masses.)

Aesthetics was a great concern for the liberal. Merton, after all, had gone to the monastery to chant *and* versify. The flowers of his *poetry* grew from "seeds of contemplation." While escaping the confines of the parish church, the liberal did not want to fall into the crudely popular style of the Fifties religious revival—the style, for Catholics, of Father Feeney and Father Lord, Father Peyton and Father Keller, Monsignor Sheen and Fulton Oursler. The liberal's tastes were more rarefied, a blend of monasticism and mysticism, done in the pale and loitering mediaeval colors of a world only half recalled, with a nunnish patina of feminine sensibility over everything.

A fussy concern with taste was, of course, as much a part of America at large in the Forties and Fifties as was the spread of religiosity. It was the time of Trilling and Tate and Ransom, of Brookes and Wimsatt and Welleck, of the Warrens (Austin and Robert Penn) and the Olsons (Elder and Charles). A time of proliferating schools—the Southern, the Chicago, the California, the Black Mountain. A refined new battle of the books went on between St. John's Aristotelians, Pound-Eliot classicists, New Critics, Freudians, image counters, San Franciscans and HOWLers, Grove Press continentals. It was a second-hand era, when men got together to Talk About Art, a time of critical expertise and distinctions, of coffee-house caution both wide-awake and watered-down—an *espresso* interval between booze and pot.

If Catholics wanted to join the world of "intellectuals," this was the only game in town. Their liberals looked hastily about, to see if they had any art of their own to discuss—and breathed a sigh of relief to find that they did. The dissertations began, cumbrously, to roll:

Duns Scotus and the "inscape" of Gerald Manley Hopkins. James Joyce's debt to the Jesuits.

The religious significance of prostitutes in the work of Bloy and Rouault.

The dramaturgy of Claudel and Gertrud von Le Fort. The novels of Mauriac and Greene.

The use of Catholic tradition by Eliot and Christopher Frye.

The Catholic Renascence Society studied such questions in its journal (*Renascence*) and kept euphoric watch on all horizons for the coming of a Catholic masterpiece.

It may look contradictory for the liberal to escape Catholic parochialism and chauvinism—what would come to be called "triumphalism" in the Sixties—by creating a cult of Catholic authors, heralding a Catholic renascence, chanting Gregorian, and trying to start Catholic farms, restaurants, film studios, newspapers, and social organizations. But the liberals' most acutely experienced urge was to prove that something recognizably Catholic need not be as cramped, ugly, and anti-intellectual as they found at the corner church. The liberal was looking for an alternative culture to that of the rectory-school complex, a culture that anyone might respect. If he was lucky, he might even prove that Catholic art is an important branch of Western art—more, that a "true" Catholicism pervades and animates our culture. In the ardor of this quest, liberals created a new chauvinism. To escape the narrow confines of censorship and the fear of "scandal," they argued that a "daring" author may actually be more Catholic than a timorous churchman unable to enter into or live out of his large heritage. One should not only read a dirty book for God—"dirty book" being what the parish priest might treat as such—but believe it had been written for God.

In this way Guardini tried to make Rilke orthodox, as De Lubac had done with Dostoyevsky. A "higher Catholicism" was formulated to which, by lucky chance, all the greatest artists belonged. It was an adaptation of the French idea that only sinners are saints. Only atheists are believers. Only non-Catholics are the truly Catholic artists—Baudelaire, Kafka, Gide. As Guardini put it, "They are living from the elements against which they rebel. . . . They cannot be understood from their own center, but only in relation to Christian doctrines." It was a neat switch. The church in America was anti-intellectual, culturally disreputable, ugly and crude?—yes, but this was not because it was Catholic; rather, because it was too little Catholic, too grubby with American materialism and industrial competitiveness, with cultural contamination. Real Catholicism is the very basis of beauty and of truth; its ideals are unconsciously sustained by people who have escaped the cultural limitations of the institutional church.

No wonder aesthetics became ever more important to the liberal Catholic. Maritain's *Art and Scholasticism* was the main intellectual guide for Thomas Merton as he came into the church. He explains the book's effect on him this way:

The word virtue: what a fate it has had in the last three hundred years! . . . When Maritain—who is by no means bothered by such trivialities—in all simplicity went ahead to use the term in its Scholastic sense, and was able to apply it to art, a "virtue of the practical intellect," the very newness of the context was enough to disinfect my mind of all the miasmas left in it by the ordinary prejudice against "virtue."

Maritain rescued "virtue" from those who meant by it a convent girl's virginity. He made it possible to use the word among sophisticates, to discourse with those non-Catholic philosophers of the Forties who used Thomistic tools of analysis, John Wild and Robert Hutchins, Mortimer Adler and Richard McKeon. As true artists were bound to be Catholic in the deepest sense, so all thinkers were "virtually" Thomist. The highest compliment Merton can pay his favorite teacher is the dubious one that he held Thomist views without having the good sense to realize it:

The truth is that Mark's temper [he is talking of Mark Van Doren] was profoundly Scholastic in the sense that his clear mind looked directly for the quiddities of things, and sought being and substance under the covering of accident and appearances.

The pattern is made complete when we remember that Van Doren showed his Scholastic rigor precisely in literary courses, in his critical perception and aesthetic sophistication.

Aesthetics allowed the liberal to come at his Thomism from an angle not pre-empted by the seminaries—one that allowed for reinterpretation, creativity, experiment; one that granted the layman a special role. The liberal thus skirted those patrolled areas where Rome's Apostolic Delegate stands guard over orthodoxy. Yet even here Rome felt obliged, in 1957, to flex a little muscle. That was the year when liberal complaints about the American church—that it was intellectually and culturally stagnant—were finally voiced in a respectable Catholic journal (Thought) by a loyal priest-scholar, Monsignor John Tracy Ellis. The response came, predictably, from Egidio Vagnozzi, the Apostolic Delegate sent by Rome to keep an eye on Americans. (Despite his excellent English, he liked to use an interpreter, giving him a conversational lag for diplomatic calculation.) Speaking to the graduating class of Marquette University in Milwaukee, he referred to the "false aestheticism" and cult of intellect that were surfacing in America. A group of young graduate students and instructors answered the speech with an open letter of protest (at the time an unprecedented liberty). Vagnozzi, with smooth Italian malice, observed that, though he knew a good deal about the American church (by which he meant he knew everything), he had never heard any of these young gentlemen's names. True enough. The liberal stayed away from the ecclesiastical establishment, so clubby, businesslike, and parochial. Liberals had gone "out into the desert" to keep their religion not only separate from politics, but from the church's more normal functions. Their liturgy had as little to do with bishops as with politicians.

But if religious orders were better than bishop-ridden pastors, the layman was best of all. Maritain and Gilson were important not only because of their acceptability as scholars. They were also laymen, who taught laymen, in the vernacular. They were not part of the dogma factory centered in Rome, clanking along in Latin, turning out priests. Maritain was the friend of Rouault, Gide, Satie, Chagall. Gilson had held a special chair at the Sorbonne. These men, and other lay philosophers following in their track—James Collins, Anton Pegis— offered an alternative to official theology much like the monastic alternative to parish ritual.

Maritain, moreover, was a convert. One reason the liberal admired converts so much, had such need of them, was that they had escaped the stultifying childhood experience of parish church upbringing, parochial school, or minor seminary. Even when converts were too Right-Wing in their politics—Waugh, for instance, or "Ronnie" Knox—the liberal admired their style, their ability to approach Catholic life "fresh," without the dull layers of used-out language and habit that encased early memories for "born Catholics." Helicon Press, a liberal publisher of the Fifties, brought out a vernacular Missal with epistles and gospels taken from Knox's urbanely "Englished" bible.

The Catholic liberal was, in fact, a kind of honorary convert. He tried, for quite understandable reasons, to cast himself out of the ghetto of his upbringing and come back at the church from some entirely new direction, sacred or secular, or both alternately. He would even be a Thomist, so long as he could be a Bergsonian "neo-Thomist" with Maritain; a mediaevalist, if it meant interesting experiences as a weekend monk with Tom Merton; a menial laborer, if it meant spending time at a *Catholic Worker* house with Dorothy Day; a "Christian humanist in the marketplace," if it meant escaping the coercive pulpit politics of Cardinal Spellman. You would never find him raising partisan religious cheers at a Notre Dame football game, or getting weepy over Barry Fitzgerald in *Going My Way,* or saying the rosary during Mass.

Thus, when religious at all, the liberal was very *very* religious; but wearing his Rome with a difference. Such intense religiosity, far from inhibiting freedom in the secular sphere, encouraged it. When Merton "got religion," he withdrew at first from the turmoil of politics: "I was no longer interested in having any opinion about the movement and interplay of forces which were all more or less iniquitous and corrupt. . . ." Such an attitude left "the world" to the layman—a satisfactory arrangement. The more otherworldly a liberal's favorite priests and monks, the less their interference with laymen's activities. Catholic intellectuals opposed any forcing of their moral views on the body politic—to outlaw contraceptives, or abortion, or divorce; to maintain censorship over Hollywood's products and ban "dirty books"; to commandeer tax monies for the Catholic schools. This was felt to be not only an imposition on non-Catholics, but a hedge on the Catholic liberal's own freedom. He did not want the puritan and arbitrary aesthetics of the Legion of Decency forced on him. He resented Catholic tactics in maintaining laws against birth control or abortion, not because he would engage in either himself—the liberal of the

Fifties never challenged "church teaching" on such matters—
but because the bishops' highhanded ways made it impossible
for the liberal to be accepted as simply another American engaged in the secular sphere of rational debate.

The Catholic liberal, it is clear, was bound to be at odds
with the hierarchy. In what sense, then, could he be called an
obedient Catholic? In the best and *truest* sense, came his
chipper reply. Just as he had worked out a higher churchiness
in the liturgy, a higher Americanism in allegiance to French
theologians, a higher Catholicism of historical taste and aesthetics, the liberal invented a higher *authoritarianism.* He went
above the bishops to the Pope, to that oracle for guiding modern man, the papal encyclical.

"What the hell is an encyclical?" Al Smith is said to have
asked, when an opponent quoted papal excerpts to show he was
Rome's stooge. Not many Catholics of his time could have enlightened him. Yet by the Fifties nothing distinguished the
Catholic liberal more than his constant (though somewhat
vague) appeal to encyclicals. His enthusiasm for these strange
Latin missives outran even his penchant for Gregorian chant
—and his heart was virtually padlocked into place when the
two allegiances merged, as when Pius XII wrote of Gregorian
in his liturgical encyclical, *Mediator Dei.* The liberal was far
more apt to quote encyclicals than to quote the Bible. In fact,
some Catholics seemed at last to have taken up the Reformation's slogan "sola scriptura" (the Bible as sole authority),
with the understanding that encyclicals were now their "scripture."

What magic was in these documents, most named after
their opening words, written in stilted Renaissance Latin of
the papal courts? Nothing intrinsic. Their prominence in this
century, like their name and format, was an historical accident.
Litterae encyclicae is Latin for "circulating Letter," that
fourth-century Greek *engkyklios epistolē* sent from bishop to
bishop to acquire orthodox signatures, anathematizing heresy.
These were not papal documents but episcopal ones, appeals
for a united front against theological opponents. By the seventh

century, use of the term "encyclical" had become a mere formality, and was allowed to lapse. When Benedict XIV revived the term in the eighteenth century, it was as a fraternal gesture to the world's bishops—yet this first modern "encyclical" was simply an open letter *to* them, a one-sided correspondence, the Pope's way of addressing bishops, not consulting them.* (It is indicative that the American journal for serial publication of the encyclicals was called *The Pope Speaks*.)

Despite the fact that this "correspondence" was a monologue, the letter form was somewhat less dictatorial than instruments of papal legislation (the bull, decree, or definition), or of curial admonishment (monitum), directive, and suppression. It lent itself to a variety of uses, and caught attention by its unpredictability. It became paradoxically weightier by being less formal. The Pope could use an encyclical to celebrate an event or anniversary, restore a devotion, praise a religious order; to warn of evil trends, or encourage worthy projects. Or he could use it to explain his actions—as Pius IX did when he proscribed eighty "modern errors" in 1864. Along with the list (*Syllabus*) of these errors, he issued an encyclical (*Quanta Cura*) to justify his action. Later, Leo XIII made a better effort at justifying that 1864 attack on continental "Liberalism." He set positive social goals in an 1891 encyclical on the condition of the working class.

That encyclical, *Rerum Novarum*, became the founding document of Catholic liberalism. When liberals spoke of "the social encyclicals," they meant a great mixture of papal teachings (including speeches) subsumable under Leo XIII's encyclical, and under Pius XI's additions to that teaching on the occasion of *Rerum Novarum's* fortieth anniversary (*Quadragesimo Anno*). By the time of *Rerum Novarum*, it could plausibly be argued that Pius IX's *Syllabus* was aimed not so much at "the modern freedoms" themselves, as at the secular-individualist framework within which they had been presented. The industrial revolution, as rationalized by Manches-

---

* More on the history of encyclicals will be found in the appendix to Chapter Eight.

ter School economics, had given birth to a whole new set of
evils, and Catholic thinkers, with great support from the
Romantic movement, were in a position to say I-told-you-so.
The church may have lingered too long with the *ancien régime*,
and "lost the working class." But now the "captain of industry"
was losing the worker; his privates and corporals were deserting him. Economic liberalism had led to alienation. The modern freedoms had "freed" man from his own work, and roots,
and past. There was a yearning back toward mediaeval times
—not only in Scott's novels, but in Ruskins's League of St.
George and Carlyle's praise for the monks of St. Edmunds-
bury.

The contract society, it turned out, was not more perfect
than the status one, and Catholic thinkers in Europe had begun to look beyond industrialism to a new era of social interdependence, no longer feudal but reviving some aspects of
the Middle Ages. There was no attempt to cancel history, despite a rather nostalgic view of the guilds' ancient function.
The industrial revolution could not be undone; but its worst
effects could be ameliorated: child labor should be abolished,
a minimum wage enacted, small merchants protected, monop-
olies broken up, private property safeguarded as a bastion of
the family unit, farm life revived, the dissipating energy of
cities somehow countered. In this way the Catholic social
movement of Europe tried to revive things from the immobile
world of status in order to salvage what was good from the
wheeler-dealer world of contract. They wanted to temper in-
dividualism with community. The movement was, in a romantic way, somewhat "Tory"—it opposed the sterility of secularized life, individualized social duty, an industrialized economy.
Yet it also had affinities with the post-capitalist Left of Marx
and Comte, Durkheim and Weber. It would be attacked as
"fascist" in its corporatist phases, and as "socialist" in its
Christian-Democrat emphases.

Perhaps the closest American parallel to this European
body of thought was, in the Fifties, the Southern agrarian
school of Herbert Agar and Allen Tate. In its literary ap-

proach to politics, it praised some "feudal" aspects of the slave South to temper the rootlessness of America's industrial North; and even its non-Catholic spokesmen recognized a philosophical kinship with the encyclicals. Thus Seward Collins, editor of the agrarians' *American Review*, published British distributists like A. J. Penty and Hilaire Belloc along with Americans like Ralph Borsodi and O. E. Baker.

Catholic liberals, imbibing some of this spirit from the encyclicals, became intense critics of the city, of materialism, and of machines. The mediaeval ideals of Eric Gill and Vincent McNabb were translated, practically, into Monsignor Ligutti's Catholic Rural Life Conference, Peter Maurin's "green revolution," and the Central-Verein's version of grangerism. Catholic publishers Frank Sheed and Maisie Ward tried to live out their distributism (disastrously) on a farm. Communitarian efforts, enriched by pageantry and liturgical symbols, abounded—Grail Farm, Peter Maurin Farm, Maryfarm, Friendship House, Joe Hill House, Caritas House, Siloe House, the Houses of Hospitality. For a while it seemed that Catholic liberalism would grow and spread from a series of such nodes.

But such literal effort at realizing the papal ideals did not prove realistic in America, and considerable "translating" became necessary in order to make an 1891 Latin document sound exciting in 1945 or 1950. The Popes, of course, had hoped to call nations back to a Christian family of nations; to win Europe back to the faith. Thus the "workingmen's associations" of *Rerum Novarum* were to be expressly religious, and to cut across class lines by including employers as well as employees. John Courtney Murray has demonstrated that the model Leo XIII had in mind was largely determined by the church's anti-Masonic crusade: the new "guilds" were meant to fight Europe's feared Lodges. In the same way, the corporatism of *Quadragesimo Anno* was meant to decentralize governments and cool off the rampant nationalism that threatened European unity.

But guilds shaped by anti-Masonic religious fervor, or "solidarist" subgovernments opposed to nationalism, could not be acclimatized in America. So liberals had to interpret the encyclicals in an American way—*Rerum Novarum* as endorsing (*tout court*) the AFL-CIO, *Quadragesimo Anno* as endorsing the NLRB. This demanded an ahistorical reading of both documents, but that was the only kind most Catholics—even Catholic intellectuals—were equipped to give them anyway. Thus the principal spokesman for Catholic social doctrine, Monsignor John A. Ryan, became known as "the Right Reverend New Dealer" (the title of his biography), and Catholic social doctrine was simply a matter, for most liberals, of the latest Democratic Party platform. This proved convenient for the church, whose immigrant members had flocked into the unions and into Democratic city machines, and who had (for the most part) only followed Father Coughlin so long as Coughlin followed FDR. This approach did not tax anybody's intelligence very much. It turned a foreign teaching into a very American one, and it gave liberals a shibboleth to protect them from charges of lax Catholicism. The Pope was with the Democratic Party, even though much of the American hierarchy found itself going to Republican businessmen for donations. And one Pope can trump any ten Cardinals or two hundred bishops. William Clancy, at the time when he was editor of *Worldview*, stated the ground rules for using papal encyclicals: "The clear, over-all direction of papal teaching on political-social problems has been in the general direction of what we in this country, rather loosely, for lack of a better term, call 'Liberal.'"

Thus was liberalism launched on its own form of papolatry. When Pius XII reserved the encyclical form for theological matters, and addressed social questions in his occasional speeches (*Allocutiones*), the Catholic liberals' leading paper of the Fifties—the *Davenport Messenger*, edited by Donald McDonald—published reams of papal remarks at audiences for political and economic and labor representatives, deriving from these largely diplomatic expressions of good will the most specific marching orders for American Catholics. Every plea for world co-operation was so much incense and holy water for the UN. The liberal press indulged in theological bullying, as when Robert A. Graham, S.J., said of UN critics that "as far as the Pope is concerned, they are unprofitable servants" (a pretty stiff biblical phrase of judgment).

In time the Jesuit organ *America* refused to accept advertisements from the Right-Wing *National Review* on the grounds that it challenged "positions we judge to be central to our faith, the natural law, or the explicit and long established social doctrines of the church." And the magazine suggested that Catholic schools ban all speakers who questioned its version of the Pope's politics: "There are some ideas and causes that a Catholic college cannot treat pleasantly. . . . Doesn't deliberate opposition to Catholic social doctrine come close to being anti-Catholic? Can anti-labor, anti-UN, anti-foreign-aid speakers be hosted and toasted on a Catholic campus?"

I have said it seems odd for liberals to stress the appeal to central authority, binding documents, and imposed propositions (it was always "social *doctrine*" when the liberal discussed papal directives in the Fifties). Yet this was an oddity shared by many non-Catholic liberals of the time. The people were Mid-Cultish and easily stirred up (e.g., by McCarthy); Congress was obstructive and in bondage to its own committee system; only the presidency looked capable of using power to enact liberal programs—except that Eisenhower was too remiss in flexing official muscle. That was Richard Neustadt's criticism of Eisenhower in *Presidential Power*, and James MacGregor Burns's in *The Deadlock of Democracy*. Kennedy was hailed as the answer to this problem. He would defy Congress, just as Pope John was—at that very time—defying the Roman Curia.

In this atmosphere of gladly surrendered prerogatives and "the cult of personality," engaging Pope John issued his first social encyclical in 1961, *Mater et Magistra*, a broad appeal for benevolent social projects in a world of increasing interdependence. The encyclical surpassed the Catholic liberal's fondest dreams; now anything and everything on the Kennedy agenda—from the Peace Corps to student-exchange programs—was stamped with the Roncalli seal of Peter. Monsignor Conway, in his newspaper column, ordered all Catholics to submit:

Have you been opposed to foreign-student exchange? To the rights of immigration? To the principles and ideals of the Peace Corps? To foreign aid? To idealistic concepts of a world community? Then you need to read *Mater et Magistra* carefully, as a humble Catholic, with deep faith in the Church as Mother and Teacher.

Herder and Herder editor Justus George Lawler wrote, in a book on *Mater et Magistra,* that the "mandate of the encyclical" reaches to such duties as opposition to *Operation Abolition* (a film supporting the House Un-American Activities Committee).

This was the period of the Cuban revolution's slogan, "Fidel, sí; Yanqui, no!" When *National Review* quoted a crack as "going the rounds in Catholic conservative circles" —Mater, sí; Magistra, no!—the liberal press rose to Savonarolan heights at the treatment of papal injunctions with such levity. Rev. William J. Smith, S.J., positively spluttered in his newspaper column: "This is the kind of stuff from which seedling schisms sprout." Moreover, the magazine's editor, William F. Buckley, Jr., had written an editorial that said of the encyclical: "Whatever its final effect, it must strike many as a venture in triviality coming at this particular time in history." Mr. Buckley was drummed out of the church in various ways. The New York *Times* headlined its story, "Jesuits Attack Buckley on Encyclical." Even such unlikely defenders of papal prerogative as Gore Vidal and Jack Paar reproved Buckley for insufficient loyalty to his own church.

Most educated liberals, non-Catholic as well as Catholic, now knew the answer to Al Smith's question, "What the hell is an encyclical?" An encyclical was A Good Thing. Another orgy of ecumenical praise was indulged in, two years later, when John XXIII issued his encyclical *Pacem in Terris,* calling for free governments within the framework of a world organization. The Center for the Study of Democratic Institutions began preparations for a great liturgy to celebrate that encyclical. World leaders and scholars would be brought to New York for days of televised speeches, tributes, and discussions. The era of the two Johns—Pope and President—had dawned, and this would be its apotheosis.

But by the time the bash could be arranged, in February of 1965, both Johns were dead. The show was still held, against a huge cloth backdrop of the Dove descending—the very spirit of Peace. But something had gone out of the meeting by then. Indeed, out of the world. Praise for the encyclical was coupled, everywhere, with praise and hope for the UN—which had just adjourned its sessions early, unable to collect dues from its own members. The Vice-President of the United States, Hubert Humphrey, extolled the UN's past way of bringing peace through war, citing the international "blue berets" that still patrolled Korea's borders. At this very time, the Vice-President's boss was authorizing the post-Pleiku raids into North Vietnam.

APPENDIX TO CHAPTER TWO: *Catholic nostalgia.*

The Catholic liberal's tastes and dreams have faded so over the last decades—changed shape and color so, or simply disappeared—that I would linger on some points mentioned in the text. It is an exercise in Catholic nostalgia.

1. First, there was the strong French emphasis. At one time, most liberal heroes were French. Foremost, of course, came Jeanne d'Arc, symbol of Resistance and special patroness of Charles de Gaulle. She was also the principal symbol in the work of Charles Péguy, another liberal hero. It was no accident that the bishop most favored by liberals in the Fifties had studied in France and acquired a number of the country's loyalties, along with its language: Bishop John Wright created a scholarly shrine to St. Joan in his Pittsburgh mansion. It had every book on her that he or his friends could acquire, along with paintings and statues, films and

relics. Ingrid Bergman herself gave him the print of her film performance as the saint.

Other heroes included Charles de Foucauld, the model for the
Little Brotherhood—some Americans planned to introduce the order in
this country. Or Abbé Pierre, the monkish male counterpart of Dorothy
Day. Or Cardinal Suhard, who took encyclicals and "social teaching"
seriously, to the dismay of others in the hierarchy. The saints of the
"socially conscious" included—besides St. Joan—St. Francois de Sales,
St. Vincent de Paul, St. Benedict Joseph Labre (the beggar of Rome),
and St. Jean Vianney (the Curé d'Ars). Even the liberal's favorite
movies were French. While others of his faith went to *The Bells of St.
Mary's* or *The Miracle of the Bells*, he went to see *Monsieur Vincent*
and *Diary of a Country Priest*. Some liberals wanted to set up a movie
company ("Maryfilms") to put the work of Bloy and Claudel on film,
along with selected plays of Henri Ghéon. America had, for a while, a
"jocist movement," to imitate the JOC of France (Jeunesse Ouvrière
Chrétienne). The journal *Cross Currents* translated key existentialist texts
from the French. The liberals' principal liturgical guides were Guéranger
in the last century, Gelineau in this, and men like Dom Columba Mar-
mion in between. Needless to say, liberals turned readily to France for
their philosophy—past (Bremond and Blondel), present (Maritain and
Gilson), or to come (Lecomte du Nouy and Teilhard de Chardin).
They read Père Sertillanges on the intellectual life, Père Régamey on the
ideal of Christian art, Père Mersch on the Mystical Body; and when they
had finished the poems of Charles Péguy, some went on to those of
Raïssa Maritain.

2. The monastic strain in liberal Catholicism stressed the idea of a
"priesthood of the laity." Since one's parish priest was so uninspiring a
spiritual mentor, people were happy to follow Dorothy Day's lead in
reciting the breviary and singing Latin hymns—she would recite *Veni,
Creator Spiritus* while driving with others. *Integrity* ran articles with
titles like "Our Work Can Help Us To Pray," and "Interior Silence," and
"Why Aren't Americans Comtemplative?" Enthusiasts at places like
Grailville encouraged new ways of observing the liturgical year at home
—advent wreaths, tree blessings, religious cards (an Eastern Icon, say,
with incongruous Latin bits from each of the three Masses of Christmas); houses darkened for Lent, eggs decorated with the Chi-Rho ana-
gram for Christ, a Lamb of God replacing the Easter bunny in candy
baskets; light-shows at Christmas, and Mary shrines in May. Such a
liturgy in the home compensated for the drab hour spent Sunday
morning at the parish Mass. Ancient symbols like the fish were used on
stationery, and letters were written in "chancery hand" by using an
"osmiroid pen"—mediaeval protest against the postwar "Parker 51" with
its fast-drying ink discovery ("Quink"). One learned in *Jubilee* how to
make the Christmas tree a "Jesse tree." *Worship* told how the father of
the house should bless it. *Integrity* made up liturgical games for children. Mary Reed Newland's 1956 book *The Year and Your Children*

taught mothers what to do on each of the twelve days of Christmas, how to make "God Loves You" valentines, and how to climax the liturgical year in Holy Week (you make a Jonah, with his whale; on Good Friday he—Jonah—goes into the fish; on Easter Sunday, the first child awake runs downstairs to take him out again, "resurrected"). When liberals did not create their own liturgical art, they could buy it from the St. Benet library or Sower Press (good agrarian title).

3. Gregorian chant—in Latin—was the most important liturgical adjunct for Catholic liberals. They knew their chant, and could talk of modes and cadences, of "neumatic" and "melismatic," of "concentus" and "accentus," of chironomy and "the Solesmes theory." They discussed the relative merits of the best chant performers—Solesmes, say, against Taizé in France; St. John's against St. Meinrad's in America. Merton had given the importance of chant his imprimatur. Choirmasters in Catholic colleges read *The Gregorian Review* and labored to break their students of the *oomp*-pah-pah strictures of bar-notation, lifting them into the "timeless" breathing sinuosity of chant-line. Manhattanville, the toniest Catholic girls' school, had a special institute, the Pius X School of Liturgical Music, devoted to Gregorian authenticity.

Those who tossed around terms like "concentus" and "accentus" made a virtue of familiarity with Latin. Communities took names like *Caritas* House or *Domus Dominae* (Baroness de Hueck's Canadian establishment). A printing venture was called *Fides* Press. A peace organization became *Pax Christi*. A musical journal was not only named after the patron saint of music, but given the patron's name in its Latin form, *Caecilia*. When the liberal was not using Latin, he might substitute Italian, as in the *Pio Decimo* Press or the *Studio Angelico* Art School. Even a journal that seemed to have an English title, *Mediator*, was actually just the first word from Pius XII's Latin encyclical on the liturgy, *Mediator Dei*. The liturgist's songbook Latinized the Greek invocation of the Mass, and was called a *Kyriale*. The pioneering liturgical journal had a Latin name (*Orate Fratres*), like its European counterpart (*Ecclesia Orans*). The magazine was shamefacedly vernaculared, after twenty-five years, to *Worship*, and its first issue under that banner cautiously suggested *some* use of English in "the Mass of the Catechumens" (what is now referred to as "the Service of the Word"). But as late as 1959, speakers at the Liturgical Week were asked, ahead of time, not to bring up the subject of English in the Mass—it would be too controversial. And when *Jubilee*, in that same year, ran an article on the Gelineau method of chanting psalms in the vernacular, the author assured the magazine's liberal audience that to think of this as "tantamount to a wish to rival, even to supplant, the Latin Psalter and the Gregorian tones, is to misunderstand" the ancillary uses first proposed for such non-Latin forms. The magazine righted the balance, several months later, with an article on Gregorian as "the voice of Christ in His mystical body." The liberal, using St. Jerome's "vulgate" Latin in chant and the Mass and the other sacraments, tended to quote scripture in its Latin form, preferring Jerome over the journeymen of Douai (who made the official English version used by Catholics) and the Greek original.

4. The liberal world was largely shaped and cared for by female heroines and attendants. There was a quiet shared admiration for Sigrid Undset and Gertrud von Le Fort, Edith Stein and Hilda Graef, Raïssa Maritain and Sister Madeleva, Dorothy Sayers and Sheila Kaye-Smith, Caryll Houselander and Carol Jackson, Lucile Hasley and Phyllis Mc-Ginley, Anne Fremantle and Clare Luce, Dorothy Dohen and Mary Reed Newland, Mary Perkins Ryan and Maisie Ward, Patricia Crowley and Jean Kerr. It is difficult to say what caused this prominence of women—partly, perhaps, the drain of ecclesiastically inclined men into seminaries, into pastoral work or technical theology. Perhaps, too, the prominence of Catholic girls' colleges had an influence; they made it possible for girls to hold offices monopolized by males in most coed colleges—class president, editor of the school newspaper, head of athletic and dramatic clubs.

Woman's influence was always strong among Catholics, since a feminine brand of piety was instilled by nuns in parochial schools. There may also have been a trace of matriarchy derived from the large Irish families of American Catholicism. But a special relationship must also be included in any survey of the specifically liberal world of sensibility—it might be called the Francis Thompson/Alice Meynell relationship, and it accounts for the presence of "earth mothers" like Dorothy Day and Baroness de Hueck in the liberals' circles. Each of these important women mothered her principal charge—Peter Maurin, respectively, and Eddie Doherty—and then mothered a whole succession of others through the years. Friendship House and the *Catholic Worker* homes were often way stations for troubled young men on their way into seminaries (or on their way out). Merton spent time with the Baroness on his way in, and men like John Cogley went through the *Catholic Worker* as they re-entered "the world." Even Maisie Ward's didactic publishing house provided a place for exseminarians like Philip Scharper to carry on a specific "apostolate."

5. Catholic aesthetes like those in the Renascence Society stressed the Catholic nature of favorite works, which could be "Catholic" either because of the author or the subject matter. Any work that excited at the time was given hopeful scrutiny, made a candidate for "Catholic masterpiece" status—*Kristin Lavransdatter*, *The Satin Slipper*, *The Song of the Scaffold*, *The Secret of the Curé d'Ars*, *The Song of Bernadette*, *The Keys of the Kingdom*, *The Man on the Donkey*, *Murder in the Cathedral*, *A Sleep of Prisoners*, *The Cypresses Believe in God*, *Prince of Darkness*, *Stage of Fools*, *The Fault of Angels*, *Perelandra*, *The Last Hurrah*, *Father Malachy's Miracle*, *Mr. Blue*, *The Cardinal*, *The Screwtape Letters*, *Don Camillo*. It was hoped that Catholics might produce a great autobiography—*Seven-Storey Mountain*, *Pillar of Fire*, *Surprised by Joy*, *The Manner is Ordinary*. Or a scholarly monument—Haeckel's

Virgil, Berdyaev's *Dostoevsky,* Guardini's *Rilke; The Making of Europe, The Drama of Atheistic Humanism, The Intellectual Life, The Mind and Heart of Love, Enthusiasm, Insight.*

The liberals' emphasis on art and criticism made Jacques Maritain far more influential as an aesthetician than as a metaphysician. Criticism had, indeed, become so important in the Fifties that Maritain's rival Neo-Thomist, Étienne Gilson, grabbed his Eric Gill off the shelf and made a belated stab at the field of aesthetics. Since he could not (like Maritain) observe the artist at work in a poetess-wife, he presented himself for the Mellon lectures (five years after Maritain had delivered his series) as the father of a painter-daughter.

6. The Catholic social movement of the nineteenth century, which found expression in *Rerum Novarum,* had been encouraged by Bishop Ketteler in Germany and Cardinal Mermillod in France, by groups like the Freie Vereinigung and the Union de Fribourg. The Jesuit cofounder of the newspaper *Civiltà cattolica,* Matteo Liberatore, helped Cardinal Zigliara draft *Rerum Novarum.* Much of twentieth-century social theory drew its inspiration from that encyclical—corporatism and voluntarism, subsidiarism (Oswald von Nell-Breuning, the Jesuit who helped draft *Quadragesimo Anno*), German solidarism (Heinrich Pesch), Italian concretism (Luigi Sturzo), English distributism (G. C. Heseltine). In America, the communitarian message of the Popes was preached, in various forms, by Frederick Kenkel in his *Social Justice Review,* by Joseph Husslein in *America,* Peter Maurin in the *Catholic Worker,* Ed Willock in *Integrity,* Ed Marciniak in *Work,* Philip Land in *Social Order,* Bishop Sheil in the CYO, Patrick Crowley in the Catholic Family Life Movement and "Cana Conferences."

· THREE ·

The Liturgical Crisis

QUARE TRISTIS ES, ANIMA MEA?
ET QUARE CONTURBAS ME?

FOR CATHOLIC LIBERALS, then, as for their secular counter-
parts, the Fifties was a time of nice distinctions, neat divisions,
of a critical liberalism and liberal criticism. One world mir-
rored the other. John Cogley's *Commonweal* was a Catholic
version of Max Ascoli's *Reporter*. Bishop Wright was the
Catholic Hubert Humphrey, and Monsignor Higgins' NCWC
the equivalent of Galbraith's ADA. Ed Marciniak was a
stand-in for Walter Reuther, and Father Murray for Professor
Schlesinger. The time, in retrospect, presents a surface flurry
of distinctions, but little deep questioning. The problem was
not whether to wage the Cold War, but how to do it with cool
rationality; not whether to accept doctrine, but how to phrase
it acceptably.

The Sixties would have little use for such scholars and
gentlemen—as little as President Kennedy had for Adlai's
older-style liberal honor. During that decade, a great change
came over the church, as over the country. I was first impressed with this fact in 1968. As I rounded a corner, they
were helping a priest out of the gutter—though he left a good
deal of his blood behind in it. He had been clubbed by a

policeman who ran; now other police tried to make amends. Their car stood at the curb, its dome light pulsing with the scene's hysteria—one cop had pulled the dash mike out on its crinkled long cord, and was radioing for an ambulance. He looked shamefaced about it all, and only snarled at us to "Keep moving!" so we would not see the man now huddled in the prismed glare of a locked store's windowed entryway. I thought back to old catechism lessons, the awesome warning that striking a priest meant automatic excommunication.

He was not a priest, though. The streets of Chicago were full of bogus Catholics that night, in 1968, of rioting around the Democrats' convention. They were not imposters, but— most of them—Protestant "men of the cloth" who had brought out or rented, purchased or borrowed Roman collars as a badge of ministry, of their mission to keep peace this night between angry cops and kids. Mayor Daley's Irish police might hesitate to club down priests—who were, after all, an expected part of scenes like this. Nuns, too, for that matter. Collars and coifs had been regular decorations of the peace and civil rights rallies and marches of the Sixties.

Not this time, however; not in this place. Chicago's Cardinal, John Cody, known to his more restive subjects as "Louisiana Fats" when he came up from the New Orleans diocese, had indicated (before he left town himself) that he wanted none of his priests involved in convention troubles. Events thus expressed the dislocation felt by Catholics today: the church is not where (or what) it seems to be. It seemed to be in the streets, but wasn't—yet it also seemed to be locked up, and wasn't (earlier use of the collar had made it a resource for non-Catholics to wear here). Just as some priests discarded their identifying symbol, other men picked it out of the dust and polished it off for social uses, as a halo to dissent. And, of course, the collar in this new role angered those who had previously been most reverent toward it. Typical. Catholics seemed constantly to be shifting sides in the Sixties, they were scrambling on such shifting ground.

Bishops who had fought for years to keep the collars on

their men would just as soon *not* see those collars on the evening TV news, bobbing under a marcher's placard. One priest from the Chicago area, an admitted revolutionary, later told me he used the church as a cover for his activities because he felt it was the one service an expiring institution could still perform. He only wore his collar in the courtroom— for priests on the picket line led, before long, to priests in jail. When two priests were arrested in Baltimore, the TV station that showed their transfer from city to federal jail was flooded with telephone calls asking why these priests were not dressed in their clerical garb. Actually, friends had taken their black suits down to them in jail, after the priests were picked up without warning; but the policeman at the desk refused to accept the clothes—and he let the visitors know (reinforcing his point with obscenity) that such men were not worthy of religious garb, and could only bring shame upon it. Nonetheless, the TV station would receive as many angry calls if the priests had been filmed in their collars. Either way, the thing had become a sign of contradiction—people resented (often simultaneously) the priest who went about "disguised" as a layman *and* the priest whose collar on a picket line seemed to give religious endorsement to a political cause.

The priest, it was argued, spoke for the church when he wore the church's livery; if he was acting simply as one American citizen, exercising any individual's political rights, he should not be distinguished from others by symbols that exact a deference irrelevant in this context. Others answered that a priest's whole life was given to the church and to his ministry; he should live and be judged, on all occasions, as a man set apart for that work. The thing could be endlessly argued. The collar opened doors, and closed them. Though it went into new places now, it received new challenge or rebuke there, also. Religious superiors were unhappy either way. I asked a priest, one who had been among the first to demonstrate, whether his bishop wanted him, at first, to stay in clericals or to picket less obtrusively in lay attire. "Are you kidding?" he answered—"That would have been like asking a

Southern redneck if he prefers to have his twelve-year-old daughter get pregnant with a white man or a black one." It was a question bishops did not want to face.

What had happened to the collar was happening to all the other signs and sacred things of Catholicism, a religion caught in an agony of lost symbols and debased associations. Whole devotions dropped from use, throwing off the rhythm of communal celebration and prayer—benediction of the Blessed Sacrament and the rosary of the Blessed Virgin, the priest's breviary, indulgences (Luther's old point of contention), novenas. Even the Mass, the central and most stable shared act of the church, had become unrecognizable to many—a thing of guitars instead of the organ, of English instead of Latin, of youth-culture fads instead of ancient rites.

The first hard-fought battle of the Second Vatican Council centered on liturgical reform. Doctrine was not supposed to be involved, just changes in the discipline of public worship. Yet emotions ran high; every change made here was a tabu broken. This was the one point where religion touched most Catholics, where they communicated not only with God but with their fellow believers and their own past; the framework in which they were accustomed to think of all things supernatural; the link in memory with exposure to spiritual things, with earlier aspirations; the holiday rite contained in every Holy Day and Sabbath, burial and marriage, Christmas and Easter. Even the Catholic who did not understand Latin was reading here a "language" both personal and shared— each rite or phrase meant what it suggested from repeated hearings in different places, different times, even different *selves* (drawing them back together into one self). Cardinal Newman described the importance of even accidental associations in building up a concept of the supernatural, creating a *history* of the soul's reach out toward God:

Nothing is so frivolous and so unphilosophical as the ridicule bestowed on the contest for retaining or surrendering a rite or an observance, such as the use of the Cross in Baptism or the posture of kneeling at the Lord's Table. As well might satire be directed against the manoeuvre of two generals concerning some small portion of ground. The Rubicon was a narrow stream. A slight advantage gained is often at once an omen and a measure of ultimate victory. Political parties, to look at the matter on the lowest ground, are held together by what are the veriest of trifles. An accidental badge, or an inconsistency, may embody the principle and be the seat of life of a party. A system must be looked at as a whole; and may as little admit of mending or altering as an individual. We cannot change one joint of our body for a better; nor can we with impunity open one vein. These analogies must not of course be pressed too far; but they apply far more to morals and politics than theorists of this day are willing to believe. It is remarkable how hidden, as well as insignificant, are these depositories and treasure houses of our most important habits.

So the shock of adjustment was greatest when the Mass was tampered with. Any new thing here posed the whole problem of change in its most poignant form. The layman, coming home, found it a strange house, cluttered with signs of an alien occupancy. He was asked to do things against which elaborate inhibitions had been built up all his life—touch the communion wafer, *chew* it, receive it standing instead of kneeling, even drink from the chalice (another old battle of the Reformation). A great part of the old liturgy had taken the form of progressive obeisance to a thing untouchable in ordinary ways. At ordination, a priest's fingers were oiled, bound, consecrated to the task of touching It. At Mass he could use only the "canonical" digits (thumb and first finger) to lift the consecrated bread. A seminarian could not be ordained, if one of his "canonicals" was missing, without specific dispensation from Rome. Lay brothers did not assign young seminarians to tasks—e.g., slicing bread loaves—that might endanger fingers destined to lift their Lord. At every Mass, after consecrating the bread, a priest had to keep his thumb and forefinger joined as he performed all other motions (paten and chalice were lifted with the third and fourth fingers). The Mass became a hierarchic dance arranged around the Host, bowings, blessings, kneelings, liftings, displayings and hidings of It. The code of untouchability was so complex that wild contingencies must be provided for: What would happen if a priest dropped dead after consecrating the bread and wine?—Another priest would have to be found to drink the chalice and put the Hosts inside the tabernacle. Even a priest in bad standing should presume automatic permission to exercise his "faculties" in this emergency. Non-priests were not allowed, without the grant of a sacristan's privileges, to touch the vessels that touched the sacred species, much less drink the blood of consecration or pick up the Host.

The Host itself was a thing unlike all other bread, or any kind of food—dough baked to a shiny thinness, then stamped out in flat circles (less than bite-size to forestall chewing); a light disk balanced on one's tongue by the priest, then lifted to the palate by the tongue, there to stick, hard and alien at first, at last dissolving against the taste buds without effect on them—chaste "supersubstantial" manna, like nothing else, plastic dew fallen from heaven. One was discouraged from touching even the unconsecrated wafer, or eating it (though altar boys sometimes did, back in the sacristy—and drank the unconsecrated wine); these sensations were to be reserved for the act of communion. The way of baking, minting, stamping the unleavened unseasoned flour did not of itself make the Host divine, but went as far as ingenuity could toward making it cease to be bread—as if helping the rite along; it might not work unless one had prepared for it ahead of time, taken bread out of the bread, so far as possible, as a magician puts the rabbit in his hat ahead of time.

One had to abstain from all other food before taking it— the fast began at midnight; an unconsidered mechanical swallow after brushing one's teeth meant no communion that day, even for a priest. Taken as sacred table etiquette, Mass rubrics were a war on crumbs. Once cut out, the crisp wafers were "cleaned" by nuns or sacristans, each one individually scraped for rough edges or for particles that might come loose. The Hosts were hard currency, negotiable stuff of salvation— most of them stamped with a liturgical sign (just like a coin), each capable of purchasing a soul. During Mass the priest repeatedly swept the cloth and his little plate (paten) for invisible specks of detached communion bread; for each part was the whole, each crumb a communion in itself. When he took the Host away from the altar, toward the communion rail, he was accompanied by an altar boy with a special crumb catcher—another gold paten, this one on a long handle, so the boy could tuck it under the chin of each person receiving communion. If the priest should drop a Host, or the recipient fail to hold it on his tongue, the boy was supposed to catch it; but I never saw this happen—either he was too late with his stab, or the Host pinged off onto the floor. The whole process was impractical; indeed, a nuisance—the acolyte rarely co-ordinated his movements with those of the priest; they bumped each other, or stayed so far apart the paten was at one man's chin while the Host was being placed on another's tongue. The gold plate was there for dramatic effect, to tell people how precious this white disk was, with the larger gold disk hovering under it, psychologically warding off the ignominy of a fall.

Actually, when a Host was dropped, the priest covered it with a cloth specially provided for that purpose, then came back after communion had been dispensed to everyone, for a thorough crumb hunt and cleansing of the area. When Daniel Berrigan celebrated a modern liturgy at Hospitality House, and used a real loaf of bread for communion, Dorothy Day was shocked that the floor was left littered with God in the form of bread crumbs.

In parochial school one used to hear stories of the bad priest who went into a bakery shop and said the formula of consecration (*Hoc est corpus meum* . . .), mocking a good priest; and the good priest had to settle down to two hard days of a steady bread diet, to prevent sacrilege. The crumb problem was never fully dealt with in that edifying tale. Indeed, the crumb problem did not bear much thought under any hypothesis—e.g., how did Jesus handle it at the Last Supper, when nuns had not stamped and cleaned ahead of time some bread coins for this transaction?

The magic phrase that could turn a bakery truck into a tabernacle on wheels was at the center of all the Mass's incantations—all of them in Latin. Unless the priest said the phrase precisely, every syllable enunciated, consecration was invalid—which led scrupulous priests to parodies of exact phonetization (*Hu-oh-cuh Es-te Cu-ohr-poos May-oom*). These words would do the job and no others—not even the New Testament phrases of institution. The biblical Greek had to become Latin before the bread could become Christ. It was by virtue of the church's language that the priest acted; his action declared that scripture was entrusted to the church, not the church to scripture. *Rome* consecrated, in Rome's language—and many things were implied in that fact. It meant that scripture was not preached (Catholics did not come to Mass, after all, to hear lectures), church announcements were made—from announcement of the Holy Name Society's activity to announcement of Rome's teaching. The Latin, and the ritual, made fresh recourse to scripture out of place here. It could not have been brought off, even if one wanted it to be. The priest not only knew Latin better than Greek, the vulgate translation better than the original New Testament; he knew his Missal better than the Bible, and the Ordo (rite book) better than the Missal. He knew his Latin rubrics better than his Latin theology, rite even better than doctrine —and he certainly knew the doctrine better than its putative sources in scripture or church fathers. He had become familiar with Torah and psalm, Testament and pericope only in the detached phrases, torn out of context and in an outdated translation, that occurred in Mass or the breviary. His preaching showed this.

The Latin Mass, in other words, did not directly offend the Latinless person; but it did steady damage to the priest, made him a man of one "timeless" language that was no language at all—a weird mix of patristic translatorese, mediaeval hymns, and Renaissance (or pseudo-Renaissance) petitions called "collects." The vernacular Mass was supposed to have been introduced for the layman, to make its words understandable to him at last. But Latin had done its real work long before one even reached the church where Mass was said. The priest saying that Mass had learned his theology as a set of Latin theses approved by Rome—the remnants of a living oral dialogue, from Scholasticism's scrappy days of creative dialecticians, now moribund. After being embalmed in books, the words were sepulchered in passive twentieth-century minds to which the whole method and its antecedents were meaningless. Such theology, derived from an historically anchored philosophy, now dragged bits of that philosophy around behind it; putative explanation had become mere obfuscation (*ignotum per ignotum*). Bits of Latinized scripture were presented within that framework—the unknowable approached from the not-worth-knowing. Having learned his theology (which was mainly an ecclesiology) this way, and only then (and partially) absorbing scripture, the priest was forced to pray an hour daily from a Latin book that was no book, but the summary of a monk's day of chanted prayer. The priest had to recite something that did not fit his circumstances, time, or place; did not equip him to deal with the writings of the ancient church or the ways of modern thought, much less bring them to a confrontation.

Trained thus, the priest arrived at the altar for Mass, where his care must be centered on valid celebration, on keeping the canonicals pinched, the formulas exact; putting together the liturgy's calendar day—its fixed, its variables—from his Ordinarium, rubrics, and Missal. The rite was satisfying as a rite, especially to those who could attend it without concern for proper recitation. The layman could pray, meditate, say his rosary, read from Missal or prayerbook—even from the Gospels; could muse, pay attention, join in the priest's words, or go his own way. For liberals like those described in the last chapter, Latin was an intermittent and exotic thing, not a daily involuntary grind. Just as the layman was free in the secular sphere by reason of the priest's churchiness—not bothered by things like the collar's symbolism, setting him apart—so he had most freedom in the liturgy.

The Mass was not brought into the vernacular for him —the laity did not ask for the change; indeed, those who understood Latin least were the ones who most resented change. The innovations were made in the name of freedom, though they had to be imposed on many laymen, and Latin was not even retained as an option, as a gesture to men's right of choice. The priest, you see, was the one being freed —the priest, with his face to the wall before him, his only contact with the congregation a brace of juveniles, snuffly and in need of prompting, who poured wine from the cruets too late or too early—so that Monsignor Ronald Knox admitted in writing: "You are tempted to regard him [the acolyte] as an unwelcome distraction." If one had to be isolated so, with set formulas every morning, better to make a virtue of solitude. Priests jockeyed to avoid the sung High Masses, with long sitting, with the choir's endless pieces, with shaky sacerdotal intonings in an early before-breakfast voice, and with altar boys unused to incense thurifers. (Laymen could go to a different Mass or different church, find a Gregorian choir, or duck out for a cigarette on the front steps if the Credo got too screechy and long-drawn.) A priest might even sneak off toward an early unscheduled Mass at a side altar, to escape the ordeal of waiting on acolytes assigned (reluctantly themselves) to serve his Mass.

Besides, escape from Latin involved for these men more than the Latin Mass; it meant the breviary as well, and— most important—it meant escape from the years of theology (and retrospective partial philosophy) learned in Latin by rote. Philosophy of a serious kind—and certainly of a modern kind—is hard enough to grasp, debate, accept, refute, or deal with in one's living tongue. Translated into a museum-exhibit semilanguage, this kind of thought dies in air before it reaches the mind. One effect, therefore, of Latin training was to make current thought and debate impossible—impossible in the formal course, no matter what younger minds did outside the classroom, tempted by thought or by rumors of thinking in the world around them.

Latin, it was obscurely (correctly) sensed at the Council, would stand or fall as a whole. Pope John made a conciliatory gesture to seminary Latin when liturgical Latin was struck down—one of those reactionary things he was always being "forgiven" because of his bolder moves: he issued *Veterum Sapientiae*, a document ordering Latin to be kept up in the courses of priestly training. It was a futile gesture. In the deepest sense, this was the real point of the controversy over Latin. Vatican II was a theologians' rebellion, that of the *periti* (expert consultants) against the Curia. The Latin of theology class was resented even more than that of the Mass —and both were resented by younger faculty and the recently ordained, not by laymen.

But the impact on laymen was bound to be immense. Priests had for years paid the price of Latin, and laymen were oblivious to its toll. Now their turn had come. It was time to pay the price of the vernacular—the layman's price. The conditioning of the priest entailed, down the line, a conditioning of the layman. The priest did not (because he could not) preach scripture; he was unequipped for that, as we found out when Vatican II urged that he try. This meant the layman had been trained to distrust "lectures" in church. He came there to *do* things—witness the miracle, and believe in it; consume the eucharist, and believe in that. Belief, as a result of the priest's formation (and of the people's expectations, formed on that), had been ritualized; it was not a thing one heard about or held by intellect, but a rite to be gone through. Change the rite, and belief would inevitably change, despite all assurances that it was changeless. A Monsignor addressing the Latin Mass Society of England in 1967 put the matter with stark truthfulness: "The Blessed Sacrament has been removed from the high altar by the simple expedient of turning the altar around." When the shrine, a thing removed, was brought down into the congregation's midst, the whole genius of devotion at (and to) that shrine evaporated. The Monsignor, Bryan Houghton, a man very learned in the old tradition, made explicit what had been implied in formulae recited endlessly: "Their use is to reduce the activity of the human mind to a minimum in order to liberate the soul for adherence to God in prayers." Prayer was a thing God did in and through you (the Spirit crying out "Abba"), not mere action of your own mind—just as the eucharist was what God did to the bread, not a human transaction.

If faith was a virtue, and doubt was opposed to it, then doubt was a sin. But sin is in the will—so intellectual objection to the faith must be *willed* away by virtue, by one's faith. That is why defined doctrines could be presented as duties, to be accepted "under pain of mortal sin." Letting the intellect dwell on any doubt was like entertaining impure thoughts. Of course, a doubt could insinuate itself into a mind off guard—just as sexual fantasies can arise unbidden. But that just means one has to learn how to head off these unexpected encounters, be prepared for them, anticipate and obviate; exculpate oneself. And if, despite all evasive action of the mind, faith was ambushed anyway, the first assault was not sinful in itself—not if one labored to repulse it. Thus doubt had to be distinguished from external temptations, for which a different term was used—"difficulties." That term, you notice, does not pose a specifically intellectual threat: what is difficult you overcome by determination, by the will. Hence Newman's famous distinction, to reassure the scrupulous: "A thousand difficulties do not make a doubt." Endless occasions of sin, honestly avoided, do not make one sin—*that* only comes when one seizes the occasion.

Doubts, therefore, were not to be argued with—that was playing the devil's game—but crushed; laughed off, or evaded. By sheer volitional assertiveness—pray harder and the doubt will go away. Or by tactical distraction—go to bed and sleep it off. (The confessor in Keneally's *Three Cheers for the Paraclete* assures an anguished young man that "Faith is merely a highly informed form of relaxing.")

So at times one had to ignore one's faith in order to retain it. Practically, this often meant that the laity had to entrust its doubts to professionals of faith, the priests; little

realizing that the clergy had its own way of going somnam-
bulistic where alertness might require the unacceptable—"scandalizing" innovation, views frowned on by the bishop, open
intellectual dishonesty or revolt; or, behind it all, a clean final
break with being schooled to think (or feign thinking) in
doctrinal tags and Latin formulae. For the priest too, faith
could only be kept at times by keeping it out of sight, away
from the light of scrutiny.

That is how priest and people tried to guard each
other's faith, ward doubts off, making the most of handy
excuses—just as each tried to get the utmost muffling effect
from the flimsy screen in the confessional, creating a barrier
where there should have been a conduit. Because faith was
in the will, and was to be preserved at all costs, by all means
—divine gift sanctuaried from rash human tampering—there
could be a certain ruthlessness in Catholics whose faith was
challenged. Wilfrid Sheed's character, Bert Flax, fights his
doubts by seeking out an irreligious friend, to bait him and
berate him, trying to revive the feeling of belief that comes
from whipping unbelievers. This might be called the Muggeridge ploy, using modernism as a bogeyman to scare up
sleeping creeds. The centering of faith on the will explains
how Catholics could go along with this strategy, trying to
prop up even second-rate faith, feigning belief in the hope
that wish would solidify as volition; submitting the will,
bypassing the mind; imposing faith, if no longer on oneself,
then on others, and especially one's loved ones ("He wanted
it to be right for her," says Bert Flax of his wife, "whatever
it was for him."). Willed virtues can be praised even by their
non-practitioners—as the roué father tries to keep his daughter
innocent. Faith *should* be forced for Catholics—Rome itself
made it enforceable, demanding intellectual submission to the
"doctrines of salvation."

But the will can only stretch the mind so far, or ask so
much of others. Trying to believe for others, make others
believe, make excuses for believing, find less belief than yours
to scourge—all this built for the mind a labyrinth that doubt

was not supposed to penetrate. And the concrete form this labyrinth took was the Latin liturgy. Rock the mind in lulling recurrences, live all one's memories of believing back into oneself, join others' reveries of faith, take faith from them (as they, presuming it where there is none, will take in turn from you), hear echoes of the creed surge up around you as you voice its phrases, not asking if the echoes come from hollowness ("We may not believe, but at least Bert believes"— *Bert* does!). The ancient liturgy was a last resort, the one thing that still worked, a place where one did not hear questions, raise doubts, submit to lectures. Here all was as it had been, proof that some things do not change, that one could go home.

That was why the Mass had to be preserved exactly. Move through it with intent fidelity, with legalistic care for validity, for volition, for what must be done—for doing it right, for rite, the last rites left in this unrecurring secular world of accident. This, at least, one saw with relief, could not change.

Which is why it had to change. Why we had to stop pretending. There were too many bogus Catholics in the streets, in the churches, at the altars. We were all too bogus. Priests had to stop worrying that people would be puzzled by their honest puzzlements; stop acting like museum curators to this Mayan ceremony of the Mass. The people had to stop making priests the custodians of their doubts. They even had to learn why some priests felt like prisoners—the prisoners of Latin, of the confessional, of their collar; why they felt the twitchings, on that collar, of an invisible leash. The bishop *had* bound their hands at ordination; their fingers *were* glued together by the sacred things they had been set apart to do daily, by rote, lest their people fall prey to doubt. It was convenient for Catholic liberals that Tom Merton stay in his monastery, the priests stay in the pulpit and off the streets— that faith be locked up, unchanging, in the liturgy's beautiful maze. But convenience, carried too far, is opportunism—what used to be called, in churchly circles, simony: the profane use (here, a use in idleness) of sacred things, use of the sacral against a final sacredness in reality. That is why, at last, the symbols could not be jostled even slightly—they were mere shells. If they had been more than that, a change in the Mass's choreography would not have shattered so many men's belief so easily. A great deal ended when the Latin sung Mass ended. Like Claudius, we sought other words for praying, and they would not come—no other Mass was "valid"; the play was over.

II · CHANGING

I believe that John Kennedy believed that his role as President was to initiate an era of hope—hope for a life of decency and equality, hope for a world of reason and peace, hope for the American destiny.

—THEODORE SORENSEN

· FOUR ·

The Two Johns: Rome and the Secular City

*For the first time since the death of Charles
Carroll, the most important, the most famous,
the most powerful American Catholic was not
a member of the hierarchy. . . . With a clearly
providential coincidence, the theology of the
Vatican Council was at the same time describing
the Church in terms which would provide
theoretical justification for the American
Catholicism of the post-Kennedy era.*

—REV. ANDREW GREELEY

IT IS CLEAR, IN RETROSPECT, the moment of triumph for Fifties
liberals of the Catholic faith. It came in 1960—that night,
September 12, when all they had worked for, over the years,
was vindicated. It was the night when John F. Kennedy
addressed a group of Protestant ministers in Houston, Texas,
and received a standing ovation. Three of the Catholic liberals'
heroes had helped draft this speech, which finally and convincingly voiced their creed: *"I believe in an America where
separation of church and state is absolute."*

The creed was henceforth public and credible. Residual
doubts would be dispelled by Pope John XXIII's encyclical

Pacem in Terris. Two men had wrought a public change in Rome's attitude toward pluralism and the whole secular realm. It is true that a fundamentalist preacher like Harvey Springer could still say, after the Houston speech, "Did you see the coronation of Big John? Let's hope we never see the coronation of Little John." But most people felt instinctively that this Pope and this President were the wrong ones to use when arguing that Catholics are hostile to freedom.

Despite the fact that "the two Johns" made an attractive combination in the early Sixties—a "clearly providential" one in Father Greeley's enthusiastic phrase—the Catholic liberal had not at first been ardent for Kennedy's election. So long as the creed was made convincing in Houston, the candidate did not have to be inaugurated in Washington. Most Catholic liberals—including one of the men who drafted the Houston speech—were on the side of Eugene McCarthy in 1960 when he called for the third nomination of Adlai Stevenson. The Catholic liberal wanted liberalism in politics, not Catholicism —that was the very point he strove to make. Politics was, for him, a world separate and quite different from religion; so the truer liberal—i.e., Adlai—had, at the outset, a stronger claim on him than a fellow Catholic with Jack Kennedy's dubiously liberal past.

Yet, despite initial misgivings, the liberal came to realize that Kennedy was a better man for office than Adlai—his defense of the secular realm's autonomy had more impact *because* he was a Catholic. And, if one were to have a Catholic President, it was better to have Kennedy than Gene McCarthy. The former was not only free *in* his Catholicism, but free *of* it. John Cogley expressed the distinction when he said Kennedy was the first President who was a Roman Catholic, rather than the first Roman Catholic President. Murray Kempton put the same thing in a less friendly way, referring to Al Smith's defeat: "We have again been cheated of the prospect of a Catholic president." It was a judgment innocently confirmed by the President's wife, when she told Arthur Krock, "I think it's so unfair of people to be against

Jack because he's a Catholic. He's such a poor Catholic. Now if it were Bobby, I could understand." Theodore Sorensen snorted: "No one who knew him believed the allegation of Jim Bishop that JFK had fallen sobbing on his knees in prayer the dawn after the Bay of Pigs venture failed."

This detachment from religion was the President's main virtue and advantage. Political man is secular man, since religion and politics have a high wall reared between them. Indeed, the effusive Reverend Greeley suggested that Kennedy be made a "Doctor of the Church" within liberalism's higher Catholicism. Kennedy represented the first tenet of a Catholic liberal by being so exclusively secular in his political judgments. The least Catholic politician was the most desirable one —there was a higher Catholicism of the statesman, as for all the great artists admired by the Renascence Society.

Balancing the secular respectability of Kennedy in office, there was the added joy, for Catholics, of a very religious man on the chair of Peter, restoring an air of saintly love to an office that had looked too harsh—authoritarian, doctrinally imperialist—under Pius XII. John was "open" to the world, not trying to coerce it, or convert, but to serve. John Kennedy was "in" the world, not trying to seduce it, to deny the evidence and norms by which it functions. It was the liberal dream come true. Catholic liberals had escaped the parish church by a flanking operation, turning both flanks (as it were) of that ugly church's ornate altar—being both churchier than the church, and more secular. They slipped cleverly off in two directions at once—to monasteries and to "the market-place." Now the world could look with approval on warm pious John XXIII at his *prie-dieu*, at cool secular John Kennedy in public office, and see the very embodiments of monastery and marketplace, of the sacred and secular. It was as if the two lobes of the Catholic liberal's brain had burst forth and taken flesh, to walk the world together, ruling it with benevolent realism. The two Johns complemented each other; they *were* church and state, not at war but co-operating; able to do so because they recognized the separateness of their spheres and responsibility. Under one John, professors went to Washington and created the New Frontier. Under another, enlightened young theologians went to Rome and created Vatican II. Vigor in the White House. "Updating" (*aggiornamento*) in the Vatican. Stuffy officials pushed into swimming pools. Gothic windows, long sealed, now thrown open. The liberal era had dawned.

Because the worlds of religion and politics were now so acceptably distinguished—a distinction expressed in all the differences between one John and the other—liberals could mix the two in whatever way they liked. A man was free to partake, as much or as little as he wanted, in the life of his parish or his political party. He could be a monk for a weekend, or a week; make retreats once a year, or more often; work for peace and civil rights with secular or Catholic groups, or both, in the proportion that best suited him. He read a mix of secular and religious journals, dealt with secular and religious universities or both; was free to go outside the "ghetto" of the parish, or the monastic "underground" of liberal Catholicism itself—the cozy little world of instantly acclaimed "intellectuals" known as *Commonweal* Catholics. He could live entirely in the secular world, like Kennedy, working for the higher Catholicism, or in an ecumenical world of "dialoguing" believers who made their religion explicit, or in the small world of liberal Catholics where one's sense of importance was easily gratified.

Though the lay liberal dutifully expressed regret that he was thus free-wheeling because free of the institutional church —i.e., that he had no real trouble with the hierarchy because he had no real contact with it, or influence on it—he did not really want lay control of the church, only recognized lay competence in the world. His lack of influence in the intellectual ghetto was just the other side of his release from priestly control. By holding the church off from secular concerns, he maintained the mobility between worlds that was the secret of his own development. He wanted (at least subconsciously) the priests and nuns to stay in their rectories and convents. He wanted (at least at this stage) to have Merton say he was incompetent for making secular judgments now that he had been removed from the world. He endorsed wholeheartedly the maxims of Kennedy's Houston speech: "*I believe in an America . . . where no Catholic prelate would tell the President, should he be Catholic, how to act . . . where no religious body seeks to impose its will directly or indirectly upon the general populace or the public acts of its officials.*"

Such a liberal rightly felt it unjust for a Paul Blanshard (in *American Freedom and Catholic Power*) to doubt his devotion to pluralism. A liberal Catholic was *super*pluralistic. He profited not only by the free play of his religious group with other beliefs in America, but by the many options thus opened up to him *within his own religion,* the different worlds of which he made his personal combination of devotion, activism, and thought. Not only was his life a meeting of one religion with others, and of all religions in a neutral (secularized) "marketplace"; it was also a choice of the particular theological, liturgical, apostolic, and charitable aspects of Catholicism he cared to bring to any of these confrontations. He was led to claim the best of both worlds, not opportunistically, but by his own deepest-held principle, that all-important principle, separation of church and state.

Yet even to say one could mix these essentially separate things is to admit that absolute division is impossible. One is a Catholic even when he is acting as voter or politician, as teacher in a public school or writer in the secular press. Does this continuity of personal commitment destroy the concept of "the wall"? Catholic liberals answered by saying that, in their secular role, they were not subject to outside domination from the church or its rulers, but only to conscience. Their conscience was, it is true, "formed" by Catholic teaching. But *everyone* has a conscience formed by the moral precepts he recognizes (upon scrutiny) as valid. Thus a Catholic is no different from any other principled man. The only authority is that of personal commitment to the right, as one sees the right—yet to admit this principle is to allow for other men's commitment as *they* see the right, and, therefore, to allow for open debate and discussion of these differing views on what is right. Church authority in political matters could not, consequently, be a matter of group or episcopal command (*"no Catholic prelate would tell the President . . . how to act"*). The only sanction was internal, and that required a proviso for the inner rights of other men. Where such consciences meet, but do not agree, they compromise, or allow for alternatives within a neutral framework. That is the essence of pluralism.

The "argument from conscience" was spelled out most explicitly, during the Fifties, by Jesuit theologian John Courtney Murray: but it had long been the implicit basis of Catholic liberalism. Murray's task was not to show laymen why they could act as they already did, but to defend their actions against Roman doubts and fears, clerical obstructionism, and the inherited maxims of seminary training. After some early setbacks, and much intramural clerical squabbling, Murray won all his battles. His approach to the rights of conscience, to the autonomy and competence of the secular sphere, and therefore to the separation of church and state, were included in Pope John's *Pacem in Terris* and the documents of Vatican II.

Thus the liberal vision was fulfilled. Paul Blanshard, making the last respectable attack on the loyalty of American Catholics (in 1948), had said church teaching was un-American: The church would, if it could, make itself an established faith in this country, dictate morals, force disagreeing consciences, and impose church doctrine with legal power. The Catholic liberal answered that church teaching, properly understood, was not only conformable to American political ideals, but absolutely identical with them—*individualist,* because based on the rights of each man's conscience; *pluralist,* protecting all men's consciences as the only way of protecting any man's; and therefore *secular,* making the division between church and state a matter of conscience. When Kennedy discussed the conflict between a Catholic President's conscience and the American Constitution, it was as an unlikely (if not impossible) thing. And when he said that, given such an unimaginable conflict, he would surrender his office rather than go against either his conscience or his oath of office, he did not present this as a problem peculiar to a Catholic, but as the duty of any man who recognizes the dictates of conscience: *"But if the time should ever come—and I do not concede any conflict to be remotely possible—when my office would require me to either violate my conscience, or violate the national interest, then I would resign the office, and I hope any other conscientious public servant would do likewise."*

The Catholic liberal was as liberal as he was Catholic; indeed, as liberal as any other liberal; just as loyal an American, and loyal because of his Catholic principles—which, it turned out, were simply American principles. The Houston speech was, much of it, penned by *Commonweal* editor John Cogley; or by Theodore Sorensen after long discussion with the liberal's intellectual in the hierarchy, John Wright—a worldly-wise Irish prelate from Boston, who had long been on intimate terms with the Kennedy family. Then, before the speech was delivered, Sorensen read it over the telephone to Father Murray, its doctrinal father, for a final blessing. One of the ministers in Houston asked Kennedy, in the public question period, if he had "cleared" his speech with his own Cardinal (the late Richard Cushing) in Massachusetts, and Kennedy answered that no bishop had authority over his political statements. The speech needed no episcopal clearance. It had a nobler stamp of approval, the *imprimatur* of the liberals' higher Catholicism. The secular John spoke with an authority the liberal Catholic recognized at once—just as, in his own sphere, the pious John spoke authoritatively.

In all this the Catholic liberal remained on easy shared ground with non-Catholics of the time. Arthur Schlesinger and others singled out Kennedy's secularity as his outstanding virtue. Liberals of the *Encounter* persuasion had proclaimed an "end of ideology," and Kennedy was the kind of "problem solver" required in such a value-free world of non-theoretical concerns. According to his Harvard professor of politics, he treated questions of state "like a young scientist in the laboratory." He shunned ideological terms just as much as he did the religious label. Asked whether he meant to be a conservative or a liberal as President, he answered, "I hope to be responsible"—a realist, what his wife called "an idealist without illusions."

John Courtney Murray had been forced, in his debate with Roman theologians, to make intricate distinctions—not only separating church from state, but state from society, and society from the individual conscience; natural law from revealed law, and the truly secular school of natural law theory from both a sacralized and an anti-sacral perversion of that theory. He broke single acts of decision down into *neutral* expertise, *political* conscience, and *religious* informing of conscience. He neatly packaged sacred and secular, private and public in their proper wrappings. He could split hairs with the best Thomists—and none of this dismayed his liberal audience, at such places as *Time-Life* editorial conferences or the Center for the Study of Democratic Institutions. The Fifties was a time convinced of the need for sorting things out—for the autonomous artifacts of the New Critics, the separate "fields" guarded by academic competence, the disjunct problems to be handled by postideological problem solvers. Harry O. Morton, of the World Council of Churches, wrote in 1963 that the task of the new politician was "to study specific problems and to work out an immediate coherent policy in a limited field." He considered John F. Kennedy the model of this politics, with "the competence to isolate a problem, to exclude from view enough of the important but not immediately relevant data in order that one may study the problem by itself, and thus find for it a workable solution."

The problem solver needs *power* to get things done. When the supreme test of a man is his efficiency, he does not welcome "checks and balances" on that efficiency. The liberals had nothing but scorn for "Judge" Howard Smith's deadlocked Congress or Ike's delegated Presidency. They trusted Richard Neustadt's argument that "The more determinedly a President seeks power, the more he will be likely to bring vigor to his clerkship. As he does so he contributes to the energy of government." More power for the President meant more power for everyone in government. The more we gave to him, the more we would have ourselves.

Thus Acton's warnings about the accumulation of centralized power no longer applied—there was no "center" for non-ideological efforts exercised pragmatically on disjunct problems. Such power set automatic limits on itself, in order to assert itself. As theologian Harvey Cox put it:

To say that technopolitan man is pragmatic means that he is a kind of modern ascetic. He approached problems by isolating them from irrelevant considerations, by bringing to bear the knowledge of different specialists, and by getting ready to grapple with a new series of problems when these have been provisionally solved.

All power was now *ad hoc* power, usable only in the concrete, gradated to specific problems. Yet this very limitation gave one "options." The Kennedy power mystique came to be symbolized in Robert McNamara's concept of flexible response, as opposed to the massive retaliation of Eisenhower and John Foster Dulles. Eisenhower's America was a musclebound giant, all power concentrated in a single unusable quantum. It could destroy the world, or do nothing. There was no third option—or fourth, or fifth. Kennedy would make response possible by making it limited, by preparing for counterinsurgency, "brush-fire" wars, war carried on vicariously through "advisers," wars fought by our own guerrillas or by those we had trained. Kennedy himself put it this way: "Our defense posture must be flexible and determined. Any potential aggressor contemplating an attack on any part of the free world with any kind of weapons, conventional or nuclear, must know that our response will be suitable, selective, swift, and effective." This was a "frontiersman" government, probing unexplored areas in a variety of ways, quick on its feet, unweighted by "the grand view" of all-or-nothing ideological absolutes. A can-do government. When McNamara was asked to join it, he called the President-Elect and said, "I have talked with Tom Gates [current Secretary of Defense] and I am confident I can handle the job." Kennedy answered, "Well, I just talked with President Eisenhower and I am confident I can handle that job."

Catholic liberals, as one can imagine, went giddy with surprised fulfillment listening to others praise "their" President. They had argued all along that recognition of separate spheres for action made a truly Catholic politics the most American kind of politics—and the most effective kind. But even they had not expected these claims to be vindicated so convincingly, taken up by others, preached everywhere as American gospel. Protestant theologians vied with "value-free" scientists in praise of Kennedy's transcendence of ideology, which was symbolized by his transcendence of theology. He won both ways, by being (officially) Catholic and by being (functionally) non-Catholic. He was the champion compartmentalizer. Arthur Schlesinger marveled at it: "One can find little organic intellectual connection between his faith and his politics." Richard Rovere also found the secret of Kennedy's effectiveness in an ability to live with his church yet ignore it: "The easy way in which he disposes of the question of Church and State—as if he felt that any reasonable man could quite easily resolve any possible conflict of loyalties—suggests that the organization of society is the one thing that really engages his intellect."

These men found that Kennedy made a better President for Catholics than Eugene McCarthy; and, even more, that he made a better President for liberals than Adlai Stevenson. Adlai was too priestly in his politics, too much the "true believer" (another Fifties term) in liberal tenets—not a man who could use them or leave them alone, as the job demanded. Rovere put it this way: "Whereas Mr. Stevenson's political views derive from a view of life that holds politics to be a mere fraction of existence, Senator Kennedy's primary interest is in politics." In order to secularize politics, Kennedy had to purge it not only of religion, but of any overarching metaphysics or system of beliefs. Harvey Cox approved: "Life for him is a set of problems, not an unfathomable mystery."

Having escaped mystery, secular man's political mastery becomes that of a technician. Cox called this the era of the "work team" that is "task-oriented," and can only think of God (if at all) as a "work partner." This is the voice of confident research. It recalls Teilhard de Chardin's approach: "What fascinates me in life is being able to collaborate in a task." So Kennedy called in the experts, Harvard with its dissertations, MIT with its slide rules, the Ford Corporation with its computers. He was "the world," just as Pope John was "otherworldly." Norman Mailer portrayed JFK's succession to Eisenhower as the triumph of city over small town. The new style was urban, cool, detached; yet mobile, appreciative, "hip." When Professor Cox sang the praises of *The Secular City*, he claimed that Jack Kennedy epitomized all the virtues of that City—was, in fact, "the first really urban President."

Cox's book gave Kennedy the secular canonization Father Greeley demanded from Rome. Most Catholic liberals were more pleased to accept it from Harvard (where Cox taught theology). For a while, in the mid-Sixties, Cox's little red paperback was a standard part of the Catholic theologian's teaching equipment—much as Mao's little book was for party workers in China. The red cover was, in fact, a lesson in itself: it was partitioned into squares by a "street map" pattern of lines, and inside each square a different aspect of city life was presented in symbolic line drawing. Facing one vertically, the cover looked like a chest of drawers, each drawer (city block) offering a different option for the urbanite (pull out the drawer that suits you)—here a pleasure to be savored, there a problem to be solved; if one drawer disappoints, close it and pull another. Isolate your "field" and conquer it. Mix your options. Vary your response. Kennedyize.

The older sociology had spoken of cities as uprooting, disorienting, causing anomie. Cox argued that uprootedness was freedom, anonymity gave mobility, disjunction made for choice. If the city was a jungle, that did not terrify the tough pragmatist—he answered the call to a new asceticism, a discipline of the secular. The tough would survive, would grow by surviving; and, having solved their own problems, would solve those of others as well—political Natty Bumppos helping tenderfoot types less skilled in the rigors of this new frontier life.

Ecological preoccupations would, in the Seventies, make us aware that men cannot effectively isolate problems in order to solve them—all problems are interconnected, one feeding on another, the seen ones on the unseen. But that had to come later. John Lindsay was elected "fresh," to be mayor of New York in the earlier time of urban hopefulness —and only learned through attrition of suave hopeful bluster that his city, like life, is one problem, an insoluble one. We do not solve our problems—we are lucky if we succeed in finding them, learn to live with them, reduce the pain. Yet there was no room for such defeatism about "the inner city" when Kennedy first came to office. Cox argued that dwelling on such difficulties was un-Christian, opposed to the gospel, since man could do all things in Christ: "The fact is that man is placed in an environment of problems which he is called to master." Thus a well-planned poverty program would solve the city's problems, just as correctly gradated force would settle the problem of Vietnam.

For no one did the secular city look fresher and more promising than for Catholics. If you had to banish metaphysical preoccupations to the utterly private realm of prayer, you were left with a technician's playroom-world, a recoverable laboratory-Eden. Theological exiles returning to this secular land might find it messy, rather overrun after long absence; but they could set all in order with the right bulldozers. Catholics thus took Harvey Cox to heart. He became a celebrity in the church press and schools, sought out for lectures and articles, constantly seen and quoted. He appeared at bouncy sessions with nun-artist Sister Corita, whose serigraphs were bright reproductions of commercial products, a happier Warholism of the supermarket. She composed advertisements for the biggest corporations; she called commercials the true art of our time, and said billboards (as the work of man and machine collaborating) were preferable to empty fields and "nature." All things secular were sacred. Her symbol for the eucharist was a serigraph of wondrous enriched bread, man improving nature with additives. Her hymn to the Virgin (as the juiciest tomato of them all) was superimposed on a soup-can design. The Virgin Mary and her plastic tomato replaced Eve and the apple in a garden never to be lost (only replanned), a paradise sown with billboard forests, with laboratories instead of wheat fields.

Catholics, too, were encouraged by the news that "God is dead." God *had* to be treated as dead if, in approaching "the marketplace," John Kennedy left his religion behind, a thing sealed up in privacy so absolute that men could not (and should not) know anything about it. The ubiquitous Greeley suggested that it would be "mortally sinful" for Catholics to speculate on Kennedy's religious views. Ted Sorensen said his boss's religion was so private he never talked of it even in private. Kennedy approved of John Courtney Murray's effort to make "the American solution" a favored opinion in Catholic theology—that is, he wanted Murray to get the job done. But (in Sorensen's words) "he cared not a whit for theology." And Father Murray, we may assume, would have reciprocated mild approval. Murray had, after all, inspired the Houston speech, which said that churchmen have nothing to tell politicians in their own realm.

If the world were to be truly secular, God must die to it, release his claim on it. The God-is-dead theologians even congratulated God on this sacrifice, on his death traded for secularity's life. We should rejoice, not be sad, at his demise, said Thomas Altizer: "All things will dance when we greet them with affirmation." God's death meant that our Eden had no overseer, no one to drive transgressors out of it if they ate the apple of technological knowledge.

This "kerygma" of the death of God resembled Marshall

McLuhan's simultaneous (and equally premature) proclama-
tion of the death of print. Rejoice in the Non-Word, said
McLuhan: print had to die, to give us TV. In the same way,
God had to die, to give us Technopolis. And Sister Jacqueline
Grennan of Webster College was glad: "The great leveling
force of Kroger's and Brown Shoe, of McDonnell and Monsanto has destroyed the tribal and feudal world of earlier
elitist societies. . . . Now in the age of technopolis we are
pragmatic men." This nun was one of Harvey Cox's great celebrators in the Happy Time. The world was, for her, a place "I
live within lyrically at age 38. . . . I want only to be a *worldly*
nun," for the world is where one works, the Eden at hand, and
she hoped to "go on being a naïve wide-eyed wonder child" of
"this magnificent last decade." She told a group she addressed
at Xavier University: "We ought to be everywhere where action is. Cox says that modern Christianity ought to be like a
floating crap game—you go where the action is."

Her advice (which Cox had earlier taken from Archie
Hargraves) points up difficulties just below the surface of Cox's
argument. Religion is to go where the action is—i.e., into the
secular realm. But where the secular action is, religion by
definition *isn't*, and (according to what Cox said earlier)
should not be. Why, then, drag it back onto the scene? Why,
for that matter, does Cox write a book whose subtitle is "Secu-
larization and Urbanization in Theological Perspective"? If a
world come of age has been de-theized, it is consequently de-
theologized. Why re-theologize it? Cox praises "demythologiz-
ing," yet imposes biblical symbols on the secular city—much
as McLuhan argued in books that books are obsolete.

The closer one looks, the more it becomes obvious that
contradictory platitudes make up a "theology" for Cox if one
only uses enough Greek words instead of plain English. You
theologize community by calling it *koinonia,* or social work by
calling it *diakonia.* The process is reduced to absurdity when
Cox offers us his four-part theory of change as a new "theology
of revolution." The first part is explained as a theory of *cataly-*
sis: "The catalytic factor in most revolutionary theories ap-

pears in the form of what might be called a *catalytic gap*, the idea that a lag exists which must now be closed, and that closing it is the action required." Taking that back out of the Greek, Cox has told us: To change, you must see some need for change.

After catalysis, we are given the other three parts of his theory, all of them neatly alliterated by the Greek prefix *kata* —i.e., catalepsy (some will resist change), catalysis (the resistance must be overcome), and catastrophe (then change will occur). That is hardly a "theory." Nor is it "revolutionary." And it is certainly not "a theology." Cox oscillates between naive fundamentalism (*scripture says* the Kingdom is ours) and a tortuous factory-Scholasticism (how many angels can dance on the head of a smokestack?). Why bring in the Kingdom of God (or, to use his idiom, the *basileia* as *eschaton*) to discuss the secular city? Cox answers, with deadpan "scholarship": Because the Kingdom of God is nothing but Jesus, and "the Council of Chalcedon held that Jesus was fully God *and* fully man." OK, but what has that to do with the secular city? "When the same [*sic*] discussion is translated into the vocabulary of contemporary social change, the issue is whether history, and particularly revolution, is something that happens *to* man or something that man *does*. . . . Is man the subject or the object of social change?" Well, which? "He is *both*" (subject and object). How do we know that? Because Jesus was *both* (God and man) according to the Council of Chalcedon. You mean we secular men must get our secular views from a combination of strained analogy and the Council of Chalcedon? Well, not exactly. . . . Then why bring Chalcedon up at all?

An unjust suspicion nags one, reading this exercise in circularity, that even though God may die, theology must not; because, if it did, Harvey Cox would be out of a job. Harvard and Emory and Temple would have to close down their divinity schools. Even the death of God could only be announced to us, you notice, by death-of-God theologians—which is like producing the Emperor of Erewhon to assure us that there is no Erewhon (who should know better than he?). There seemed to be a proprietary interest at work, as in the oil-depletion allowance: The oil is gone from here or there, but you have to keep paying the firm that drilled for it. In the same way, even when God could no longer demand intellectual tithes, the God-drillers could.

The suspicion is, of course, unjust. Nothing so open or planned as venality lay behind this clumsy grope of the mind back toward God through his own death. For that is what it was. The death-of-God movement was religion's way of crying from the tomb; a confession of lost energies. An ache was felt, though it seemed like pains "in" an amputated limb. Though God had died, man's need for him lived crazily on, only half acknowledgeable. Not to admit the ache was impossible. To deny the amputation would be dishonest. There was nothing for it but to graft life onto the hurt spot (or try to graft it, however ineffectually). Thus, though the liberal world was divided into secular and sacred spheres, President John's domain was pre-eminent, reversing the precedency of Pope over Prince in mediaeval arrangements. In the framework of the Catholic liberal's symbols, Rome (as well as Cambridge)—the Vatican (as well as Harvard)—looked to Washington. Theology on its own no longer convinced, nor did liturgy console. So the secular world's unquestionable liveliness was channeled toward our moribund religion. The death of God was to be the life of worship, for it let wild secularity's life break in, with billboards and profits and a fizz of salesmanship.

Theology had nothing to offer the secular world—definitions of the Council of Chalcedon are not required texts in Harvard's sociology department. Religion came not to save the jazzy swinging with-it world of the Sixties, but to be saved by it—perhaps Chalcedon could be retrospectively introduced to a class as relevant by making Tönnies and Weber principal texts in the School of Divinity. The real purpose of Cox's book is revealed in his last chapter, which addresses itself to Dietrich Bonhoeffer's question, "How do we speak in a secular fashion of God?" No longer, Cox answered, in terms of myth or metaphysics, since they are dead too. Only politics had stayed alive. "In secular society politics does what metaphysics once did. It brings unity and meaning to human life and thought." Politics was the only way left to talk of reality. If we talk of God in these terms, perhaps even He will seem (somewhat), real; reality will rub off on Him; something of what men used to mean by Him be vestigially retained.

The White House lawn had become the true campus for Harvard professors. The church was not serving the secular city—whose pride was in taking care of itself, solving its own problems. John Kennedy did not ask bishops for advice. But perhaps, just maybe, the secular city could serve the churches —as John Kennedy lent a new respectability, shrugged off on them almost as an aside, to Catholics. Religion in the age of Cox was a parasite on politics, trying to live off the surplus of young Washington energies, a pious corps applying for relief to the Peace Corps. In the old days, nuns had said, "Keep commerce out of Christmas." Now they tried to resuscitate the gospel with brash salesman pushiness. Jacqueline Grennan told her students to imitate the enterprise of Monsanto investors. Sister Corita found the message of the Christ Child in seasonal commercial messages: "He cared enough to send the very best."

But many people felt, on November 22, 1963, that God or fate or history had taken "the very best" away. The bullet in Dallas—how did one isolate that problem and solve it? Men tried to, of course. The problem solvers now had a crime to solve, and they fought against despair with charts, precision, measurements, photos, a labyrinth of footnotes. Better conspiracy than craziness—one can solve a plot, but not mere "unsecular" uncool madness, released so soon into our new garden of reason.

Their computations gave no solace. All those who had been glad at the death of God were sad at the death of Kennedy. God's death had been the death of mystery—Cox said so: "Life for him is a set of problems, not an unfathomable mystery." But Kennedy's death signaled the rebirth of mystery—the mystery of evil. The sacred John's sphere might not be much, any more; but the secular John's had crumbled in one gunshot-instant. The death of Kennedy must eventually kill the death-of-God euphoria. Even Harvey Cox would soon be writing: "I used to believe, and even hope, that mankind might someday outgrow its religious phase and live maturely in the calm, cool light of reason. But people have been predicting the end of religion and the death of God for centuries. And I no longer seriously believe it will happen, nor do I hope it will." He too had rediscovered the irrational—though, typically, he tried to limit it to irrational celebration and festivity. As in the Poe tale of masquerade, the dance would get wilder because of threat impending.

· FIVE ·

Omega, the New Frontier

*I tell you the New Frontier is here
whether we seek it or not. . . .
I believe the times demand invention,
innovation, imagination, decision.*
—JOHN F. KENNEDY, *Nomination Speech*

IN THEIR NEW YORK PROVINCE, Jesuits are buried at the novitiate, St. Andrew's on the Hudson. In 1955, that upper part
of the state had not thawed by Easter; the casket of a Jesuit
foreigner, shipped up from New York City, had to be stored
until a grave could be carved into the ground. Lay brothers
finally lowered the plain box, and put up another in the row
of identical stones. The name on this marker meant nothing
to novices caring for the grave; but more and more laymen,
in time, came asking after the man's burial spot—and approached with the air of pilgrims. By the early Sixties the
place had, with no other ornament, become a shrine. The
name on the grave was distinction enough: *P. Petrus Teilhard
de Chardin.* He died in the unresented obscurity of lifelong
exile; and was buried, as he might have wished, in transit.

Yet he also died, without fully realizing it, in his true
spiritual home. It was America that broke the atom, built the
great public universities, pushed out scientific frontiers, and—

as a necessary precondition to such progress—made lots and lots of money. And it was Père Teilhard who wrote: "Gold, which is blameless so long as it is busy in service and so long as it helps along the current of humanity, becomes corrupt as soon as it stands still. It is lack of motion that makes gold—a thing good in itself—first fester and then infect other things." Money was almost sacramental for this priest, "material energy in an easily handled form"—it got things done, fueled human progress, gave men power.

When Eisenhower was elected President, "I shed a tear for Stevenson," said Teilhard. But he would have greeted the reign of the two Johns with an enthusiasm matching that own period's regard for him. Many people called Vatican II the vindication of Teilhard, considered him its absent but presiding genius. Robert Speaight wrote, with enthusiasm outrunning grammar: "Nothing that Teilhard said in public or in private—and much that he did not say—was left unsaid at the Second Vatican Council." Religious and secular leaders alike praised him; he merged their spheres more intimately than anyone else, even Harvey Cox. Cox, appropriately, called Teilhard one of the most important teachers of the future, because of his emphasis on man as "that point where the cosmos begins to think and to steer itself," Man the Cosmic Problem Solver, for whom pragmatism means constant adjustment to the unforeseen out at the edge of evolutionary advance. Kennedy's dynamic Secretary of Defense, Robert McNamara, put Teilhard on his list of most valued authors, and thenceforth the Jesuit's name was mentioned with awe in the White House.

The phenomenon of Teilhard was, in the first place, an unexpected wonder of the publishing world. Books by and about him sold briskly in the Sixties, despite their lofty and abstract style. *The Phenomenon of Man* alone sold over half a million copies in hardcover. His name and work were everywhere, for a while—and his face, in the striking Philippe Halsman photo: the bent long profile palely glowing (with wilder eyes and hair, it could have been a saint's face by El

Greco). He became a kind of court philosopher for the Johannine era, and would have found in this development a justification for his views.

Thus, though the man was dead, his time had come; a time, as Henri de Lubac said, to which Teilhard's thoughts were "perfectly attuned." No politician, not even the Adlai he bewailed, could have been more congenial to him than John F. Kennedy, secular Catholic, celebrant of intellect and power. Kennedy was the President who committed America's vast resources to the exploration of space; threw our collective hat over the wall, opened new horizons, shunning no challenge, bearing any burden. It was typical of Kennedy to choose a slogan for his regime easily grasped by all, yet with special meaning for the learned. To the common man, "frontier spirit" was a thing compounded of TV westerns and old John Wayne movies. But the *new* frontier was also a deft reference to Frederick Jackson Turner's theory of American history as shaped by the old frontier (and menaced by its closing). It was, naturally, Camelot's house historian, Arthur Schlesinger, Jr., who suggested the concept—he had given a lecture in March of 1960 called "New Frontiers of American Liberalism." Five months later, accepting the Democratic nomination in Los Angeles, Kennedy told the convention, "I stand tonight facing west on what was once the last frontier. . . . Today some would say that those struggles are all over, that all the horizons have been explored." Turner himself had feared that. But now the young candidate gave him this answer: "We stand today on the edge of a new frontier—the frontier of the 1960s, a frontier of unfulfilled hopes and threats. . . . Beyond that frontier are uncharted areas of science and space, unsolved problems of peace and war, unconquered pockets of ignorance and prejudice, unanswered questions of poverty and surplus, . . . I am asking each of you to be new pioneers on that new frontier." This use of Turner to transcend Turner matched Teilhard's use of geological strata (barysphere, lithosphere, hydrosphere) to transcend mere "stratism" with a liberating new "envelope" for the earth, a thing exploding outward as well as containing—the Noosphere; horizons opening eventually on an ultimate horizon, the "last thing," Omega. "For every circle of the world," he wrote, "mystery lies in the next circle."

Despite what he himself called "the ambitious splendor of my ideas," Teilhard was by temperament retiring and unassertive. All who met him were impressed by his exquisite manners, the well-bred combination of poise with deference. He was the fourth of eleven children, born in 1881 on a modest country estate in Auvergne—his father practical, mother pious, the stern and the serene, their spheres clearly marked, merging only with the formal nod that such worlds give each other (as when farm workers clattered in for evening devotions, presided over by Teilhard *père*). Teilhard *mère* kept a picture of the Sacred Heart at the home's front door, the talisman of entry there; and Teilhard—whose religious imagination lacked all other iconography whether of crib or crucifix or Pantokrator—remained devout all his life to this crude symbol (Jesus pointing to his own heart, worn on his shirtfront, lumpy as a clown's satiric war medal).

Young Teilhard was an obedient son, as he would be an obedient religious all his life. There was never a break or rebellion with his parents, or any but fond memories of home. His brother Albéric described the family astringently as "the glass-encased kind," but Pierre either did not notice or did not resent its museum atmosphere. He later wrote of his years at home, "I doubt that one could be happier on earth than I was during that time." As a child he had worshiped an iron ploughshare, his *dieu de fer*, as "everlasting"—until he learned, with sadness, about oxidation. His affections were redirected from iron to stones, which held magic for him, not for what they did, but what they did not do: "the cherished substance," he remembered as his life was ending, "had to be resistant, unassailable, hard." Flowers he thought of as "scandalously inconsistent and destructible." The only insects that caught his fancy were hard-shelled beetles, miniature tanks, slow and stolid but enclosed and tough. He must have liked turtles, too, surviving in a clamped-up state disguised as stones. At the age of eleven, when he entered a Jesuit school (where Henri Bremond was one of his teachers), he had become something of a turtle himself: Bremond called him "disconcertingly well-behaved" and impenetrable: "The most backward and thick-skulled member of the class occasionally came alive. . . . But he, never."

Under the shell, a wound had been given—one around which all his thought would, like layer on layer of scar tissue, be built up in ridged intricate hardness: "I was five or six. My mother had snipped off a few of my curls. I picked up one and held it close to the fire. The hair was burnt up in a fraction of a second." It was bad enough to know his *dieu de fer* was quietly succumbing to its own red fires of rust. He lived in a world being consumed. Even his stones would fade. And what of him?—he was closer, obviously, to frivolous destructible butterflies than to iron or rocks. He could be taken in a gulp. Compared to iron and stone, he *was* being hourly devoured; his breath was fuel to his own fires, became the fire—*he* was a fire; the quicker he flared, the quicker he would fade: "A terrible grief assailed me; I had learnt that I was perishable." Frequently he argues, in his later work, that a world without an outcome—or, rather, out*go* (French *issue*)—is suffocating, unbreathable, without psychic oxygen.

When he was nineteen, Teilhard entered the Jesuit order and, after his first years of formation, went to Egypt to teach science at a mission school. He greeted the unknown in his old way, from inside a shell of caution and politeness: "The students were very nice. . . . I have to withdraw rather so as not to lose my prestige in the familiarity of vacation time." He was often assigned the task of showing visitors around, and regretted that they preferred a seething Cairo to the desert—where he repaired whenever he could. Others found human artifacts there, from the periods of Greek and Roman occupation, but he preferred collecting crystals, fossils, beetles. In his letters, the students are referred to affectionately, but in the mass; nameless, no person singled out. Insects are individuated, with scientific and poetic description lavished on prize specimens. He encountered "the East, perceived, and avidly 'imbibed,' not at all from the point of view of its peoples and their history (as yet without interest for me), but in its light, its vegetation, its fauna and its deserts." At times he felt he should be taking interest in the peoples and their history: "These Orientals are big children, and I cannot forgive myself for not knowing Arabic; it would be so easy to make friends with them. . . ." Learning Arabic was a noble ambition that was to go unfulfilled. He concentrated on his entomology.

Teilhard's advanced theology training took place in a Jesuit house in England. His letters from there do not mention theological matters, nor once bring up a faculty member or course by name—though, in his rambles through the English countryside, he reports that a herd blocking his way had numbered sixty-three. He made scientific friends, and was allowed to participate in the search for remnants of the fraudulent Piltdown Man (he found a canine tooth). Excited by this discovery, he has been unfairly taxed for credulity—he was, after all, a scientific novice amid convinced experts. What is most important, from this period, is the confirmation in his own mind of a vocation within a vocation—to preach Christ by preaching evolution. He notes that this made him "hard," like the very stones he pondered: "All I remember from then on (and more about this magic word 'evolution' which kept coming back to my mind as a refrain, a delicacy, a promise, a call—), all I remember, I say, is the extraordinary hardness and power that overtook me at this time in the English countryside especially when I was lying in the sun, when the forests of Sussex were filled with the fossilized life for which I was searching on the cliffs of Wealden clay."

Teilhard had been ordained a priest by the time he was summoned to war as a stretcher bearer in World War I. He was thirty-three years old, and had spent almost half of those years in his Order. He rejoiced in his priestly ministrations—

Mass in the trenches, confessions of the dying, anointing of
the dead. He did calm brave service to the wounded, was
promoted to corporal and decorated. But he received more
than he gave in this experience, the most vivid of his life,
brighter even than his memories of the ploughshare or the
fire. Those first experiences, occurring in the under-glass placid-
ity of home, had brought terror to him. The war's impact,
felt in the mud and squalor of serving mangled men, was
oddly consolatory; he would always look back with fondness
on those days.

Up to this point Teilhard had groped for a solution to
his twin problems of change (the iron rusting) and death
(the hair obliterated); he sought the answer in evolution.
Though this concept was popularly thought to be at war with
conservatism, Teilhard took evolution as a principle of conservation: everything serves, all things are saved, nothing lost
—down to the smallest lock of one's hair. Our hairs are numbered, as men number the fossil lines in rock—marks of things
gone treated as still present in the mind, giving us a history,
forming us, giving us ourselves. But this is an ancient message
of comfort, and none too effective. We may pass; but the
world's atoms, even though shifting, stay. It is Shelley on
those "whose transmitted effluence cannot die," or Whitman
saying "All goes onward and outward, nothing collapses."

This makes man serve the cosmos, not the cosmos serve
man; leaves him lost in the vastness of time and space; useful,
but not essential. The aspect of evolution that Teilhard received most grudgingly was the idea that progress comes
about by random trial and error, accidentally. He preferred
Lamarck's concept of the higher species' self-determination by
"appetency" instead of Darwin's "natural selection"—and when
scientific orthodoxy made him show Lamarck out the front
door, he tried to sneak him in the back: "Properly understood
the 'anti-chance' of the Neo-Lamarckian is not a mere negation.
On the contrary it appears as the *utilization* of Darwinian
chance." What Teilhard needed was a linear undeviating process, in which all things are necessary, yet in which man

remains central. He would soon be constructing models that answered to this need—e.g., that of a pyramid, the whole structure focused from its widest base toward a narrowing point. Yet this must be a pyramid whose mass works with an inverse gravity of upward thrust, so that the wider its bottom, the sheerer its slope, the more will all weight throw its energies at and into the topmost point, carrying that point (man) *beyond itself.* The metaphor was satisfying: it got the best of both worlds, maintaining man as the culmination of nature (the value in old stable world-views) yet leaving him a further goal (the comforting aspect of progress philosophies). The larger space was seen to be (unthinkably) large, and the farther back time stretched (into abysses), the more important was man. Far from being lost in this immensity, he centered it all in him, in a union all the richer for the range of multiples focused in his consciousness.

This mental scheme of things, though useful, remained at some distance not only from evidence but from experience. It satisfied conceptually, without offering tangible solace. A personal element was lacking, an experience that summed up the theory—until Teilhard was given that experience in explosions of vision under artillery smoke.

Teilhard was a patriot from a line of patriots, entirely convinced of the justice of the French cause. "The present war is basically a struggle between two moralities. . . . It's Christian justice that we're fighting for." In this great work of God, he would rather bear a gun than a stretcher:

I assure you that I'd rather be throwing grenades or handling a machine gun than be a supernumerary as I am now. What I'm going to say may not be very orthodox—and yet I believe there's a core of truth in it: I feel that doing so I would be more a priest. Isn't a priest a man who has to bear the burden of life in all its forms, and shows by his own life how human work and love of God can be combined?

Teilhard criticized the doubters of the war for taking a too distant and intellectual view of it, rather than plunging into these birth throes of a future order. The doubter "can't admit that anything is impatient of his penetration and analysis." Disgust with the war he held to be a temptation. When his friend Jean Boussac warned him not to confuse "the brutal doings of military men and the insincere clap-trap of diplomats with the noble and silent transformation of Nature," Teilhard responded that his own view of evolution made it "essential to establish the validity of this comparison."

Teilhard lived with danger and men dying at the front, himself trodden into "the mud in which mud-colored figures were moving," ducking into shell holes "from which, all too often, if one wants to make room for oneself, one has to turn out some corpse, Boche or French." He was exhilarated by all this, and not downcast: "All whom I have seen die, died so simply"—and did it "in the finest of causes and on the most magnificent of stages." He was only dispirited when drawn back to the rear lines, where raucous and bawdy vitality in "ordinary" men offended him: "At such moments I long to dismiss all this world to its bottles or its bunk and build myself an ivory tower." He wrote to his cousin at such times, "In itself, the mass of humanity is profoundly inferior and repulsive." But this was only when men were allowed to relax, to pull apart, go separate ways, yield to the temptation of multiplicity (his favorite word of condemnation in this period). All was changed when they moved together back toward battle, sharing a common purpose and danger. Then Teilhard felt "the joy of forming part of a whole greater than oneself," the "excitement of battle," and "the healthy joy of death." He could almost feel evolution at work, himself and all round him turning, together, into something else.

To understand how much these sensations meant to Teilhard, the key work is his "Trois histoires comme Benson," translated as "Christ in the World of Matter" in *Hymn of the Universe*. This is the most intimate and revealing thing Teilhard ever wrote. Composed on the eve of an assault in which he fully expected to die, it is cast in the form of reminiscences about a friend who does die in that particular battle. He later apologized for sending it to his cousin, aware that he must have alarmed her with his ecstatic anticipation of death.

"Histoires *comme Benson* . . ." It is widely acknowledged that Teilhard came out of the war with his basic concepts formed; that he formed them from reflection on experience, not by studying other philosophers or theologians—or even other scientists. It is not as widely known that a key part of that war experience came from the books he lived with daily through those crucial years, all of them works of English fiction, largely futuristic or militaristic—the novels of Kipling, H. G. Wells, and Robert Hugh Benson. And the deepest impact was Benson's.

It is hard to recreate, now, the spell Monsignor Benson cast on English youth in the first years of this century (years when Teilhard was studying in England). A son of the Archbishop of Canterbury, he was an aesthete of the *fin de siècle* at Cambridge, reading the fashionable decadents, having the fashionable nervous breakdown, fashionably toying with the lure of Rome. What sets him apart is the sudden deep seriousness with which he took his conversion, and went off in quest of other converts. He engaged in quaint literary research with the romantic humbug, "Baron Corvo," then descended on Cambridge again, "fingers twitching" (as Shane Leslie wrote) "to baptize the next undergraduate he could thrill or mystify into the fold of Rome." (Ronald Firbank's was one of the first souls he bagged.) Benson's early work had the faery quality of a more orthodox Yeats, with touches of swashbuckling out of Robert Louis Stevenson. (When Benson wrote of Elizabethan priests being racked by Topcliffe, his own limbs thrilled with the pain.) As Benson toiled on at top speed, his work coarsened toward mere theological propaganda. By the time he died, burnt out at the age of forty-three, his life had become a veritable seizure of apostolic scribbling.

One of Benson's main themes was the power and burden of the priesthood, a theme which Teilhard dwelt on at his ordination just before the war, and in one of his earliest essays, "Le prêtre," written in 1918. Teilhard felt the priesthood was symbolized by his middle existence between the front lines and the rear, as courier between the living and the dead. The hero of Benson's collection of stories, *The Light Invisible*, says, "Years ago I was set apart as a priest to stand between the dead and the living. It was meant that I should be the meeting-place, as every priest must be, of Creation's need and God's grace—as every Christian must be in his station."

Another strong element in Benson is a belief in prayer, spiritual aspiration, and the strivings of the mind as palpable presences. Thus a church for him is thick with all the prayers breathed into and from it. Anything man has used is still in thrall, as it were, to his spirit: "I never can look at a piece of old furniture without a curious thrill at a thing that has been so much saturated with human emotion." A wooden confessional box breathes forgiveness over old mutters of guilt, since "human emotion has a power of influencing or saturating inanimate nature." This became an important principle to Teilhard—that lower things can be taken up into higher ones, which "envelope" and save them. There are direct reminiscences of Benson when Teilhard finds that a house he is billeted in used to be a Jesuit residence: "I have the feeling that a whole accumulated store of strength is around me, within these walls." And when he enters the Strasbourg cathedral, he writes "I had seldom realized what spiritual power is concentrated in a church loaded with whole centuries of prayer."

Another aspect of prayer's physical palpability emerges from Benson's "In the Convent Chapel"—a story Teilhard singles out for comment in his letters. The hero sees a cloistered nun at worship in a lonely church, her life set apart from life, useless in any practical sense—until the pulleys and conveyer belts of this spiritual plant become visible to the narrator, the Virgin's revenge on Henry Adams's dynamo:

First I became aware suddenly that there ran a vital connection from the Tabernacle to the woman. You may think of it as one of those bands you see in machinery connecting two wheels, so that when either wheel moves the other moves too. Or you may think of it as an electric wire, joining the instrument the telegraph operator uses with the pointer at the other end. At any rate there was this vital band or wire of life. . . . There ran out from this peaceful chapel lines of spiritual power that lost themselves in the distance, bewildering in their profusion and terrible in the intensity of their hidden fire.

Here is the germ of another Teilhardian image—that of "filaments" running through all creation, into and out of the node of highest energy, man's consciousness: "Traced as far as possible in the direction of their origins, the last fibres of the human aggregate are lost to view and are merged in our eyes with the very stuff of the universe. . . . Each of these fibres traverses each one of us, coming up from far below and stretching beyond and above us."

Even when Benson attacked science, it was in terms that Teilhard would incorporate into his view of science. There is nothing more Teilhardian, for instance, than this sentence from a story called "The Traveller": "The scientific view is that you are not justified in committing yourself one inch ahead of your intellectual evidence; the religious view is that in order to find out anything worth knowing your faith must always be a little in advance of your evidence; you must advance *en échelon*."

The obvious place to look for Teilhard's themes in Benson is the well-known (but late) apocalyptic novel, *The Lord of the World*. Teilhard did in fact read the final chapters of that novel at the front (they were translated in the *Revue Hebdomadaire*), and Speaight implies that "Trois histoires" was a result of this encounter. But Teilhard did not come across the *Revue* issue until late summer of 1918. (The book did influence his visionary tale, "The Spiritual Power of Matter," written at that time.) The *histoires* had been composed almost two years earlier, and he gives as their source the group of stories I have been quoting from, *The Light Invisible*, more especially that book's initial tale, "The Green Robe." The robe is earth's foliage seen as God's own garment, sweeping up to a vision of Him through and in its folds—what

Teilhard would later describe as the green film of our "biosphere" opening out to the Noosphere.

Teilhard in 1916 gives us three visions recounted to a disciple by a wise priest at the end of his life. In each vision, personal memory and passages from Benson merge and blend, always centered around a physical object—a picture, a monstrance (the sunburst vessel used to expose the large eucharistic Host in processions or at benediction), and a pyx (the wafer box in which consecrated Hosts are carried by a priest taking communion to someone outside a church).

The Picture: The hero of the tales tells the narrator, in this first one, of a problem he had felt, "partly philosophical, partly aesthetic"—how to depict Christ without giving him an individuality too exclusive. He was looking at a painting of the Sacred Heart as he meditated on this difficulty (one that had vitiated this very painting), when the features began to disjoin, become jumbled, fall out of focus. What replaced the vulgar particularity was not diminution or mere blur, but new richness. He closes this tale by saying that the picture's blend of all pain and joy in an aureoled non-specificity was glimpsed only one other time by him, "in the glance of a dying soldier."

Teilhard was coupling two experiences here, the childhood one of gazing at his mother's Sacred Heart picture, and that of watching men die in battle. In one of his letters he describes such a moment:

The only man who knows right in the innermost depths of his being the weight and grandeur of war is the man who goes over the top with bayonet and grenade. In that moment training, of course, and a sort of intoxication play a large part; but even so it is still true that the infantryman leaving his trench for the attack is a man apart, a man who has lived a minute of life of which other men have simply no conception. . . . My best friend in the regiment, and the finest soldier I've yet known, poor Commandant Lefebvre—to make sure that his Africans followed him, he was the first out of the trench, waving his *képi* and shouting, "En avant, mes amis, c'est pour la France!" Twenty paces further on, he fell, making the sign of the cross. . . .

These events gave Teilhard the sensation of walking the very borderline between life and death: "Thus, the day before yesterday, one of our best captains was badly hit; it was then more than at any other time perhaps that I felt the power of the priest." The war gave Teilhard an experience not unlike that undergone by Dostoyevsky when he faced the prospect of execution and was at the last moment reprieved: the presence of death heightened all aspects of life, gave them deeper color, new reality. One becomes conscious of the basic miracle of minimal being in such crisis situations. Much of Dostoyevsky's work, with its almost Keystone acceleration of complex encounters, tries to recreate the weird beauties that lie in danger—a world in which, as Chesterton's Ogier sings, "the barest branch is beautiful/One moment, while it breaks." Prince Myshkin, the epileptic, feels this as his nerves sharpen blissfully toward seizure. Here was the horizon experience that made him seek, "at the vague line where earth and sky meet, the solution of it all." He indulges in delicious anticipation of his fit:

He wanted to be alone, so as to give himself up entirely and passively to this agonizing feeling of insufferable strain, without seeking to escape it. . . . His sensation of being alive and his awareness increased tenfold at those moments which flashed by like lightning. . . . He clung with all his mind and memory to every external object. . . . The moment by itself was, of course, worth the whole of life. . . . "At that moment the extraordinary saying that *there shall be time no longer* becomes, somehow, comprehensible to me."

Teilhard resented the stumbling into battle unexpectedly, without prior concentration on approaching danger. "When that happens, the mind can no longer dwell on any distant prospect, and you gradually find yourself living as though you were no longer of this world. At Ypres we were thrown into battle without having had the time to realize what was happening to us; this time we could savor at leisure the slow approach of the great day—and to all those who were capable of reflection, this anticipation brought a ripening of the soul."

But Teilhard did not feel death as mere dissolution, making his farewell to life intensely sweet. Death was a border against which man must fearlessly press, to enter a higher state. This was the healthy joy in death—a living forward into evolution's next stage. For Dostoyevsky, too, the thrill of death had a positive side, a merging that would come only from surrender of one's separate identity. Thus, in the elated mournfulness of Father Zossima's death, Alyosha feels bound by Teilhardian "fibres" to each farthest thing in the universe, tingling out to the very stars by this vicarious absorption in their processes:

Alyosha stood, gazed, and suddenly threw himself down on the earth. He did not know why he embraced it. He could not have told why he longed so irresistibly to kiss it, to kiss it all. But he kissed it weeping, sobbing and watering it with his tears, and vowed passionately to love it, to love it forever and ever. . . . In his rapture he was weeping even over those stars, which were shining to him from the abyss of space, and "he was not ashamed of that ecstasy." There seemed to be threads from all those innumerable worlds of God, linking his soul to them, and it was trembling all over "in contact with other worlds."

Here was the experimental answer to Teilhard's problem of finding spiritual comfort in the doctrine of evolution. Though life's processes merely use man on the way to higher things, a man can enjoy those future things, have foreglimpses of coming good, by an act of loving abandonment to history's workings. Grind however hard they will, the wheels of the machine merely aid one in the task of self-transcendence. In that way, the war was beautiful, an instrument of personal delivery and fulfillment. Teilhard would shortly be writing his essay "La nostalgie du Front," a paean to the trenches and the dying men: "I feel as if I had lost a Soul, a Soul greater than my own that inhabits the front line." His experiences there allowed him to conduct a laboratory test, as it were, in the crucible of his own body, on the concepts he had worked out in an abstract way. Benson had written, in the story Teilhard relies on most, that "spiritual perception . . . is the faculty by which we verify for ourselves what we have received on authority and hold by faith."

The creation of new spiritual worth out of human suffering is figured often enough in Benson's *Light Invisible*—e.g., when the hero brings news of tragedy to a woman and glimpses her angel's face above, a face on which "the intensest pain and the intensest joy lie together. . . . Anguish and ecstasy were one." Such experiences are likened by Benson to "the first steps on the other side of death." But the focal point in Teilhard's story is the transfiguration of Christ's picture, which pulses with a shimmering quality derived from Benson's "The Green Robe." There the priest sees physical and spiritual worlds (what Teilhard would later describe as the world and one's interpretation of it) "as if on the same plane . . . as if when you looked at the sky, you saw both the sky and your own thought at once, on the same plane." Teilhard's hero, looking at the particularity of the Sacred Heart portrait and at his aesthetic objection to such overparticularity, sees the two merge: "It was as though the planes which marked off the figure of Christ from the world surrounding it were melting into a single vibrant surface whereon all demarcation ceased."

The vision is sudden in both cases, and gives hints of a personal beauty beneath nature's woven robe. Teilhard writes, "It was, then, as I was deeply pondering over these things and looking at the picture, that my vision began. To tell the truth, I cannot say at what precise moment it began, for it had already reached a certain degree of intensity when I became conscious of it." (Benson: "*Now I cannot tell you how the vision began. . . . It must have come upon me and enthralled me so swiftly that my brain had no time to reflect.*") Teilhard describes Christ's vibrant robe, in which "I could see the stitches running on and on indefinitely . . . marvelously woven by the continuous co-operation of all energies and the whole order of matter." (Benson: "*Right in the center lay a pale agate stitched delicately into the robe with fine dark stitches; overhead the blue lining of this silken robe arched out. I was conscious that this robe was vast beyond my con-*

ception, and that I stood as it were in a fold of it.") "And always, beneath this moving surface, upholding it and at the same time gathering it into a higher unity, there hovered the incommunicable beauty of Christ himself." (Benson: *"But clearer than any other thought, stood out in my mind the certainty that this robe had not been flung down and left, but that it clothed a Person. And even as this thought showed itself a ripple ran along the high relief in dark green, as if the wearer of the robe had just stirred."*)

Teilhard's own personal note remains strong through all these borrowings—especially when, to account for the glimmering throb of the picture, his mind is drawn again and again to the Sacred Heart as source for "all this movement." The crude symbol has been made subtle: the heart is generalized in a way that the face can never be. And in all depictions of this heart, there is a wound in the side, and fire bursting out above. Things broken release a fire that is both their inner self and something better than the self. The Sacred Heart had become, for Teilhard, a continual death from which streams life.

The Monstrance: Though Teilhard's fictional narrator is recounting things said to him before a death in battle, the scene of these discussions is the romantic dark room as necessary to Yeats as to Poe for telling such tales. In "Poena Damni," another *Light Invisible* story, Benson's hero is startled into a train of thought "by the red lamp on the table," glowing like the fires of hell. In Teilhard's second tale, a vision of the past is called up when the narrator turns on a lamp "made of diaphanous sea-green glass" which diffused light through "the entire mass of crystal."

What the lamp reminds Teilhard's hero of is the eucharistic Host in a monstrance, a Host hypnotically bloated with white energy, silvering all things in its milky translucence—until "through the mysterious expansion of the Host the whole world had become incandescent, had itself become like a single giant Host." Here, too, Teilhard draws on a war experience, that of his "solitary, and how romantic, 'noctambulations'" at the front: "Yesterday evening, in particular, I was favored by a wonderful moon. . . . I savored as a rare experience this veil of poetry flung over the formidable array of two civilizations, at grips, right before my eyes, with one another." In the story, once the divine whiteness has spread illimitably out, over, and through all things, its fires turn back upon themselves, drawing all that is "savable" back to original unity, volatilizing off certain indigestible "dross" in the process. This recalls another battle evening: "Solitary and majestic, the moon, which a fortnight before had been invisible, disengaged itself from the ridges of black soil, and seemed to glide across the barbed wire. Is it the moon that rises over the dark trenches this evening, or is it the earth, a unified earth, a new earth?" The earth, and what the earth will be; the real and, simultaneously, its own self-transcendence—that is what he saw in an earth he both stood on and yet saw above him in its moon-mirror, reflecting back into present time its own perfected future, the eucharistic sublimated world.

The Pyx: Teilhard often carried consecrated Hosts at the front, to give communion to dying men, or those risking death. The immensity of the little thing he carried, the casualness of a transaction normally reserved for solemn rites in church, impressed him often. He wrote to his cousin: "This morning, as I thought about the Master so close to me and yet still so incompletely united with me, I was so entirely filled once again with the infinite mystery of the contact and fusion of beings." In his third story, Teilhard's hero recounts this same experience, but reflects on the fact that even when he gives himself communion out of the pyx, "though the Bread I had just eaten had become flesh of my flesh, nevertheless it remained outside me." The deeper "the divine particle" sank into his mind, the more it fled before him: "Its center was receding from me as it drew me on." As in the second vision, one looks up to the moon one is also standing on. The Host could not be enveloped; its effect, rather, was to open the hero out toward all things. The wafer was all smooth elusive surface, contact with which was frustrating, a repulse—but if one did not try to strain and beat at the surface, other energies radiated from within. Paradoxically, the "outside" could not be touched; only the "inside," responding to his own interior longing. The straightest way was therefore a detour—to the surface from behind it; to that supreme Within by way of all other "withins." In the trench, Teilhard felt he could not reach the Host placed up against him in the pyx, because the only way to it was through all other beings. The Host of the world had to be lifted up (with him in it) in order to become the Host so deceptively near and small in his pocket.

Benson's 1903 stories had tried in many ways to suggest that "the other side" of life, of death, of the obvious, is closer to us than the hither side. When his hero sees God's mantle, all its external embroidery, he does so by standing inside one of its folds. The same man looks outward to find his thought, as on a pane of glass; the world reflecting depths *off* its surface if we refuse to focus solely *on* that surface. His priest lifts the Host at Mass, and sees all the world's scenes in it. One must look past the surface always: "Across this material world of light and color there cut a plane of the spiritual world, and where the planes crossed I could look through and see what was beyond." The seen world is mere shadow of the unseen, a shadow that falls crookedly, always slightly off true balance. In one story an angel is seen "leaning at a sharp angle to one side; but it did not appear to be grotesque. Instead the world seemed tilted; the chestnut tree was out of the perpendicular; the wall out of the horizontal. The true level was that of the man." Here is the hint for Teilhard's constant talk of progress along an axis that is placed aslant man's more limited strivings. Our acts are insensibly bent *from* the bias, *toward* the true.

All these insights came home to Teilhard as he pressed the pyx close to his chest, held the Host in his hand, took it into his mouth. He could not possess by grabbing, only by giving; or by being given up. He had wanted the ploughshare to be whole, and his, and immune to rot. But one cannot possess the smooth completed separate things of surfaces. One can "have" the iron only by mingling one's own aspiration with the fire-rot of its self-transcending rust. One "keeps" the lock of hair by following it into the hearth, where its reality is released by fire, as one's heart is freed by suffering, one's mind cleared by war, one's faith strengthened in the presence of death. The fire could not win, after all, if one became the fire. He would later write, "Throughout my life, *through* my life, the world has little by little caught fire in my sight until, aflame all around me, it has become almost completely luminous from within."

Communion, therefore, is not a rub of surfaces, but the breaking open of inner springs, fiery springs. To be is to be consumed. This paradox was also a solution—it gave Teilhard the polarities of all his later thought: outer vs. inner, surface vs. radial, position vs. axis, stability vs. change, appearance vs. reality. One finds one's higher self in the beneficent destruction of all lower selves. Teilhard's hero ends the three tales with an ecstatic certitude that he goes toward his own center when he flings himself outward into the army's struggle:

In a few days' time we shall be thrown into battle for the recapture of Douaumont: a grandiose, almost a fantastic exploit which will mark and symbolize a definitive advance of the world in the liberation of souls. And I tell you this: I shall go into this engagement in a religious spirit, with all my soul, borne on by a single great impetus in which I am unable to distinguish where human emotions end and adoration begins. And if I am destined not to return from those heights I would like my body to remain there, moulded into the clay of the fortifications, like a living cement thrown by God into the stone-work of the New City.

The question posed by a premonition of human suffering (the lock of hair discarded and consumed) was answered for Teilhard in the presence of human suffering and death. All the rest of his work would be an attempt to express this answer in new language, recalling the experience to himself, trying to share it with others, casting it in less personal terms, weaving it into his scientific activities. And so, using a British popularizer, this strange priest in the French army was preparing the rationale for a weird American optimism, voiced half a century after Benson's vogue and a decade after Teilhard's own death. By anticipating that death, forging proleptic comforts against its mystery, he became the posthumous theologian to Camelot.

SIX

The Two Jackies

Dwight Eisenhower, the painter, declared that
he wasn't too certain what was art, but he knew what
he liked, and Harry Truman, the pianist, said
of something he didn't like that if it was art,
he was a Hottentot. Jacqueline Kennedy, the
connoisseur, makes both look like Hottentots.

—WILLIAM MANCHESTER

IN 1961, AFTER THE GLITTERING VERSAILLES DINNER with De Gaulle, President Kennedy told newsmen, "I am the man who accompanied Jacqueline Kennedy to Paris." It was gracious exaggeration of a truth. Much of what was called the "Kennedy style" was in fact a kind of Bouvier style. The President's wife did not like Hyannis Port, touch football in the sand, or what she called "going on corny sails." She meant to bring to the White House as much of Versailles as she could, and as little of Boston. All Camelot's princes had to dance attendance on her. While Jack ruled, Jackie reigned. Norman Mailer, smitten yet suspicious, called her both "the nation's Muse" and "an institution being put together before our eyes." Even more than her husband, she symbolized, for a while, an America of vast wealth and power well used, of healthy young self-esteem, of glamor mobilized to get things done. The old Left had been a dreary bunch; now liberals possessed a diamond with cutting edge, a princess even paupers could look up to.

Catholics had the Pope, their own John, to balance against "secular John" in the White House. But for a while they had no Jackie. By the rules of the game, Mrs. Kennedy—though formally a Catholic—could not be theirs; she and her husband represented "the world" as a Catholic option, not the church. The sensitive women of Fifties Catholicism—and especially the Earth Mothers—were not at home with the cool contemporary style of newer liberals. There were, of course, plenty of Catholic women to advise the Kennedy administration, from Barbara Ward to Sister Francetta Barberis (first head of the Women's Job Corps). When Sargent Shriver had trouble with rumored immorality around a job-training center for girls, Francetta would descend on the place, irreproachable herself, to quell the excitement. But that was the trouble—the competent nun-administrator was, like the lady scholar, just not exciting enough. There was Sister Corita, of course, perhaps too excitable, unable to contain herself at sight of a catsup bottle. For a while Soeur Sourire sang "Dominique" on the Ed Sullivan show—but she could not even speak English. The job was still vacant.

Sister Francetta solved the problem by introducing to Washington circles her successor as President at Webster College in Missouri, a woman whose very name (*Jacqueline* Grennan) and age (mid-thirties) fit the mood of the times and went with the role she wanted to play in them. If Providence could arrange for two Johns, why not for symmetrical Jackies? She soon became the New Frontier's favorite nun, the other Jackie, "Sister J." She loved the life of commuting and committeeing, picking up honorary degrees on the run, a flying nun in the first "jet set" of Kennedy days, the kind that wanted to turn the nation around. She talked with jerky hand gestures about options, "multiple alternatives," and "orders of magnitude." As flexible response became the keynote of Kennedy's foreign policy, she told her girls to become "guerrilla fighters of the grace life." Neustadt had blamed Eisenhower because "he exchanged his hero's welcome for much less than its full value in the currency of power." Sister Jackie urged Webster students to "put your power on a value basis," as the only appropriate form of gratitude to those who "trust power into us." Formally opening her first year as President of Webster, she promised to get things moving again: "History records. Men do. Let us begin."

Her love affair with the Kennedy administration did not go unrequited. JFK himself inscribed his picture for her: "From one frontiersman to another." She was appointed to his advisory panels on education and urban affairs, and became a consultant to Headstart and the Peace Corps. *Life* did a picture story on her as "a woman who could run U. S. Steel as easily as a college." She joked about her White House "clearance," and retailed Kennedy stories picked up in Washington corridors. All the fads of the time were guides for her soul:

—The Pope's election had made 1958 Year One: "These wonderful kids . . . have a nineteen-year lead on me [*Sister J. had become thirty-nine by this time, and was talking to twenty-year-olds*] because they are twenty in the post-John XXIII world."

—"One of the men in whom I recognize a little piece of myself is Karl Rahner, the great Jesuit theologian and philosopher."

—"Harvey Cox, in his very illuminating book *The Secular City* . . . defines his role as the role of prophecy [*she means the role of a prophet*]."

—"Another exciting book, written many years ago but suppressed for a long time by my own church and now republished [*she means published*] is *The Phenomenon of Man.* . . . Teilhard is probably the one who has had the most profound influence on my own thinking."

—But her highest and first hero was, always, Kennedy: she compares that "line I think all of us love from the Kennedy inaugural"—*The torch is passed to a new generation*—to the Spirit's fiery coming at Pentecost, when "God, indeed, passed on his life to the future of man."

So devout was her Jackolatry that she revived for him an old art form, the hagiographical parable, a *genre* fallen into disuse since Bill Stern stopped broadcasting his shaped little vignettes from sports life:

When John Kennedy called a press conference one Sunday afternoon in the White House, a CBS cub reporter made a terrible mistake. You are always supposed to be on instant call if you are on White House duty, and the young reporter forgot to tell them where he would be. Kennedy called the press conference. The reporters came and the news broadcast was video-taped. And, as the poor cub reporter ran into the White House, the ABC and NBC reporters were going out and the film was finished.

The cub reporter went in and moaned to Pierre Salinger: "I'm finished; do you realize, I'm finished! No man makes a mistake like this! Not only do I lose this job but I'll lose any possible job in television in the future." As Salinger was trying to console him, the President of the United States strode into the room and asked what the matter was.

The young reporter, still in emotional anguish, poured out his story to the President of the United States. And John Kennedy smiled and said, "Suppose we do it again." Then, with no one knowing it, the President gave the press interview completely and exactly as he had done it a few minutes earlier, and no one on the news broadcast that night knew the difference. He did it to save one cub reporter who was trying.

This is, as Sister Jackie puts it, a lovely little tale; it should be included in the Kennedy "fioretti." To appreciate its supernatural character, one must study its details. A cub reporter (the very term puts us in storyland) is given the White House as his beginner's assignment, yet manages to miss his first press conference, from which ABC and NBC depart with their video-tapes (so our poor hero is a cub *camera*man, not a reporter—or, rather, both: he is the only man from CBS who can cover the event). But the bad luck of missing the public appearance is matched by the good luck of getting Kennedy all to himself ("with no one knowing it") immediately afterward. The saint's majesty is emphasized at first ("the President of the United States strode into the room"), to be played off against his humble softening: "John Kennedy smiled." The President then "gave the press interview completely and exactly as he had done it a few minutes earlier." What does that mean? Were reporters' questions, as well as his own answers, recalled verbatim? Or had Kennedy just filmed an announcement, for which there would be press-release copies in abundance? But the character of the pericope is not fully authenticated till the end, when Jesus (as it were) claps his hands and the clay bird comes to life: though the cub reporter still does not have a videotape to match the ABC and NBC ones, "no one on the news broadcast that night knew the difference." Apocrypha do not traffic in the probable.

Though Kennedy's death shattered the nation, it had special impact on Sister Jackie. Even three years later—when Camelot had begun to dim, for some, under criticism of Vietnam—she stayed loyal and affirmed that "I need to believe in Robert MacNamara [still Secretary of Defense] in these troubled days." In 1967, during a long and revealing speech, she took the University of Missouri into her confidence about the most important thing that had ever happened to her. It is a tale of life rising out of death, Cuban triumph out of disaster, laughter out of ordeal, comfort out of intimacy, the tears of life out of barren disorientation. A chain of events and memories leads to the rebirth of Jackie (after being entombed in St. Patrick's, and in herself) to new consecration and a path marked out for her. The mantle has passed on. The successor, knowing her duty, faces life:

The most important anecdote [*she seems to mean episode*] of my own personal life took place in two settings [*and so was two episodes*]. One was in the Executive Office Building of the [*she means next to the*] White House on the day after the Second Cuban Affair. Dr. Jerome B. Wiesner, who was Mr. Kennedy's science advisor, came into a meeting that I was attending and said, "Jacqueline, walk down the corridor with me. You and I have often talked about humility and courage," he continued [*she means he opened*], "I still don't know how to define them, but I want

you to know I'm sure I watched them yesterday." He had watched
Jack Kennedy look nuclear warfare in the face to know it was
there [*well that's one way*], to know it was possible, to know
there existed some moment in time that was better than any other
moment in time [*for making one's move, she seems to mean*],
some degree of force that was better than any other degree of
force [*she goes back to the doctrine of flexible response*], some
juxtaposition of that moment and that degree of force that was
better than any other juxtaposition, to know that he was the
President of the United States and that he had to make a decision
and he didn't have a hell of a chance to hit it [*Sister!*], but that
not to make a decision was to make the worst possible decision
[*a doctrine that was Neustadt's worst bequest to Kennedy, and
the cause of the crisis in the first place*]. Wiesner said: "I can't
define humility and courage, but I know I watched them yesterday."

Thirteen months later, I was in a hotel room in New York
City alone when I heard the first terrible announcement that the
President of the United States had been shot. I went through
all those hours unable to cry. I walked the streets of New York
and went to St. Patrick's and tried to pray, came back and glutted
myself with the television playbacks, trying to make some sense out
of the world. Late into the night, some station replayed the
Rocking Chair Conference in the Oval Room of the White House.
Earlier in the interview, one of the network men asked: "Mr.
President, were your advisers wrong in the Bay of Pigs?"

"I don't know," Kennedy said. "I was President of the United
States, and I obviously took bad advice."

About ten minutes later, Sander Vanocur, who was his friend,
played the role a friend always plays, the compassionate, loving,
supportive role [*so much for the cub-reporter ethics of the press*]:
"Mr. President, were your advisers right in the Second Cuban
Affair?"

Kennedy, with that beautiful sense of humor that one wishes
all presidents shared [*so much for then-President Johnson*], said:
"I don't know, I was the President of the United States, and I
obviously took good advice."

And with that, all of the grief and all of the terror welled
up and I wept in my hotel room alone, and I remember beating
the pillow and saying aloud, over and over to myself, "My God,
that's the kind of human being I want to be."

Mere apocrypha yield, at this point, to active Imitation of the
Saints. Kennedy ceased, in death, to be "the secular John."

Now Catholic poet Brother Antoninus could compare Mrs. Kennedy standing over the casket to the Virgin of *pietá* convention holding the dead Jesus in her lap. Sister Jackie, accepting the mantle of the fallen leader, felt a new urgency to reach out toward the world:

If I share at all in the power which is God, then I ought to be the greatest gambler in the history of mankind. I ought to go where nobody else will go. I ought to look at what nobody else will look at. I have often said to our own students at home that a prostitute ought to be able to be most comfortable with a Roman Catholic sister because it was the Christ who went out to the women of the Pharisees [*sic*], the women [*she means woman*] taken in adultery, the woman at the well.

Sin had, after all, come into the secular city (so recently an Eden)—Kennedy's death was a second fall of man. The whole City of Man was stained now, needing to be cleansed. Sister Jackie still talked of the exciting challenges she faced as a nun reforming her church; but she also sensed that more crucial issues had arisen: "Young Negroes, I think, are perhaps the one group that has even greater privileges and greater challenges than I. If I had a reincarnated life to live, I would love to be one of those students in the seventh row." Convents were no longer "where it's at." Ghettos were. The pace was picking up. Committees and commuting were no longer as much in the news as marches, picketing, shootings down South, and good men gone to jail.

The change was seismic, it shook even Thomas Merton in his cell. The Trappist's message for the Fifties was that men should flee the world, entirely; or, if they could not do that, retreat from it often, live as much apart, as insulated from its evil, as possible. Merton had given up the duties of citizenship along with some of its privileges—e.g., the duty to be misinformed by radio or newspaper of politicians' comparative mendacities. But now he yearned back toward the struggle, spoke of apocalypse and evil's time, of the spreading darkness that had swallowed Kennedy. He ached to join the March on Washington, envied the religious ardor of black militant orders (like reincarnated Knights of Malta or St. John). He said men should read the new "Moses and the Prophets—Martin Luther King, James Baldwin and the others," and admitted to Baldwin: "Humanly, there is no hope [for racial peace], at least on the white side—that is where I unfortunately am." He, like Sister J., would trade places with those blacks "in the seventh row," if only he could. He told white liberals that any counsel of moderation was now implicitly fascist, an argument that "revolution must be prevented at all costs; but demonstrations are already revolutionary; *ergo* fire on the demonstrators; *ergo* . . ."

Whither Merton only yearned, unconfined priests and sisters could go—and Jackie, too, was on the move. She had begun with a determination to engage in dialogue (she called it "intertalking") with the world. She wanted teachers from "outside" to give courses at Webster College, and Webster's Catholics to teach in the secular schools. But then the question occurred to her (as, in time, it was bound to do)—why *inter*talk, when one can just talk? Why think in terms of outsiders and insiders, this side and that side? Isn't the very existence of specifically Catholic colleges an insult to other schools, a suggestion of rivalry (however friendly)? One should not stand over against people in their need, but with them, fully in and of them. So she "laicized" Webster College—brought her Order to surrender control of it into laymen's hands. She still talked like a Kennedy, but was adding harsher notes—of admiration for the Free Speech movement at Berkeley, for antiwar poet Dan Berrigan, and for "participatory democracy" (the slogan of SDS, the Students for a Democratic Society). She was "with it"—though "it" was getting harder every day to stay with.

Younger Catholics were too nimble for her. The SDS itself had strong Catholic appeal from the outset. Its founding document, the Port Huron Statement, was written by Tom Hayden, a Catholic by birth and education. Though he no longer considered himself a member of the church by 1963, he could still quote Pope John in his famous Statement, and that Statement in turn prompted Father David Kirk to join the SDS and, later on, to found Emmaus House in New York, the creator of liturgies to have a revolution by. Catholics were in the very thick of things. Their own church had finally admitted to the need for change, and vivid (belated) realization of that need pushed priests and nuns into the forefront of groups seeking change throughout society. Catholics were the first to burn their own draft cards and to vandalize selective service records. The toughest fair-housing movement of the mid-Sixties was led by a priest in Milwaukee, James Groppi. The harshest critic of any bishop's stand on race was a priest in Los Angeles, William Dubay—he reported Cardinal McIntyre's attitude to Rome, and was driven from the exercise of his priesthood. A Josephite priest, Philip Berrigan, went on trial as the leader of "the Baltimore Four" (which raided a draft board). With his brother, Jesuit priest Daniel Berrigan, he was convicted a second time with "the Catonsville Nine." Three Maryknoll missionaries, expelled from Guatemala for revolutionary attitudes, ended up in American jails for anti-war actions. A diocesan priest from Detroit joined seminarians of "the D.C. Nine" in actions against Dow Chemical, manufacturer (at the time) of napalm. A Dominican priest argued natural law with his prosecutors as a member of "the Milwaukee Fourteen." Other priests were involved in "the Rochester Ten" and "the New York Eight."

Priests and nuns did not stream onto the streets all at once, of course. Like Sister Jacqueline herself, they started close in toward shore and moved by stages out to rougher water. In 1961, when a priest was arrested in Oklahoma during a civil rights demonstration, his bishop established a rationale that would be often used over the next few years: while calling open political protests "the forum of the laity," Bishop Victor J. Reed excused the priest's participation as a rare but exemplary act that can be tried "in the absence of sufficient lay activity." He had prodded a bee's nest for his brother bishops —the issue of approval by superiors became the first battleground for clerical activists. When Philip Berrigan tried to join a freedom ride in the South, his superior publicly recalled him en route, and he turned back. Daniel Berrigan was exiled to Mexico for his activities as a founder of Clergy and Laity Concerned About Vietnam.

This surge of street activity and protest put Sister Jackie in two minds. By the end of 1966, though she could still praise "purists" like David Harris for their contribution to public awareness, she made it clear that those who actually achieve the goals desired are the people willing to work in responsible positions, "tacticians" like Robert McNamara and herself. She was willing to grant purists their use, as keeping pragmatists honest: "Because I am a tactician, I am in danger of being a fink." But she was increasingly testy at the way Left ideologues denied *her* any useful role, smugly dismissing "the responsible game of action." She lectured the Movement that "there is no way to go back to the sanctuary or to Walden Pond," and criticized them for not being where the real action is, in decision-making offices: "Having chosen not to decide what play to call on Saturday or Sunday afternoon, we must not smugly stand on Monday morning and say if we had only been coaching we would have done it all the right way." She still offered as the supreme idea, combining purity and tactics, Jack Kennedy's "rare paradox of ambition and humility: ambition to say, 'Where can I make the greatest impact? Where can I be the most powerful?' and then to take the awfully humble position of saying, 'I will try for it!'"

Other Catholic liberals also felt embattled. Monsignor George Higgins, "labor priest" of the old National Catholic Welfare Conference, thought younger Catholics had fallen victim to "the Selma Syndrome," a belief that all problems can be solved in the streets, with shouts and placards. Monsignor Daniel Cantwell, once a champion of clerical activism, asked: "Is the trend among clergy to envision themselves as ward committeemen any healthier for religion or politics than the distant unhappy situations in which we recall knight-bishops, cardinal-chancellors, or the voice of Royal Oak, Michigan?" Father Andrew Greeley, would-be canonizer of Jack Kennedy, became Daniel Berrigan's leading denigrator.

To criticize the political system itself (and not merely some particular decision made within it) was to deny John Kennedy's "capture" of the secular for God. The System was now God's system, and not to be challenged. As Teilhard wrote of those who doubt the gradual progress of all things toward enlightenment, "There can be no place for the poor in spirit, the sceptics, the pessimists, the sad of heart, the weary and the immobilists." It is the same protest that Harvey Cox had made against those who doubt that the System can be made to work: "For the Bible, there are no powers anywhere which are not essentially tameable and ultimately humanizable. To deny this, in word or deed, is to 'worship the creature rather than the Creator,' to open the door and readmit the banished furies, to genuflect before some faceless Kismet." In the past, idolatry had been interpreted as bowing down to Caesar. For Cox, it became just the opposite—a refusal to trust the machinery of modern urban and secular power.

Liberals had, then, finally realized (as they settled into power themselves) that Power Purifies. The whole mystique of the two Johns was based on a belief that awesome responsibilities sober those who bear them, instill a wisdom not granted men of lesser sway. These latter people are mere sideline critics, not tested by experience in the game. "Decision-making," according to Sister Jacqueline, "must be the essential human act"; and those not in a position to make the big decisions could not even be true critics, merely writers of ridicule and "empty satires":

The satires, I think, belong to the nineteenth-century romantic poets who wrote ivory-tower satires that offered no resolutions, no first hunches, no first approximations, but condemned all of society around them. The poet took on the role of the high priest without the commitment of the priest. This, I think, would be terribly dangerous in our society. On the other hand, the responsible involvement of one who is willing to go in and make some of the hunches and to live with the hunches and to say he made mistakes if his hunches turn out wrong, and remake some others [*sic*], could reshape and remake the American society.

The cult of power, of the decision-making process as a purifying one, is expressed—along with all the other fads of the early Sixties—in Morris West's novel, *The Shoes of the Fisherman*. There a Pope of tomorrow, modeled on John XXIII, deals with a Premier and a President modeled after Khrushchev and Kennedy. The three of them bring peace to the world, on the basis of a deep mutual understanding granted them along with their tremendous power. The Pope is made to say that "all men who arrive at authority have certain attitudes in common," and that even the Communist Premier, "having thrust himself up so high, has begun to breathe a freer air." The new authoritarianism had been born, one in which Lyndon Johnson could justify his actions by saying, "I am your President," assuring others that they could not know all the things that went into a decision affecting Vietnam.

Another character in West's novel is Père Jean Télémond, S.J., a silenced palaeontologist who has written a book called *The Progress of Man*. West is correct in his iconography, at least: Teilhard was the deepest celebrator of power, since advance and evolution are for him "irresistible" and "irreversible" (two of his favorite words). To advance is to succeed, to be on the winning side; one's very success is the pledge of one's solidarity with God. "Life cannot be mistaken," he had written from the trenches, "cannot develop successfully other than in the direction of the true (from which it follows that the true must exist), in the number of, in the direction taken by, the things that succeed." Sister Jacqueline had found models for her own action in the enterprise and risk of businessmen, in the large anonymous force for good to be found in corporations like Monsanto. In the same way, Teilhard wrote to a businessman: "You are still having some difficulty in justifying to yourself the euphoria of a soul immersed in 'business.' I must point out to you that the most important thing is that you *do* have a feeling of well-being. Bread was good for bodies before we knew about the chemical laws of assimilation. . . . Because your undertaking—which I take to be perfectly legitimate —is going well, a little more health is being spread in the human mass, and in consequence a little more liberty to act, to think and to love."

No wonder Robert McNamara swore by Teilhard, and Sister Jackie swore by them both. McNamara was the very type of that teamwork Cox had praised, suggesting that "the organization principle entered Western history with the Christian Gospel." It is this teamwork that made Teilhard offer scientific research as the pattern of all future human activity, saying of those who smashed the atom: "Nothing in the universe can resist the converging energies of a sufficient number of minds sufficiently grouped and organized." With McNamara, the worlds of business and the academy and government and the foundations converged on each problem he undertook. He had taken the academy's abstract discipline and computerology into a corporation, and the corporation's tough remodeling competitiveness into the Pentagon. He was the ideal of administrative wisdom, of force and restraint, quick acts and long views. He ran a war by day, and went home to read Teilhard at night. He was an enthusiastic participant in Bobby Kennedy's Hickory Hill seminars (a kind of Great Books for Great Men course). Men like these might err, but that was just the price of progress, the necessary side effect of having energetic decision makers where we needed them. The worst thing that could be done was doing nothing. Henry Trewhitt, in his book on McNamara, quotes a Pentagon associate's judgment: "McNamara felt that inaction was almost always a mistake." McNamara himself, on taking office, told the television cameras: "I've always believed and endeavored to follow the active leadership role as opposed to the passive judicial role." Such a man would learn by any mistakes he might commit along the way, mistakes which would thus be put to use, no action being really lost, all things "saved" by the self-correcting nature of man's superintending judgment. With Kennedy, the Cuban missile showdown would redeem the Bay of Pigs. With McNamara, the C-5A would redeem the TFX. With Maxwell

Taylor, strategic bombing would redeem the Green Berets. With Cabot Lodge, Big Minh would redeem our bad bet on Diem. With Ellsworth Bunker, a Thieu would redeem a Ky. Defoliation would be redeemed by interdiction, and strategic hamlets by resettlement, and pacification by Vietnamization. The System staggered on through successive dark "redemptions," with McNamara and his men computing through it all, until nothing but Lyndon Johnson's resignation could redeem the Tet offensive. The System had not only broken down, but given up; confessed its failure.

For a while, celebrators of the two Johns could pass off what had happened by pointing to the two demon successors, Pope Paul and President Lyndon. They did not have the Kennedy charm or Roncalli charisma. Still, if power purifies, why did these men not grow in office? Both had taken up the same burdens, and pursued the same programs—Paul completing Vatican II's sessions, Johnson pursuing the war on poverty at home and "flexible response" abroad. But, under new direction, the programs themselves were suspect. The church somehow seemed worse off after the Council than before; the nation was almost as scarred by the war on poverty as by poverty itself. Kennedy had brought "vigah" to foreign affairs—and the result was a presidential war rubber-stamped by Congress with the Tonkin Gulf Resolution. Pope John restored the power of his office and widened the scope of encyclicals—and the result was a papal condemnation of contraceptives in *Humanae Vitae*. Even the triumphs of the Johannine era took on a dubious air. Sister Jacqueline was comforted, at the time of Kennedy's death, with the way he calibrated his response to the threat of Russian missiles eighty miles from our shore. But soon those missiles, sheathed in Russian submarines, cruised even closer to us, and we learned to live with them—as well as to doubt the wisdom of nuclear brinkmanship the first time they showed up.

Our trouble was not with one man (LBJ), or one mistake (Vietnam). The mistakes came in a train, connected; not self-correcting, but cumulative. We did not learn from them, but compounded them. McNamara's folly led to—McNamara's folly: the TFX to the electric "wall" for fencing off North Vietnam. Something was wrong with the whole process—and one of the things wrong with it was our refusal to think anything basic *could* be wrong with it. The System could not be judged except from within, by those able to speak *from* power *about* power.

Besides, in what other terms could the System be judged? Cox had taught us that even God could only be talked of meaningfully in terms of the System, of politics and progress, of tangible solutions. This System could not be talked of in terms of something else—of mystery or metaphysics, ideology or over-all assumptions, from the outside. But once one was on the inside, he would not *want* to deal in such abstractions, but with discrete problems, curable because isolable. One was not allowed to make large assumptions except on the basis of *results* emerging from action, results converging into new problems at a higher level, working themselves out on the moving edge of reality. The process judges, by way of trial and error; it is not judged.

But one had not, in this pragmatic world, escaped from large assumptions. One had simply made them untouchable. One could debate this or that problem involved in Southeast Asia, but not the basic assumption that American power should be maintained there. One could debate whether McNamara's doctrine of "commonality" gave us a better strike force, but not whether we should have a better strike force. McNamara would say, about Vietnam, "If we can learn how to analyze this thing, we'll solve it." But he did not mean "analyze" at other than the technical level, even when he had lost all heart for the war. On leaving office, he would say: "I think the actions that this government has followed, the objectives it has had in Vietnam, are wise. I do not by any means suggest that we have not made mistakes over the many years that we have been pursuing those objectives." The goal was fine; we had just not known the proper instruments for reaching it. Yet that had been his claim to eminence all along—that he *did* know, or could find, the technical means for us to solve problems; that we had unlimited power at our disposal and new ways of disposing it toward good. Only our technique had failed. But if McNamara did not know technique, what did he know? At times he consoled himself with the thought that the technique had not failed, after all—only our willingness to use it. We had the power, and knew what to do with it; but for some perverse reason *would* not do it, would not listen to him. In 1967, he revealed his bafflement to Congress: "Are we running out of money? The answer is no. The only thing we are running out of in this country is will." But the national will had to do with national goals, not means. It was a problem not accessible to problem solvers. McNamara's attempts to find technical (secular) answers for moral problems got more bizarre as time went on, as brand-new gadgets for sniffing and listening and registering footsteps were sent into the jungle and finally a magic electronic wall was built, the computerologist's Maginot Line, to fence in human spirit with technology.

It was for this expertise, then, that the churches abandoned their separate critical stance apart from "the world," their skepticism over Caesar's claims. The mechanics of this surrender were symbolized in 1969, when Jesuit seminarians in protest against the war turned in their draft cards, surrendering clerical exemption by way of a challenge. The cards were passed on to a Congressman of the students' own Order, a prominent critic of the war, elected despite his liberal record and his priesthood, Father Robert Drinan. The seminarians were dismayed when Father Drinan refused to accept the cards; but they should not have been—his reason was the one they had all applauded back in the happy days of Jack Kennedy and the Houston speech. Father Drinan would not let his coreligionists affect the way he kept his oath of office. He had sworn to uphold the law, and was now bound—as Kennedy had promised that *he* would be. On these terms, America's voters would not only put a lay Catholic in the White House, but a priest in the Congress. But some Catholics were reconsidering those terms. Father Drinan had all the old arguments—

that he could work better for peace from inside a position of power, that the way to change the System is to join it and use it for one's own purposes. Nonetheless, when called on by his brothers on a pressing issue, the Congressman now had to answer, not the priest; and the answer must be a No to any criticism directed at the System's very basis. It was his System now—or he was its man.

Those who deal in power must go where the power is, maintain it in order to use it, serve it before it will serve them. McNamara, by streamlining the Pentagon, strengthened it. Robert Kennedy, by giving J. Edgar Hoover's empire a wider berth, let it grow. John F. Kennedy, by exalting the Presidency, made it strong enough to carry Congress and people into half-war and full defeat. Liberalism was not the enemy of the System, but its best friend, despite all its claims to the contrary.

Liberalism professes an opposition to "the status quo," to the reactionary's mere conservation of present institutions. But the reactionary usually stands guard over a status quo *ante*, over yesterday's positions (now beleaguered), ideas whose time has gone. Indeed, the one thing a Tory like Samuel Johnson cannot forgive "Whiggism" is its need to win, to move with the wave of history, with ideas whose time has just now come. Liberalism fights yesterday's status quo in the name of today's, savoring a victory assured.

That is precisely why Teilhard de Chardin, despite his own piety and selflessness, made so perfectly acceptable a Sixties liberal. He spoke of man in control; man possessing power, and not possessed by it; solving problems, and trusting history. Teilhard's views had been constructed out of personal need for solace, and they offered hidden counsel of *resignation*. If one sings hymns to one's victor, how can he be considered the victim? The fire cannot defeat you if you become the fire. And (circling back) if you *become* it, you cannot criticize it. So all things work together unto good for those who trust power. Teilhard praised Woodrow Wilson's view of the First World War, as a war to end war. But when the Second World War came, he had to welcome it, too, as a war beyond war, something to make us even *more* perfect: "Peace is not the opposite of war. It is war carried above and beyond itself in the conquest of the trans-human." He greeted all the plagues of the twentieth century as blessings, ever resigned, ever triumphant. Fascism, despite evil excrescences, was at root bringing us deep truths about the need to be fused in a superhumanity. Overpopulation raises the "psychic temperature" to a "boiling point" that promotes fusion. Unemployment will release more purely mental energy, "so that to attempt to suppress unemployment by incorporating the unemployed in the machine would be against the purpose of Nature." One is not to question Nature's will, even when one is led into Nature's depths and frees the energy of the atom: "There were those, on the morrow of the Arizona [he means New Mexico] experiment [at Alamogordo], who had the temerity to assert that the physicists, having brought their researches to a successful conclusion, should have suppressed and destroyed the dangerous fruits of their invention. As though it were not every man's duty to pursue the creative forces of knowledge and action to their uttermost end! As though, in any event, there exists any force on earth capable of restraining human thought from following any course upon which it has embarked! . . . In the glow of this triumph how can he feel otherwise than exalted as he has never been since his birth. . . . In exploding the atom we took our first bite at the fruit of the great discovery, and this was enough for a taste to enter our mouths that can never be washed away: the taste for super-creativeness. . . . War will be eliminated at its source in our hearts because, compared with the vast field for conquest which science has disclosed to us, its triumphs will soon appear trivial and outmoded." Power purifies.

In her own measure, Sister Jacqueline tried to maintain a similar hopefulness toward any new situation; and to prove her trust for the new, the secular, the powerful, by always *joining* it. Thus, as early as 1964, she was trying to get rid of her nun's habit because it kept her from the marketplace of

general human endeavor: "I am begging that religious con-
gregations do something about these mediaeval habits so that
we can again assume our citizenship, and that we may, on the
free and open market, again volunteer to make our investment
in the mainstream of American society" (i.e., join the System).
But why merely take the habit off, if one was going to maintain a religious school? Secular substance should go with the
secular style, since "the Christian grace is translated into every
secular institution in civilization today" (from Krogers to the
Pentagon). And why "laicize" her school without laicizing herself? Which, in 1967, she did; and for a typical reason—because a nun's vows circumscribed her *power*: "I had given
someone else the authority to limit or veto my decisions." She
kept the name she had taken in religion, had become widely
known by; but added to it a husband's name—so that it was as
Mrs. Wechsler that she took up the new responsibilities of
President at New York's Hunter College. She had kept true to
her first insight, though it made her abandon so much of what
she first stood for. Through it all, she had gone where the action was, floated with the floating crap game of power and decision. Her response was flexible enough to satisfy even Robert
McNamara.

But at the same time she was living by McNamara's standards, he was falling by reason of them. A prime example of
tools created for flexible response was the TFX, whose mov-
able wing would make it the very model of "commonality"—it
could be flown for all purposes by all military services. This
was what McNamara was best at. The Ford executive, brought
into Kennedy's Cabinet to build the equivalent of his company's successful model, the Thunderbird (sports car as conventional car), he had given birth to an airborne Edsel. Built
to do everything, it did nothing; to please, it only angered; to
open options, it closed them.

Sister Jacqueline still trusted him, but some students did
not. She praised McNamara when he stood up to anti-war heck-
lers, vindicating the idea of academic freedom. He even used a
frontiersman's boast, of the sort she loved, shouting back at

Harvard students, recalling his school days: "I was a lot tougher and lot more courteous than you. I was tougher than you and I am tougher today." He had spent years signaling that message to Ho Chi Minh. Now the students were no more impressed than Ho had been. Camelot toughness wasn't the only game in town any more. It wasn't even the most interesting one.

Mrs. Wechsler did not know how tough one might have to be till she met the pressures of a real secular campus, not just the half-secularized little Webster College in St. Louis. In the heady old days on Kennedy's education panel, when she discussed the fate of Harvard and MIT, the panel chairman called her a "Joan of Arc of Education." By 1970, some students were ready to burn her in effigy, Joan at the stake. Campus graffiti called the flying nun of the jet set Hunter's own "Lying Nun." She had come to Hunter welcoming trouble ("If we don't ask for some trouble today, we're not going to play any part in healing society") and promising to meet it with reason instead of coercion ("One must never resort to force, psychic or otherwise"). But she had to back off a bit from her praise of participatory democracy, calling it a naive and nostalgic idea. She advocated, instead, a *procedural* democracy, with "some form of honest bureaucracy." From rebel to tactician, and from that to "honest bureaucrat"—it is the price of power. She disbanded the student faculty grievance committee when she came into office—and that in itself became a grievance, with no channels for its own settlement. When Hunterites sat in at the administration building, she swore out an injunction against them. When they defied it, she not only called in the police, but asked them to patrol the corridors henceforth. It was becoming clearer to her every day that no criticism of the System from outside the System could be justified: "You see, to unbuild a bureaucracy through constitutional means is to get that bureaucracy to unbuild itself and to reconstitute itself." Demands from outside just interrupted honest bureaucrats in this effort: you must not "alienate . . . the ones who have to effect the change." Like Andrew Greeley, she had now become a critic of Father Berrigan: "Dan knows I disagree with him in the way he's gone in the last two years." At the end of her first year at Hunter she locked herself in her office while student delegations tried to reach her, pounding on the door and shouting, "Hey, Wechsler! Hey, Wechsler!" It was almost enough to send one back to the convent. Something had gone wrong with the dream. Camelot was never like this. "Let us begin?" No, no—she must have felt like screaming—let it stop.

III · DOUBTING

The means that allow men, up to a certain point, to go without religion are perhaps, after all, the only means we still possess for bringing mankind back, by a long and roundabout path, to a state of faith.

—TOCQUEVILLE

· SEVEN ·

Secular Incompetence

The "adult" state, conscious of the autonomy
proper to its adulthood, is not merely
impatient of any political tutelage exercised
from without by the Church, but rightfully
free from such external tutelage because the
means for its self-direction to right spiritual
and moral ends exist within the political
order itself—I mean the whole range of
democratic institutions.

—REV. JOHN COURTNEY MURRAY

WOODSTOCK COLLEGE, FOLDED INTO THE HILLS of Maryland, is a
historic place—the first, and for long the best, Jesuit school of
theology in this country. Its main building, hewn of native
white stone over a hundred years ago, is very impressive, each
wing of it backed by semidetached high bell towers. The story
goes that plans for the seminary had been drawn up and sent
off to Rome for approval, but that construction had already
begun when Rome sent back a query: *Suntne angeli?* ("Are
they angels there?"). The plans had not included toilet facilities, which were belatedly concentrated, floor by floor, in the
towers, whose steamed upper windows hold no bells after all.

The College became a center of scholarship (here *Theological Studies* was edited, here John Courtney Murray forged the theological basis for political liberalism in the Fifties)—but the College's widely scattered neighbors found the seminarians, who walked in twos and threes through the hills, approachable and easy-going. These boys knew all the younger farm children by name, and watched them grow, passing acquaintance with them on to new arrivals at the College. It was hard to perform any "community service" for this independent group of farmers, but the seminarians found a way: they manned a County fire engine from the College. The engine crew lived in a single corridor, gear hooked in careful folds outside each door, where a clangorous alarm bell called them from classes or out of sleep. Most of this ministry was to small brush fires in the autumn; but each trip out earned its crew a case of cold beer (rare treat in old seminary days).

Now the fire engine is gone, and so are the Jesuits—all but their dead, who lie in their cemetery, which they could not take with them. (One stone, still white from its cutting, reads: *P. Johannes Courtney Murray.*) Prickly neighbors, who welcomed their presence, now bitterly resent their departure. It was late autumn when I drove out past a ruined parish church, just off the College grounds, to a local tavern (always off-limits to the students, though run by a Catholic family of the area). It was strictly a beer bar, well populated in the early afternoon, as one set of chores was finished and men braced themselves for the next set. Their faces have the midafternoon ashenness of steady bar customers, with that flush (underneath the ashes) of men who work outdoors—powder of deadened skin over chafed elbows. Everyone knows everyone here, and the stranger feels marked.

The woman at the bar is the owner's wife, easy at trading banter with her regulars, relaxed as sediment—till she is stirred by mention of the College. "I suppose they had to leave"—I mean it as a question.

"*Had* to," she mutters. "Did they have to sell the College to the government? Did they have to have all those girls hanging around? They didn't have to stop being priests. But that's all they want." She explains that when their church burnt down (the ruined one I had passed), parishioners attended Sunday Mass at the seminary: "It made me sick to find so many girls living in a house of priests. I've been here all my life, and they never had to have girls around until just last year." She was describing a group of political activists—including some "Jesuit groupies" of the peace movement—who had brought sleeping bags out to Woodstock and lived on the grounds, or in parlors, close to their fellow conspirators, defendants, and radical pamphleteers. *Suntne angeli?* Not any longer—not, at any rate, in the bar lady's books. The woman knows what their trouble was. It was Woman. But for that, "They wouldn't have gone away and left us."

Oddly enough, Gabriel Alexander Bennett agrees with her. "Gabe" as everyone calls him, was the Jesuits' chef for sixty-five years, and he has been left behind to die at the College, where he lives, a recluse cared for by his son-in-law, in the old laundry building. He has no reason to feel surprised at being left behind. His great-grandfather was shipped over from Algeria as a present to the Jesuits, and all his family were slaves to the Order until 1865. In fact, in the last days of the war, when sly merchants were buying black babies and shipping them out of New Orleans to slave islands, Gabe's eldest four brothers and sisters were sold by the Father Minister; their mother, a devout Catholic, stayed up all night praying the rosary, then went in tears to the superior and he relented.

Gabe is not rancorous about these memories, or shaken in his own faith: that is just the way things are. Though he ruled the seminary kitchen for well over a half-century with his great height, impressive physique, and surprising knowledge of French cuisine, he had to master resignation early on in his ninety-nine years. He approves of the Jesuits' belated capitulation to reality. Why, I asked him, did they leave? "They all want the opposite sex," he said matter-of-factly. (Gabe is patriarch to a huge family, which has ramified out into almost fifty great-grandchildren.) "Don't think some wasn't gettin' it before, without marrying. Their life was going against nature. God made man and woman for each other." I asked him what he thought had brought this realization home to the Jesuits, after so many years. "The automobile. When I came here, there was no automobile. This place was hard to reach; and when you did, it had a gate locked bottom and top. The auto changed all that. People came and went too easily. They couldn't lock the world out no more."

Gabe is the bar lady's kind of Negro. He was part of "old Woodstock," which had locked the world away. The Jesuits served as a buffer against harsh aspects of Baltimore (ten miles away) and Washington (twenty miles off). The blacks who worked for them were well-behaved, servants where their fathers had been slaves, good Catholics filing into the back of that church that burned down in 1968, knowing their place, not (apparently) wanting to move out of it, masters of resignation. (The bar lady does not realize that Gabe tried to make it in the outside world, and found that impossible for a teen-ager with no education; he came back to Woodstock because there was nowhere else to go.) It is strangely fitting that the College now trains black teen-agers for better work, since the state has leased it as a Job Corps Center. That, for the bar lady, completed the Jesuits' treason. "Once they've gone, they let all the trash in. What do you expect that to be, up there, with a lot of black teen-agers, but a glorified you-know-what-house?" It was the Jesuits' job, in her eyes, to keep priests separated from women so that this countryside could stay separated from the city, whites from blacks.

It was, then, in a whole context of separations, that Father Murray worked, with his sharp conceptual tools, on dividing church from state. He lived to see his arguments vindicated abroad, at Rome's Vatican Council; and fortuitously died (in 1967) before he saw them violated on his own campus. His whole point had been to locate the secular order as something separate, having its own expertise and proper autonomy; but the actual effect of his work was to make the secular respectable even for churchly people. Whence the double invasion—

of priests and seminarians at Washington demonstrations, peace marches, draft-board raids; and of their young associates trailing back to "boot camp" around the seminary, a Cox's army of the moral wars. Even before he died, Murray was complaining of this—and the first arrests of Woodstock personnel had not been made. It was in Murray's own headquarters that a visiting radical, spotting grapes on the community's dining table during the Cesar Chavez strike against vineyard owners, ostentatiously seized the offending bowl, marched the length of the hall during its most crowded dining hour, and flung the grapes over Woodstock's neatly tended grounds.

Murray would not have understood the young peacenik priests turned out by Woodstock in the late Sixties. His own position, toward the end, was that Vietnam may have been a mistake but: "We are there, and that is the starting point of any discussion now." The decisions that took us there were made by proper authorities, duly elected and legitimate—the church, after all, cannot depose rulers, acting from some higher vantage point of power. Our own rulers had drawn on all the proper centers of secular expertise, and had the competence for making these decisions, which are irreversible even if mistaken. The state's claim is not to infallibility, but to autonomy (always within its own sphere). The debate over Woodstock's move away from Maryland had begun during Murray's life—in fact, he had helped make the first decision, to incorporate Woodstock into the Yale Divinity School. That, too, had a campus set apart, a scholarly mini-Yale far out from New Haven's blighted center, in the vicinity of the little Catholic college, Albertus Magnus. But second-generation admirers of the secular were already surpassing their elders in desire to go "where the action is." A counterproposal was raised—to take Woodstock into New York, where it could share classes and faculty with Union Theological Seminary on the upper West Side. An advantage much bruited in the basement discussions of this move was the presence, almost on Union's doorstep, of a million New York Puerto Ricans: "Think what an apostolate that would offer our theologians!" That was too much for the ailing Murray, who muttered before leaving: "How many gawd-damn Puerto Ricans can one seminarian service?"

He lost, of course; and all of Woodstock's academic apparatus was moved piecemeal into New York—faculty, students, library, and Theological Studies (old forum for "the Murray thesis" through a hot decade of liberal debate). In general the liberals were losing; radical young men took their old causes into the streets, turned their distinctions into protests, their carefully guarded praise of the secular into active politicking. Perhaps the turning point, the high tide of liberal engagement, after which liberals recoiled, aghast, at the radical wave that overlapped and raced beyond them, was the Civil Rights Act of 1964. That engagement began in May of 1963, when John F. Kennedy quietly summoned religious leaders, along with labor and civil rights spokesmen, to the White House. Kennedy, you remember, had pledged not to be led by bishops in his purely political decisions; but he could justify himself by reflecting that he meant to lead (and use) them, not vice versa. And they could justify themselves—how? By inventing the concept of the moral (i.e., suprapolitical) issue. Senator Richard Russell was mocked when he said the Civil Rights bill passed because "those damned preachers got the idea it was a moral issue." But he was speaking of a very specific idea and strategy; and many of the "damned preachers" themselves would live to regret that idea they had "got."

President Kennedy was properly skeptical about his chances of getting civil rights legislation out of Congress. The Southern leaders would call in all their debts, jockey and finagle, and resort at last (as they always had) to a filibuster. Senators who might vote for the bill itself would hold back from voting cloture, in which the issue was not simply racial rights but the sanctity of Senate debate. This was especially true of midwestern Senators, who had no strong civil rights constituency; without pressure from home, a man has the luxury of humoring Senate grandees, whose power will be useful to him later. Yet how create a constituency out there? No Eastern liberal sentiment could be stirred up by the ACLU.

The labor unions' more liberal spokesmen cannot mobilize rural areas. The answer was obvious: religion. Whether Bible Belt or scattered Catholic, these Middle Americans take their religion seriously. So Joseph Rauh (speaking for labor and liberals) and Clarence Mitchell (speaking for the blacks) turned to the National Catholic Welfare Conference (represented by Father John Cronin) and the National Council of Churches (represented by James Hamilton) to create a religious constituency in key states—e.g., they would aim at a state like Nebraska, channeling new kinds of mail into the offices of Carl Curtis and Roman Hruska. This meeting at the White House was to co-ordinate strategy: Kennedy's bill was to be *criticized* by Rauh and Mitchell, lobbying for civil rights; they would propose a "dream bill" supported by clergymen of all stripes—and this would lead to passage of the first (embattled) proposal.

Thus was the "moral issue" born—something neither partisan nor political, but overriding all such considerations. As Dr. Eugene Carson Blake would testify before Congress, "The religious conscience of America condemns racism as blasphemy against God." In the face of that opposition, what are lesser wars of mere Republicans with mere Democrats? And already the rallies had been held, the organizations created, the mail got out—in Nebraska alone, an NCC gathering in Lincoln was followed by an NCWC conference in Omaha. Father Cronin also arranged an ecumenical Washington meeting at Georgetown University to insure efficient lobbying when the bill came to a vote.

All this may not, as it turned out, have been necessary. Kennedy, who feared he would not get the bill through while he lived, insured its passage by dying. After his assassination, the civil rights law was expiatory; any religious leader's own doubts now vanished, as the nation did penance for its leader's death. A Southerner had entered the White House, intent on proving that his part of the nation (and he personally) was as stricken as the other sectors. When Father Cronin and Mr. Hamilton went to see Everett Dirksen, the Senate minority leader, a key figure in achieving cloture, they found him entertaining tactical doubts about the Rauh bill, not about Kennedy's original! They could scarcely repress their glee till they got outside his office. The nation would get a "dream bill" that had been at first no more than a dream—or, rather, part of a very practical scheme for the "realistic" bill's passage. By the time the bill reached a vote, riding this wave of popular and religious sentiment, bishops and priests and rabbis were openly lobbying in the halls of Congress. No important Senator lacked his visits from the major faiths' delegations. Rauh, the old pro, said he had never witnessed such a powerful lobbying effort.

The preachers who had tasted this first victory were not ready, yet, to go back to their pulpits. Johnson sent his civil rights director, Lee White, to meet with clergymen at Airlie House and suggest that legislation had been pushed as far as was feasible for the moment. But these men, originally summoned to be consulted (i.e., used), now had their own demands to make. They would push further, for a voting rights bill—also as a "moral issue." They got what they wanted in 1964—while Johnson got much of the credit. Father Cronin and others picked up their second presidential pen at the bill's signing—a new religious pennon of victory.

The preachers were prepared, now, to overreach themselves. When the Office of Economic Opportunity, under Sargent Shriver, looked around for a way to sponsor "Headstart" programs in Mississippi, it asked the National Council of Churches for guidance. The NCC, which had set up a Mississippi "Delta Ministry," channeled the government's funds to its contacts there, organized under a new acronym as the CDGM (Child Development Group of Mississippi). So far, so good. But the inevitable overlap of personnel meant that Delta-CDGM volunteers would also be among those leading a voter registration drive for the insurgent Mississippi Freedom Democratic Party. It is easy to guess what Southern Democrats thought of this—the federal government, under a Democratic administration, seemed to be funding the most serious challenge to the Democratic Party. Southerners were being had by those preachers again.

Mr. Shriver was caught in the middle, and no wonder: he had boasted, in 1965: "Three or four years ago it was practically impossible for a federal agency to give a direct grant to a religious group. Today we have given hundreds without violating the principle of separation of church and state." The civil rights revolution had begun in black churches, led by preachers of the SCLC. Now white churches and halls and schools were being opened to the movement. The CDGM funds—sixteen million dollars, for a starter—were directed to a Presbyterian college, instead of any state schools, to keep the program free from interference by state officials. Among Catholics, Mr. Thomas Henton co-ordinated applications from each diocese to get the maximum in federal money for parochial schools engaged in Headstart and other programs—another cause for Southern concern.

Senator John Stennis responded to this new treatment of the church-state problem by calling the OEO before a Senate appropriations subcommittee, to explain why a $30,000 check, meant for tutoring Mississippi children, was cashed in New York by the National Council of Churches. Mr. Shriver supported his program at this hearing; but alarm spread through the churches when, in 1966, he tried to cut back on CDGM funds. Church lobbyists went straight to Vice-President Humphrey, their ally in the battle for the 1964 bill, to threaten withdrawal of support from President Johnson if OEO funds were curtailed.

Thus, in less than three years, the churches had moved from co-operation with the White House (on civil rights) to outracing the White House (on voting rights) to defying the White House (on poverty funds). They had assumed a regular bargaining position on what now seemed an established permanent floating "moral issue." But to bargain you need credibility; to gamble, you need chips. The threat to withhold support would have no effect unless the lobbyists could trade church support for OEO funds. And that support was no longer to be mobilized at will. The moral issue had not only floated, but bloated out in several directions. Young church-men were interested in a dizzying variety of moral issues by now—party reform, and campus violence, and the war. The Delta Ministry itself could not be bought off merely with CDGM funds, after having Fanny Lou Hamer's MFDP delegation repulsed at the Atlantic City convention. Besides, while some were bargaining with Humphrey, others would never trust him, since he and Rauh had protected Lyndon Johnson's nomination from Fanny Lou Hamer's challenge. And, in the interval, a moral issue to dwarf all the rest had unexpectedly arisen—other church groups were ready to follow the lead of preachers like William Sloane Coffin, Richard Neustadt, and Daniel Berrigan, who founded Clergy (later Clergy and Laymen) Concerned About Vietnam.

The moral issue had worked too well for the preachers—like too much magic for a sorcerer's apprentice. Indeed, the liberals' moral issue, a thing above politics, now became the radicals' "non-negotiable demand," a matter of such urgency that it would be compromised by any discussion of its merits. Liberals, in horror, began to denounce their own offspring. Right-Wingers no longer frightened men like Norman Podhoretz so much as shaggy radicals who refused to be controlled by elder critics of society.

So a new kind of Catholic book began to come out by the end of the Sixties—the liberal defense of old arrangements. It took several forms—e.g., Andrew Greeley's *Why Can't They Be Like Us?* or James Hitchcock's *The Decline and Fall of the Catholic Liberal.* (Hitchcock confused "liberal" and "radical" throughout his text, while himself taking the side of conventional liberalism.) But perhaps the first of these books was the best, since its continuity with an older liberalism was so carefully traced. Ed Marciniak's *Tomorrow's Christian* (1969) reprinted the text of Kennedy's Houston speech, and the New York *Times* advertisement taken out by prominent Catholics during Kennedy's campaign. That ad stated: "The principle of separation is part of our American heritage, and

as citizens who are Catholics [Father Murray's kind of dis-
tinction] we value it as an integral part of our national life."
Marciniak attacked clerical activism as an encroachment on
the role of the layman, who is the secular "insider," the initiate
of an expertise quite different from the clergyman's. If conscience is to mediate between moral teaching and politics,
while preserving the wall of separation, laymen must be the
mediators. The clergy speak too directly of moral imperatives,
making churchly claims too little negotiable, too unyielding
for the pluralistic marketplace.

Marciniak, who had long been an activist for civil rights,
realized what had happened in the ecclesiastical breakthrough
of the 1964 bill; but he tried to make that a rare exception—
based, of course, on the isolable extreme case of a "moral
issue"—and to return things to the pre-1964 state of separation:

During the 1964 debate in the United States Senate over the
passage of a civil rights law, Southern senators bitterly resented
the wave after wave of religious leaders who flooded Senate
chambers in support of the legislation. Without threat or bluster
the clergymen and their allies insisted that racial discrimination
was a moral evil and that to root it out, everyone had to do
his part—"and what was the Senator personally going to do about
it?" The Dixie senators and Northern holdouts argued that a
civil rights law was a political matter. In their own ways the
clergymen and the recalcitrant senators were both right. The
decision to do something was the moral question [*Murray's "informing" of conscience*]; what to do, how to accomplish it, was
the political issue [*left by Murray to those with secular competence—but the clergymen who met secretly at the White House
were very much involved in "how to accomplish it"*]. The law
was finally approved by the Senate after the religious leaders
were able to open enough senators' eyes and—let us never forget
it—those of their constituents back home to the moral issue at
stake. The claim that the Negro's civil rights were *solely* [*my
italics—Marciniak is cutting the actual campaign back again*] a
political question had been destroyed. It was one of those rare
occasions in the United States Congress when, during an intense
national controversy arising out of a legislative proposal that aban-
dons an age-old tradition, an overwhelming national religious
consensus [*the clergymen focused on roughly six senators in their*

campaign to create this "national consensus"] uncovered enough votes for passage [*not directly—the religious campaign was aimed at votes for cloture, not passage*]. The lesson of this victory has been misunderstood by some [*and, we might add, misrepresented by others*]. It is not the typical situation [*it became that for some years*]. A categorical moral imperative is the exceptional case.

Religious pluralism meant, for the older liberal, a benign neutrality between church and state. Romanist theologians had argued against this on the ground that "error has no rights." Murray answered that they were confusing categories: error of itself can neither have nor not-have human rights; only men can—and all men do, even "erring" men. Murray won that battle when Pope John wrote: "A man who has fallen into error does not cease to be a man. He never forfeits his personal dignity; and that is something that must always be taken into account" (*Pacem in Terris,* par. 158). But it dawned on some men, even in this moment of victory, that Murray had battled the old theology on its own ground, circumscribing the kind of victory to be won there. This frequently happens in theological debate, where there is such concern for doctrinal continuity and for persuading those in authority that new things are not dangerous or heretical.

When a difficulty arises in the church, a theologian's instinct is to distinguish his way around it. The distinction may be, in some measure, an evasion; but at least it soothes men's doubts in a time of spiritual crisis, so "pastoral" considerations rush to the aid of academic prudence to admit the circumvention. However, once the distinction is sanctioned, it goes into theological handbooks, ticking away there like a time bomb, ready to go off some time in the future. The escape from one problem becomes a new problem in its own right. This was the framework in which Murray operated. When the challenge of the secularized state arose, the church resisted it, working itself up to the grand condemnations of Pius IX's reign. The nineteenth-century liberal Cardinal Dupanloup, attempting compromise, granted the mediaeval doctrine of the church's monopoly on religion, but said it was not applicable to present circumstances. He gave the old formulations his assent as abstract ideals (the "thesis"), but said the church in this imperfect world, can only approximate that idea. The actual arrangement (or "hypothesis") would therefore be the result of church bargaining with political authority and other religions. As much of the thesis would be preserved as the traffic would bear.

The trouble with this solution was that it merely held the thesis in abeyance. If Catholics breed apace, argued Paul Blanshard in the Fifties, and reach a bare majority of voters in America, they will introduce a Catholic regime like that of Franco or Salazar, outlawing all Protestant and other religions. To prove that American Catholics were not merely opportunistic in their devotion to pluralism, Father Murray had to go farther than Dupanloup—he had to challenge the thesis.

He did it by standing the old argument on its head. He ransacked church history for statements of the legitimacy of secular power in its own sphere. The mediaeval arrangement violated this principle, but only because of historical circumstance—the barbarian invasions had destroyed education outside the monasteries; all education therefore became clerical education, and "clercs" took on the vacated functions of secular authority. But as the world came of age, the autonomy of the governmental sphere could again be recognized. In other words, the ideal relationship of sacred and secular authorities —stated by Jesus as "Give to Caesar the things that are Caesar's" and by Pope Gelasius as "Two (powers) there are" —was not realized until European culture reached its maturity in modern times. The mediaeval world was, thus, the hypothesis, that imperfect and transient period during which the ideal must be held in abeyance. And the "thesis" is—the American Constitution!

I should add that this [present state] is not hypothesis—the simple product of a factual state of affairs in which the Church is somehow shorn of power, compelled in expediency to make only minimal demands, etc. On the contrary, it is thesis—the full development, by theological reflection and political experience, of the central datum of the distinction of the two powers and their hierarchic collaboration for the total good of man and human society. Anything less than this is hypothesis.

It was a very nice ploy. Murray used his opponents' own norms and out-theologized them. He had better proof-texts. He could grant their assumption that the church is permanently "mature" while the world fluctuates in its degrees of competence. He even found mediaeval authority for his views (in John of Paris). Nor did he have to disturb the thesis-hypothesis framework of the discussion; he just reversed its application. And he could do this while making his conclusions sound very liberal and enlightened—as no doubt Dupanloup's had sounded in his day.

And that was the trouble. Murray was so perfectly suited to the times that he could not step outside them, could not criticize the spirit of the age:

I am inclined to see a striking testimony to the fact that the doctrine systematized (incompletely, if you will, and with some fragility) by John of Paris is the traditional doctrine of the Church in the further fact that it is so perfectly adapted to our contemporary situation.

He, no less than his opponents, thought in terms of a single and extrahistorical ideal toward which church and state should strive; but for him that ideal was best realized in the modern democracies. And what does one do, in this situation, if even the "mature" secular power goes astray (as in Vietnam)? The argument will, of course, allow for exceptions and deviations—the rare case of a "moral issue" where secular power must be rebuked. But too many exceptions destroy the rule, break down the autonomous sphere of political "competence."

Murray had carried his questions farther and deeper than Dupanloup; but not far or deep enough. This is explained by his almost total concern with the problem of church *establishment*. He trained all his artillery of argument upon that problem, leaving himself exposed to assault from any new direction. Young churchmen of the Sixties did not feel that establishment

was a real problem any more—they did not want to join the
government, but to oppose it. After all the seminar talk of mature pluralistic deference, of grown-up agreement to disagree
politely (Murray called this "creeds at war intelligibly"),
priests wondered if their voice must always be the lowered
one of an outsider at the board meeting. Had prophets observed such decorum in the past? Or could prophets only interfere with kings' actions back in the "immature" period of
Murray's "hypothesis"?

Prophets are not summoned; they come unbidden—and so
they irrupted into Murray's postwar liberal world. These
young disturbers of the ecclesiastical peace, once they began
to doubt their liberal elders, found much to object to in those
elders' world. Catholics, indeed, repeated the experience of
secular radicals, who discovered that much of their parents'
liberal ventures had been financed by the CIA, or by interlocking elites from government, the academy, and the foundations.
"Establishment" no longer meant, for them, a state-endorsed
church, but this secular caste of "clerks" with the shared belief
that American standards of "self-determination" should be imposed on the rest of the world by coaxing or judicious coercion.
Their cold war was the anti-McCarthyite form of anti-Com-
munism; "cold" indeed in its rationality, opposed to any hysterical use of force, but not to "reasonable" use of it against Communist regimes. Father Murray himself, often on call to deliver
papers at foundation meetings, was this kind of cold warrior.
He even argued that publicly forswearing a nuclear "first
strike" was unwise, as was even partial "disengagement":

Only the very opposite policy is safe—a policy of continuous
engagement at every point, on all levels of action, by both tactical
and strategic moves.

It was in his best-known work, *We Hold These Truths*, that
Murray justified brinksmanship:

Our policy should envisage a minimum of security and a maximum
of risk. Only by such a policy can we seize and retain the
initiative in world affairs. And it is highly dangerous not to have

the initiative. On the premise of this balance we did, in fact, enter the Korean war, which was right. But then we retreated from the premise to a policy of minimum risk, which was a mistake. Moreover, it would be prudent even to create situations of risk for the Soviet Union—situations in which the risk would be too great for it to take.

Much of youth's disillusionment in the late Sixties came from the discovery that liberals were only the left wing of the Establishment, and that they conceived of no position leftward of their own as legitimate. American liberalism was just not a very daring thing; and Catholic liberalism was even less venturesome than the non-religious kinds. Its principal journal, *Commonweal*, would in later years boast that it never fell for McCarthyism; but only a staff member's last-minute tampering with Edward Skillin's copy kept that magazine from saying, back in 1953, that so much McCarthyite smoke around Owen Lattimore must be the sign of real fire somewhere. The "distributist" and agrarian bent of so many Catholic liberals made it easy for them to slip into anti-intellectual forms of American "conservatism"—an arc that a Centra-Verein journal like *The Wanderer* had traced back in the Forties. Even at *Commonweal* a distributist stockholder, Philip Burnham, toyed with the idea of selling his key bloc of shares to *National Review*, where his brother James was a senior editor. William Buckley was interested, and had drawn up the tentative editorial board for a new and conservative *Commonweal* (he hoped to get Christopher Dawson as editor-in-chief), but the crisis came and passed while Buckley was in Europe.

It is no wonder that Father Murray's last pupils at Woodstock thought his brand of liberalism simply obsolete or irrelevant. In the year after his death some of these seminarians questioned the secular competence of those manufacturing the antipersonnel weapon, liquid napalm; and after they were arrested for destroying Dow Chemical files, it came out that the Jesuits' Maryland Province owned $45,000 worth of shares in Dow Chemical. Nothing wrong with that, in the Murray view of things. Businessmen have their competence, and government has its; and the church should not dictate to such legitimate concerns how they contract for each other's services. Still, it embarrassed the Order to be on both sides of this criminal trial —having a proprietary interest in the prosecution and filial ties with the defendants. So Jesuit superiors made a typical liberal compromise: they decided to sell the stock as an expression of brotherly solidarity—but not of ideological agreement—with the seminarians facing trial.

Yet the time for admiring such compromise had passed. The defendants were not grateful, but indignant, at sale of the stock. They wanted to use that part-ownership as a lever for stockholders' actions against Dow management. Murray's scheme of separation would not permit such questioning of Dow in its own area; if there was doubt of its legitimacy in serious actions, he would simply have withdrawn church ties from the secular endeavor. Young protesters saw all this as mere evasion—taking profit from the secular order, yet refusing to assume stewardship for the consequences of that action. Their challenge was meant as a call to responsibility, to an involvement that already existed at a hygienically neutral (yet profitable) level, but not at the level of moral accountability.

More and more, during Woodstock's last days in Maryland, arguments between such factions reached an impasse. Just as the bar lady claimed, it was an entire old ideal that was being left behind, not just a physical site. It was a fragmented community that scattered off, in stages, from the Maryland countryside. A pilot group of faculty and students moved to New York. The library was eased toward its new location. The college half-lived in two places while bits of it were dismantled, some saved, some left behind, some given away. Individual Jesuits carted off things otherwise fated to be lost—desks, a chandelier, the parlor inlay, bits of altar furnishings; historical knickknacks, sentimental emblems of unity taken one by one to new places. Even the fire engine was returned to the County, some months before the last contingent of seminarians left for New York. That is why the church I drove by, on my way to the neighborhood tavern, was a ruined one. On the night it caught fire, the alarm rang uselessly in the College corridor. A bridge was being repaired (had been repaired, but was still blocked off for a grand opening), so the County could not get its engines back out to the College. Woodstock, caught in midtransit, was helpless to do anything; so everyone just gathered and watched the church burn down.

· EIGHT ·

Paul in Chains

The church, instructed by the teaching of
humility, does not command as though by
authority, but persuades by reason.

—POPE GREGORY THE GREAT

SOME TIME AFTER VATICAN II the secular city enthusiasts lost
their faith in the World; and with that mainstay gone, it was
hard to believe in anything—how could faith in the church,
which had become a parasite on political optimism, outlast
that worldly hope? The very weakest things, in the postconciliar era, were what preconciliar liberals had felt surest of—two
things, especially: the liturgy, and papal encyclicals.

No conciliar victory was more evident—nor emptier—than
reform of the liturgy. The Liturgical Conference in this country
succeeded itself right out of business. It became prosperous
and wealthy (from the sale of ever-changing liturgical guides
and texts), but soon found itself with nothing to do. Its annual
bash, the Liturgical Week, veered uncertainly back and forth
from the grand to the bare, from monster rally to hotel-room
intimacy, from casual to theatrical; too jaded with the exotic
to find anything really daring, yet unable to fall back on the
familiar. In 1966, the Week became a seminar on secularity; in
1968, reflecting the national change in mood, on revolution. In

1969, the best-known speakers were some Black Panthers, Dr. Benjamin Spock, Wayne Morse (former Senator from Oregon), and the SCLC's Andrew Young—none of them Catholic, despite the fact that eucharistic celebration is basically (though not exclusively) a gathering of one's fellows around the hearth of the faith—those called by Saint Paul *hoi oikeioi tēs pisteōs* (Gal. 6.10). Ecumenism backfired when *Protestant* observers attacked the meeting's lack of real concern with liturgy. The major audience response was given to Rabbi Abraham Herschel, who refreshed the delegates with novelty by daring to speak about God. When something liturgical was offered, it was in the trendy vein of that year's borrowed hippie idiom; and when some participants felt this was alien to their personal style, the director publicly called them "stiff-assed honkies." So much for the banquet of charity. Five members of the Board resigned. As a Cause, the liturgy was dead.

The whole effort had been based on a chain of false premises—that there was large-scale demand for liturgical change among the laity; that the liturgical mystery these laymen failed to understand was the Latin language; that one cannot participate in music or spectacle without being an active musician or spectacle-maker; that resisting bishops had to be forced to grant new freedom in this area (whereas in fact the bishops were maneuvered into forcing new things on their resisting flocks). The results dismayed most of the faithful in one way or another. They were presented with something neither new nor old, just a muddied intermediate third thing (or non-thing), with songs no one sang, tentative English-language pieties one did not hear or did not want to hear, and sermons as lifeless as before but with different clichés ("People of God" for "Mother Church"). The thing that most needed change was least changed. "Breaking the bread of the Word" meant, in the patristic era, close public study of scripture—some of the greatest ancient commentaries are merely the collected sermon-cycles of an Augustine (on the Psalms, on St. John) or a Chrysostom (on Genesis, on Romans). Readings and hymns were arranged around this continuing meditation on the community's own biblical origins.

But older Catholic priests were unequipped to speak of scripture before an educated audience, and most younger priests tried to be "relevant" as a prelude to preaching, and never got beyond the prelude. Thus politics replaced parish finances in the Sunday sermon. The problem, it turned out, had not been Latin or too little singing, but faith itself, and Catholics' inability to discuss that faith with one another in convincing ways (a difficulty not entirely caused, but certainly symbolized, by priests' inability to lead such discussion). The liturgical movement was supposed to call liberal "drop-outs" back from monastic retreats to the revitalized parish, reuniting the faithful in a single rite that could speak to all, clergy and laity, experimenters and traditionalists. But liberals soon found that the intellectual impoverishment of the neighborhood church was even more apparent in the new English than in the old Latin. (Under the old system, feats of Gregorian or mediaeval vestmanship could give aesthetic cover to intellectual resourcelessness.) So they dropped out again, this time not toward monasteries but into "underground" liturgies that were often mere branches of the youth and peace-movement "counterculture." The "sign of unity" had divided men, done so more dramatically than the Latin Mass ever did. As a last insult to the very concept of freedom, American bishops "outlawed" the Latin Mass and created a short-lived "underground" of pre-Tridentine nostalgia.

But if the fate of the liturgy was disheartening to some men, the papal encyclical became a disaster in almost everyone's eyes. With *Humanae Vitae*, his encyclical condemning "artificial" contraception, Paul VI did to his reign what Lyndon Johnson did with the Vietnam war. From that moment everything seemed to run downhill, till it looked as if Paul could do nothing with his papacy but what Johnson did with his presidency—surrender it, resigning as a gesture of reconciliation.

Pope Paul, no more than President Johnson, deserved such cruel recompense for his stewardship. It is not merely that both were unfairly compared with their predecessors, as lack-luster successors to men of glamor and "charisma." The basic injustice to their reputation lies in the fact that both were following the policy of the preceding regime when they took the actions that made them unpopular. Kennedy had committed himself to an activist presidency, symbolized by the willingness to enter "brush-fire" wars—and his own foreign-policy team stayed on under Johnson to play out these commitments in Southeast Asia. It is less widely recognized that Pope John, too, had marked out the path that led Paul to the catastrophe of *Humanae Vitae*. John had reserved the question of contraception to himself, not letting Council fathers discuss it at Vatican II; he appointed his own commission to study the problem, one that Paul expanded and made more inclusive. There is no sign that John XXIII was receptive to doctrinal innovation—he was very traditional in his theology and piety (he even tried to canonize his reactionary predecessor Pius IX). As a lifelong diplomat, his genius was for humanizing the existing system, for placating, making things work.

John was not the holy fool men made of him—no one survives a lifetime career in the Curial diplomatic corps without learning the tricks of his trade (one of which, for him, was suggesting to others that he was a holy fool). When he suavely baffled Curial initiatives at the Council, it was with skills only one of their own could use against them. So "aggiornamento" meant, for Pope John, mere adjusting—not basic reform. This is signified in the emphasis he placed on the Council's task as "pastoral" and not "doctrinal." At first this stress was welcomed by church liberals, who resisted any Roman moves toward doctrine, since that had for a long time meant stricter doctrinal enforcement (as in Pius XII's *Humani Generis*) or doctrinal additions (as when Pius "defined" the Virgin's physical ascension to heaven). No one, at the outset, dared hope for doctrinal *revision* to come out of the Council.

But Paul inherited a Council accelerating past these early expectations, and he had to deal with a postconciliar restlessness even John could not have charmed away with charismatic diplomacy. The demand was no longer for warm pastoral attitudes, but hard doctrinal statements, for changes made without equivocation, for admitting mistakes with intellectual honesty. Paul, beset from two sides, had to resort to the biggest weapon in his arsenal—which was, in practical terms, the encyclical. "Definitions" would be suspect now. But liberal allegiance to encyclicals had been carried to new heights by John's famous letters, *Mater et Magistra* and *Pacem in Terris.*

Yet even here John's "liberalizing" moves had odd side effects. Men praise him for addressing *Pacem in Terris* not merely to Catholics but to "all men of good will." This seemed to open the church out toward the world. Considered, however, in the light of encyclical history—which had been, symbolically at least, a consultation of the Pope with his brother bishops—the encyclical moved away from the collegial sharing of authority.* Furthermore, John's letter anticipated—with the college of bishops assembled already in Rome—conciliar statements on the relation of the church to the world. John did not speak with or through the bishops, but outran the debates and sessions in his own statement. Liberals, of course, were in no position to resent this—his letter put pressure on the Council to advance their own opinions; and they had for years relied on encyclicals as weapons against the very bishops whose "collegiality" they now advocated. All this left Paul with an ambiguous situation.

Paul took his task to be both pastoral and doctrinal—through the Council to "update," to modernize within the ancient framework; and through encyclicals to affirm the stability of that doctrinal framework. He assumed this latter task in his encyclical on the Eucharist, *Mysterium Fidei*—and the theological community showed it was not ready to compromise further: the Aristotelian concepts of substance and accident, in which Aquinas had enunciated the doctrine of Christ's presence in the Eucharist (by way of "transubstantiation"), could no longer be accepted. There was quiet resistance to the encyclical, precisely on the grounds of its outmoded basis in

*For more on the history of encyclicals, see the appendix to this chapter.

one philosophy, the anchoring of gospel mystery (Matthew's account of the Last Supper) to scientific opinion (Aristotle's, in the *Metaphysics*).

This first encounter should have been a warning to the Pope, since opposition to the church's attitude on contraception had already arisen, in seminaries and universities, as a protest against narrow readings of old "natural law" philosophy. Here, as in reform of the liturgy and new versions of the bible, the laymen had not first grown restive—though the use or non-use of contraceptives seemed to affect them most intimately. The doubts came on the priest's side of the confessional veil, or in the pulpit; and therefore in clerical studies and classrooms. The issue was one of intellectual honesty; of the whole intellectual structure within which faith was to be grasped and taught—its demands laid upon others, its claims rationally vindicated. The church's stand on contraception did not even blend dubious philosophy with gospel mystery; it simply had no basis in the New Testament or in the Old. The crime of Onan, who "spilled his seed upon the ground" (Gen. 38.8–10), was once considered to be contraceptive—a form of coitus interruptus; but modern scholarship is agreed that the crime involved is a tribal one, the withholding of heirs (and so of inheritance) from a dead brother's line.

The Pope's ban on contraceptives, as an extreme case of papal teaching claims, became a test and a symbol of all his other claims. Many seemingly peripheral issues were closely bound into this one—the question of a church tradition as separable from scripture (one of the first fights at the Council had been over this "two sources" view of doctrinal derivation); the question of the relationship between faith and morals (can a moral duty not directly taken from revealed doctrine be a subject of church law at this level?); the question of rescuing past papal commitments (Pius XI's *Casti Connubii*, already weakened and whittled at, would collapse entirely if contraception were permitted now); the question of the faithful's trust or credulity (if they had been misled for so many years, at the cost of so many daily sacrifices, in this matter, why take the church's word on anything?); and even the question of the bishops' joint or collegial authority (they had united with the Pope in explicitly condemning contraceptives for at least three decades). So, just *because* this was the weakest part in the church's moral "line," a weakest-link way of thinking made it the most crucial point. Let this line break, and the whole chain would give. Indeed, so well was the trap laid for Paul that extremists on both sides used the weakest-link approach. Right extremists used it to assert maximal claims for the church to pronounce on all kinds of moral issues. The church's extreme Left used it to say that, since all authority was at issue in this case, and the Pope had clearly erred, the whole doctrine of "infallibility" was destroyed. British theologian Charles Davis took this latter position, and left the church. Hans Küng took it, and stayed within to reform the church. Both theologians agreed with disciplinarians like Washington's Cardinal O'Boyle that *Humanae Vitae* was a sufficient and supreme test of traditional faith. In a debate so structured, if the Pope listened to *either* side in drawing up and trying to enforce an encyclical against contraception, he was lost—and, as it turned out, he had been listening to *both* sides.

The result can be read in reactions to the encyclical. Most of the faithful tried to ignore it, most theologians tried to minimize it. Exceptions, modifications, "hard-case" loose applications were instantly invented, in the manner of casuist moral theologians—which just raised again the difficulties of intellectual honesty among teachers and preachers. The only ray of hope for some men was the fact that the Pope had not "defined" the doctrine with those *ex cathedra* formulae demanded by Vatican I for infallible (*de fide definitae*) doctrines. But the extremists scurried and bustled to close even that loophole.

Both Right and Left—by synecdoche, *Triumph* magazine and Hans Küng—argued that the encyclical merely put a seal on the church's agelong opposition to contraception. *Triumph* found multiple infallibilities hedging everything to do with the subject; and even Küng, who knew better (as the words I italicize indicate), could write: "And yet, because—as we have shown—it [the prohibition of contraceptives] had *always*, or *at least for half a century* before the Council, been taught unanimously by the ordinary teaching office of the Pope and bishops, it belongs to the universal infallible Catholic faith." This way of sneaking generally accepted things up the scale of authority to "practical" infallibility is an old trick of the Curial theologians, and sounds very odd in the pages of a "liberal" writer. Even the abrupt shrinking to "half a century" stretches things, since the only solemn papal statement on the books was Pius XI's *Casti Connubii*, written just thirty-three years before the Council. (Sixtus V's bull *Effraenatam*, had condemned contraception; but it was rescinded after two years.) Of course there had been a cultural consensus against contraception through the ages, one often strengthened by the objectionability of means proposed—things such as magic, potions, or spells. (These were the *maleficia* condemned by Sixtus V.) Even Pius XI's letter had been superseded by the "rhythm" method of contraception which was just being introduced to the medical world in the year (1930) when *Casti Connubii* appeared. And everyone now agrees that the 1930 encyclical's strongest argument—from scripture, over which the Pope has a greater claim to speak with authority than in the field of natural philosophy—was based on a mistaken understanding of the Onan story. (Paul did not repeat that argument in *Humanae Vitae*.) Thus the whole papal "tradition" banning contraceptives is based on a 1930 encyclical that erred on its strongest point and fell into almost immediate desuetude (though this latter fact was disguised from laymen).

Another position the extremists had to shore up was the problem of contraception's moral gravity. Vatican I, in setting forth the doctrine of papal infallibility, said the Pope could speak *ex cathedra* on serious matters of Christian faith and morals. How can the birth-control pill be subjected to Christian revelation? What specifically theological importance does it have? *Triumph*, of course, attaches a prurient importance to the whole subject of sex, and then asserts: "It is difficult to imagine a more likely battleground on which her [the church's] fate will be decided. . . . If the Church does not own this key, it does not own any keys at all." Thus are the "keys of the kingdom" reduced to mere smithying of intellectual chastity belts.

Dr. Küng tries to skirt the problem of contraception's theological importance with a series of misleading rhetorical questions:

"Is not the Catholic morality of marriage based precisely on dogmatic arguments?" Partly—especially the arguments for monogamy and against divorce. But *Humanae Vitae* itself stresses that the whole and the sole argument against contraception arises from "natural philosophy."

"How are the requirements of Christian revelation and those of natural law (if we want to make use of this problematical expression) to be adequately distinguished from one another?" Dr. Küng knows perfectly well how they are to be distinguished; he is just not, for the moment, saying—as the next question indicates.

"Doesn't the Bible also contain 'natural law'?" No, not in the technical sense given the term "natural law" by those condemning contraceptives. Küng grants this point *sotto voce* when, to save some pretense at theological sophistication, he is forced to put quotation marks around "natural law" and to call it a "problematical expression." The "law" adduced is a particular form of one school of philosophical speculation; and the gospel is not bound to one school of philosophers.

"And isn't the Decalogue for the most part both [i.e., both revelation and natural law] *in one?"* The answer is No, and Küng knows the answer is No. The Decalogue, so called, is a covenant treaty between God and his people, contracting for specific obligations on both sides. To treat it as a general statement of all human morality is absurd; it is the sort of thing that made old "examination of conscience" manuals derive the most unlikely imperatives from particular clauses of the Jews' treaty. Thus all sensual indulgence was lumped together under the prohibition against "coveting thy neighbor's wife," an approach which made gluttony, laziness, and drunkenness di-

rectly sexual offenses—offenses where, according to Catholic moralists of the old school, there was "no parvity of matter," all sins were automatically grave or "mortal." I knew a scrupulous young man who was literally driven mad by this line of thought, one that Küng now glibly advances for his purpose.

Even by Rome's nineteenth-century standards, the problem of contraception does not qualify for infallible church pronouncement. It is not one of the great interconnected mysteries that make up what Cardinal Newman called "the circle of the articles of faith." It is not a revelation on the nature of God, like the doctrine of the Trinity. It is not a revelation of the nature of man, like the doctrine of human redemption. In fact it is not a supernatural subject at all, nor one treated in scripture; not one on which another doctrine depends as its premise, nor one that is derived from such a doctrine. It is not even a subject on which there is a clear and useful church tradition.

Yet even when Pius XII was stretching the infallible claims of the Pope to their utmost, when defining the physical assumption of the Virgin Mary, he felt obliged to justify his action by noting that this was a strictly theological matter, "truth revealed by God and contained in that divine deposit which Christ has delivered to His Spouse to be guarded faithfully and to be taught infallibly . . . which surely no faculty of the human mind could know by its own natural powers." The ban against contraceptives does not, as Pius said of the Assumption, "form a complete harmony with the other revealed truths"—how could it, when it is not itself a revealed truth?

There is, of course, an adventitious importance lent to this subject, one not arising from its own nature but from the fact that church authorities have chosen to defend their prerogatives on this ground. What is at issue, then, is the question whether these authorities can define anything as of ultimate importance if it involves their pretensions. This tactic falls right in with Küng's counterstrategy, so that he quotes with approval the minority ("conservative") report of the papal commission on birth control:

If contraception were declared not intrinsically evil, in honesty it would have to be acknowledged that the Holy Spirit, in 1930 (*Casti Connubii*), in 1951 (Address of Pius XII to midwives) and 1958 (Address of the society of haemotologists in the year of Pius XII's death), assisted Protestant churches, and that for half a century Pius XI, Pius XII, and a great part of the Catholic hierarchy did not protect men against a very serious error, one most pernicious to souls; for it would thus be suggested that they condemned most imprudently, under the pain of eternal punishment, thousands upon thousands of human acts which are now approved. Indeed, it must be neither denied nor ignored that these acts would be approved for the same fundamental reasons which Protestantism alleged and which they (Catholics) condemned or at least did not recognize.

We cannot let the Holy Spirit be more on "their" side than on "ours"—not, that is, on the side of the Anglicans' Lambeth Conference, against which *Casti Connubii* was directed. It is the argument of churchmen who had to maintain the case against Galileo for so long. Any error made by church authority must be sustained by a thousand subsequent and reinforcing errors, each more egregious as reality becomes ever harder to oppose.

Küng naturally sees the force of these parallels, but joins the minority report in discounting them: "The Galileo condemnation was concerned with a peripheral question (world picture); the condemnation of the Eastern Patriarch Photius, which was withdrawn by Paul VI after 900 years, was only an excess in the mode of procedure." Yet the Galileo thesis was hardly "peripheral." It was challenged as unscriptural, as an attack on the reliability of the bible, on the very possibility of divine revelation as it was understood at the time. Taken in those terms, not only was it more properly theological in scope than anything having to do with contraception, but more within the competence of church teachers *and* more important in the practical religious life of men. The mere "procedural excess" of condemning Photius led to the eventual sundering of Christian unity and—again in terms of that day—the denial of the very sources for supernatural life to a large part of the world. Next to these, the recent and admitted errors of the church in the whole matter of contraception are minor things. Küng only wants them to be major so that every kind of authority can be involved in the ruin of this straw man.

Needless to say, the *Triumph* editors are in entire agreement with Küng's position (though for entirely different motives). They, too, see this teaching as important because it is precisely here that "the Church is ready to take a stand for her own life." By "Church" they mean of course (as theological "conservatives" usually do) the church authorities—whence expressions like "the Church says" or "the Church teaches" or "the Church is always right." If the arguments in *Humanae Vitae* are not valid ones, then this church is in error—which Catholics must consider an unfortunate situation. But the opposite assumption is no more pleasant for them—might, in fact, be a good deal worse. For if the Pope is right, another "church" is wrong—the majority of the faithful, lay and clerical, amateur and professional (even *Triumph* admits most theologians are at odds with *Humanae Vitae*), including many bishops (perhaps a majority of those who hold a reflected-on position, as opposed to the bishops who regard implementing the encyclical as a simple administrative problem). And which "church" matters more? The defenders of "church" in the narrow sense (church *rulers*) should think back on the ancient theological maxim that "firmest judgments are those most widespread in the Christian life"—*Securus judicat orbis terrarum*, as St. Augustus put it. Vincent of Lerins, in another statement used as a touchstone ever after, called true doctrine that which had been accepted everywhere, always, and by everyone (*quod ubique, semper, ab omnibus*).

It was John Henry Newman's meditation on these standards that took him out of the Anglican church (which seemed too parochial) into the large communion of Rome. He did not consider this step, primarily, as an act of submission to the Pope, but as entry into a complex life of the whole (Greek *to holon*), that which gives the church its catholicity (*kath-holou*, "through-out the whole"). And he came to differ with Roman authorities over the very episode that had led him to historical catholicism: during the Arian heresy, Newman argued, church authorities erred oftener than not—papal authority as well as conciliar—and the greatest continuity of orthodox belief was maintained by the laity. Newman saw nothing unusual in this; he argued that the Spirit's promise was to the whole church, in which authority has had various "distribution and allocation in the ecclesiastical body" without destroying the faith's unity of impulse: "A triangle or parallelogram is the same in its substance and nature whichever side is made its base."

These are the norms St. Augustine used in criticizing the parochialism of Donatist bishops: "As Christ sits in glory at his Father's right hand, the possessor of the whole world, these Donatists have the audacity to say to him, 'Here is your kingdom,' and instead of the whole world, they give him—Africa." The papalists of today must be shaken at times when they consider the difference between "the church" in their sense (Pope and Curia) and in Newman's or Augustine's sense. These people, in their attempt to maintain a spurious consistency in recent papal documents, rather than a unity of impulse through the whole Christian body, have forced Pope Paul into the position of justifying his stewardship in the church much as Donatists did in the fifth century. Instead of the whole world, Paul is rendering back to Christ—*Triumph* magazine.

APPENDIX TO CHAPTER EIGHT: *The Early Encyclicals*

At a time when all liberals, secular as well as religious, were celebrating the weight of encyclicals, the New York *Times* ran a background story on Pope John's *Mater et Magistra* with this headline: "Encyclicals Issued 20 Centuries." Actually the *engkyklios epistolē*, or "circulating letter," arose as a distinct form in the fourth century. It was a polemical instrument used by and against the Arians. In the orthodox see of Alexandria, the bishop Alexander (helped by his brilliant young secre-

tary Athanasius) wrote to other bishops for endorsement of the anti-
Arian position:

> Brothers, beloved, one in spirit, show yourselves at unity with our
> view, against the crazed audacity of these men; follow the example
> of our colleagues in the ministry who, indignant against the sect,
> have corresponded with me to condemn it and have added their
> names to my document—names I have already sent you by my son
> the deacon Apion, names from all Egypt and the Thebais, Libya
> and Pentapolis, Syria and, even farther off, from Lycia and Pam-
> phylia, Asia, Cappadocia and those regions. I trust you will accept
> these as an example for yourselves (82.909).*

Alexander fired off some seventy letters, acquiring a formidable list
of names in this effort at holding a quasi council by mail. The Arian
Eusebius of Nicomedea tried to head off this epistolary excommunication at every postal pass, sending letters and eliciting signatures for the
other side. Alexander warned his correspondents against these heretical
encyclicals:

> Since these men have been anathematized by our brothers, do not
> receive them, nor accept speeches or letters from them, with their
> seducing lies and general lack of truth. They visit cities for no other
> purpose than, by pretext and wheedling, under cover of amity and
> show of concord, to give and take letters with which to fool the little
> victims of their lies, "silly women laden with sin, etc" (82.908).

The air of the fourth century was thick with anathematizing missives—
an epistolary warfare that became so heated it was parodied in theaters
(62.52). But Alexander defended his use of the encyclical as an instrument of peace:

> In all my efforts to find a cure for those wounded, I came on this
> antidote for a people deceived by them—since men follow the gen-
> eral concord of our colleagues in the ministry, which leads them to
> desire repentance (82.909). (The idea of true doctrine as the soul's
> medicine became a commonplace: cf. John Chrysostom *Peri
> Pronoias* 1–4).

It is not surprising that Alexander's secretary, who became his
successor, used the encyclical in his own behalf when Arian bishops
procured his exile. Athanasius asked his colleagues in the ministry
(*sylleitourgoi*) to join with the people (the *laoi*, faithful to him throughout all his troubles with the court and the episcopacy) in restoring him
to Alexandria (25.225). He is repeating the call to all twelve tribes in
Judges 19. 29: He sends his letters of unity as the Levite sent around
lopped-off limbs of the murdered woman, to call Israel up against its
violators (25.224).

---

*References are to volume and column of Migne, *Patrologia Graeca*.

For over a century, authenticating letters were a testimony to orthodox faith. But as the heresies were conquered and power was centralized in Rome and Constantinople, the initiative of local bishops dwindled. It was now a Pope (Martin I) who called his letter to Carthage *encyclica nostra epistola* (the older Latin term for the bishops' missives had been *litterae communicatoriae,* as in Augustine *Epistle* 43.7). The form was neglected after the eighth century, and largely forgotten until—a whole millennium later—Dominic Bencini wrote a two-volume study of early encyclicals. Twelve years later, Benedict XIV, prompted apparently by Bencini's study, decided to use the bishops' ancient form in addressing them: in 1740 he wrote the first modern encyclical, *Ubi Primum.* It was another century, however, before the issuing of these letters became a regular practice. Since then, Popes have varied in their approach to encyclicals—Leo XIII, for instance, first used the letters to discuss political and social problems in a broad way; while Pius XII by and large saved the encyclical form for strictly theological matters, and made his major political statements during an annual Christmas address.

For the most part, the idea of consulting the bishops was maintained only as a courteous formality; but occasionally the Pope has asked for response and opinion by way of an encyclical. Thus, before defining dogmas by their papal right, Pius IX and Pius XII sent encyclicals requesting the bishops to consult local clergy and laity on the state of the church's belief. Pius IX's encyclical, *Ubi Primum,* asked bishops "that you be willing to report to Us how warmly the clergy and faithful are devoted to the Virgin's immaculate conception, and how earnestly they desire that such a matter be defined by the Apostolic See." Then in the Bull that contained his definition, Pius explained the process of consultation: "Although the view of most of our episcopal colleagues was known to Us from the petitions they sent asking for an eventual definition of the immaculate conception of the Virgin, nonetheless we addressed an encyclical and other correspondence to our revered episcopal brothers, one and all throughout the Catholic world, in order that, along with their prayers addressed to God, they might also report to Us in writing the state of the faithful's pious concern for the immaculate conception of God's Mother." So the "preconciliar" church, even during its most extreme exercises of authority, treated the encyclical as an open channel of communication with the entire church.

· NINE ·

═══════════════

Prisoners of Sex

───────────────

Sex, I think, is a frightful trouble,
and I consider, myself, that marriage
only becomes bearable when that element
is largely eliminated.

—MALCOLM MUGGERIDGE

WHY DID PAUL VI FALL SO READILY into the birth-control trap? There was a confluence of motives, arguments, and reasons. The deepest prompting, however, was instinctual, and emerges almost as an aside—but it does emerge, persistently, from the text of *Humanae Vitae*.

Paul gives the apparent reason for writing his encyclical in these terms: he means to give an answer (*responsum dare*, par. 6) to certain *quaestiones* (3) that have arisen, questions that necessitated a profound reconsideration (*nova et altiora consideratio*, 4) of the church's position. He claims he was helped in framing the *responsus* by two groups—the commission appointed to study this subject, and the body of bishops (5). But their "help," as it turns out, lay solely in the prodding work of opposition. He had to mention these two groups, in an age of professed "collegiality" and of praise for "public opinion" within the church. But his expressions of gratitude are empty, and just draw attention to the isolated stand he finally took.

The aim of the papal commission was to bring together various kinds of expertise (in biology, chemistry, gynecology, psychiatry, philosophy) within the context of faithful acquaintance with church teachings. The group was therefore made up of reputable Catholics, episcopal and theological, lay and clerical—bishops and theologians consulting with scientists and those in the lay apostolate. Yet the Pope says he had to reject their findings, for two reasons—first, because the commission did not reach unanimity (*plena sententiarum consensio*); second, because changes recommended by the majority went against what the church had proposed "with constant firmness" (6).

On the lack of unanimity, it should be remembered that unanimity is rarely reached on a controversial issue; that it was not reached in Vatican II's debates, though that did not prevent the Council from issuing documents approved by a majority. The commission on contraception did reach a majority of three-to-one among bishops and four-to-one among theologians. It did this against all the heavy weight of expectation, habit, training, and external pressures. More could not be expected from a group deliberately set up to include the whole range of opinion (and therefore containing diehards from the Curia). To expect absolute accord from such a group would be unrealistic. To use the lack of such accord as an excuse for setting aside the whole report is an astonishing move. Especially if we add one special circumstance.

The subject of contraception is, by the Pope's own account (11), a matter of the natural law—not a revealed mystery, not part of a special deposit of truths entrusted to the church; but a teaching in accord with all men's natural reason (*doctrina humanae rationi consentanea,* 12). An area, then, in which the counsel of competent laymen is most appropriately sought and heeded. Yet the commission did not arrive at what the Pope presents as a fundamental position of natural morality. Here is a truth that the mass of men, given a certain degree of good will and of attention to the subject, should be able to grasp. Not only that—it is a truth the Pope says our age is especially able to grasp (*nostrae aetatis homines aptissimi ad perspiciendum*, 12). Yet the Pope's own commission of Catholics, brought up in the church, trained to the old position, given all the presuppositions that went into that position, could not, with all the expert advice at their disposal, reach the same conclusion as the Pope. They were people of manifest good will, as their records show. They possessed better than average intelligence and training, and they were called upon because their particular fields of concentration were involved (*disciplinarum ad hanc rem attinentium studiosi*, the Pope himself calls them, 5). Yet if even these people could not grasp a truth available to all men's reason, and could not do so in an age best suited for grasping it, what hope is there that the mass of men will ever do so? For the Pope to set aside the report, and yet to maintain that his conclusions are perspicuous to human reason, is absurd. If these men and women were wrong on this issue, how can mankind at large ever find the truth about it?

Paul's second reason for rejecting the report was that it went against what the church had consistently maintained. That judgment is itself disputable; but assume for a moment it is right—why set up a commission at all if it could not reach new findings? If its decision was foreordained, then its procedures were a mockery. The Pope, by his action, seems to say that the *quaestiones* to which he is responding must not be taken seriously as subjects which the human reason, following *its* own inner dictates, can deal with in *their* own proper terms. Yet, all this is done in the name of natural reason. Either the Pope had nothing to learn from specialists in the field of natural morality—and then why did he ask for their help? Or did he have something to learn—and then why did he reject their conclusions? The dilemma is irresolvable.

What of the other group he thanks for their advice? He says that various bishops offered him advice and counsel, some at his request, others spontaneously. He does not expressly say that he put such help aside (as he did the commission's findings), but this is implied when the Pope moves directly from the thanks for both groups to an assertion that he had to solve the problem all by himself (*per Nosmetipsos,* 6). It is known that some bishops counseled against release of the encyclical. Others were patently embarrassed by it when it did appear. What is more to the point, Paul did not consult other bishops in the obvious way—at the Council—when they were conveniently assembled at his doorstep for considering the needs of the church. So far was he from consulting them that he ordered them not to bring up the *quaestiones* which, the encyclical says, need reconsidering by the church (4). In this matter, Paul not only restricts "church" to mean the teaching church, he limits it to himself: *"L'église, c'est Moi."*

The Pope writes that his decision was an agonizing one. Why, then, did he not share the burden with others? But with whom could he share it? With the expert commission, whose report advocated change? With the mass of the faithful who, according to the public polls and petitions and lay congresses, favor change? With the *schola theologorum,* whose *periti* were active for change at the Council? With the bishops, who were being convinced by the arguments of the *periti,* and whose document On the Modern World goes far, despite the papal ban on discussion of contraception, toward changing the old view of Christian marriage? Paul showed how much he trusted the bishops when he tried to insert his personal statement into their documents, on the condition that they not debate the issue. The Pope could turn to no one but himself, because it was unlikely that any representative body would reach his foreordained conclusion. Even *Triumph* magazine, in defending the Pope's actions, admits that by the time of the cncyclical "those who were willing to defend the Magisterium [teaching authority] were reduced, in fact, to a beleaguered minority." The magazine boasts that it was the only national publication to greet the Pope's letter with full assent upon its appearance in America.

What prompted the Pope to go out on this limb and, in *Triumph's* words, "take on the whole world"? What were the *quaestiones* he felt he had to answer at such risk to his personal standing and the discipline of the church? The encyclical lists four important changes that must be dealt with in our present situation—the population explosion, higher expenses for child support and education, the changed role of women (with a consequent change in the view of marriage), and new means for controlling nature.

This is a remarkable list, both for what it includes and for what it excludes. No one will deny that the first three points are generally relevant; but they had been pressing concerns for many a decade without affecting Catholic belief. They were, in fact, leading considerations at the Anglicans' Lambeth Conference, which elicited *Casti Connubii*. They explain the fact that our country has for a long time been "egged on by the agitation of proliferating birth-control societies" (in the ungracious phrase of *Triumph*). What was it that, when added to these things, caused Catholics to change their attitude so abruptly? "Technology," the Pope suggests in his fourth point— and that is, at one level, a reference to improved techniques of contraception, notably anovulent pills (which are not, however, expressly mentioned in the encyclical). It is true that "the pill" forced a reconsideration of Rome's position. But that reconsideration was based on the argument from natural law, closer scrutiny of which soon ran into massive difficulties on its own, so that doubt spread far beyond the pill's licitness. In the end, the papal commission's majority report made no distinction between the pill and other contraceptive devices. The opposition to contraceptives had crumbled "across the board."

Given this situation, why did the Pope specify the occasion (the pill) rather than the grounds (natural law philosophy) of Catholic reconsideration? Part of the answer is an animus against technology itself, an attempt to blame the new moral insensitivity (which apparently makes it hard to grasp old verities) upon the pretensions of science. The letter is almost obsessed with man's aim at achieving total control over his own situation (*moderationem ad totam suam vitam, 2*). We are warned that men must not deal with their sexual life arbitrarily (*se arbitratu suo gerere*) as if the right course were left to their autonomous decision (*modo omnino proprio ac libero,* 10). Intercourse during infertile periods is allowable because the act's barrenness is not then within the will of the spouses (11). Man is not to separate sex and procreation on his own initiative (*sua sponte,* 12). It is against the divine will (*voluntati primi vitae humanae Auctoris*) that man should aim at complete mastery over the sources of life (*dominum se confitetur fontium vitae*), since man does not have unlimited power over his own body (*corporis sui infinitam potestatem,* 13). It is the infertility achieved by man's *industria* that is illicit (14). An underlying horror is expressed at the idea that the generation of life might lie within man's choice (*hominum arbitratu concedatur,* 17), suggesting that man will take total possession of his own body and its natural functions (*potestas quam homo in proprium corpus in eiusque naturalia munera habere potest,* 17). Man must not place a Faustian confidence in his own scientific skills (*technibus artibus sese committens,* 18).

Why is this confidence wrong? Are the skills to be feared in themselves? Apparently not, for sure dominion over things becomes laudable when it is a question of physicians seeking a foolproof basis (*certum fundamentum*) for the rhythm system, a thing which the *medica ars* is to accomplish by doctors' deliberate effort (*sua data opera,* 24). Science is resisted when it extends the use of sex within marriage, supported when it limits that use—a pattern we find discernible in all parts of the encyclical.

I said above that the encyclical's list of *quaestiones* is as remarkable for what it excludes as for what it includes (e.g., the strong emphasis on man's rampant technology). The problem it excludes is the main one—the impossibility of maintaining old "natural law theory" as applied to the contraception issue. That is not put among the problems to be considered, things to which the Pope makes his response; yet it was the thing most needing treatment. The external pressures of population and cultural change had beat on the Catholic position for decades and made no appreciable dent. It was only when the debate over natural law became intense that change took place—and then it happened rapidly. The Pope's own commission, hardly a radical group, entered on its deliberations predisposed against change, accepting the maxims of theologians about "the end of the act" and "the integrity of the act" —yet as soon as they questioned these maxims, they were forced to new conclusions, disconcerting the Pontiff who had called them together.

Since the Pope does not place these difficulties among the new matters calling for response, he does not give new justifications for the old theory, or even trace its argument. He simply states its conclusion: *necessarium est ut quilibet matrimonii usus ad vitam humanam procreandum per se destinatus permaneat* (11). "It is necessary that each marital act remain intrinsically intended to beget human life." *Destinatus*, which means "intended" or "aimed at" or "designed," is softened in the first English text that was released—"remain *open* to the transmission of human life"—as a way of fudging the problem of "rhythmic" intercourse during the infertile period, carefully scheduled acts which are *not* intended to beget life. Some, using this mistranslation, tried to justify the rhythm method as "open" to life because it is inefficient—as if the morality of the act would change when 70 per cent predictability edges up to 80 per cent, or 80 per cent to 90 per cent. Yet Paul himself asks doctors to give rhythm a *certum* (100 per cent) *fundamentum*.

The Pope's judgment is based on a weird Catholic reading of "natural law" theory, one largely shaped to provide a basis for condemning contraceptives, but drawing on Aristotle's biological teleology as it had passed through the Stoics' moral reductionism. The argument is that "natural acts" have their unity from a singleness of aim (*telos*), to which all other side effects or uses must be subordinated as ancillary. Unless these secondary uses subserve the primary aim, they are disordered and "unnatural." Thus the natural aim of intercourse is procreation, as that of eating is nutrition, that of seeing is to receive knowledge, and of speaking to convey knowledge—any pleasure or other use of these acts must be subordinate to the natural aim. Pleasure from food is a biological bribe toward self-preservation, and each act of eating or drinking must be designed to promote nutrition or it is immoral.

This biologistic approach to morality had the paradoxical result of making the most moral aspect of an act its most animal side. Man might put natural necessity to a higher use, but only if he *subordinated* this human innovation to the functional first uses of biology. The feast of fellowship, for instance, the breaking of bread in amity, the creation of spiritual symbols out of what had been mere physical compulsion—all this was not to be considered a sign of man's spirit, something to separate him from the beasts; since he must justify such "indulgences" precisely in the name of bodily necessity.

Actually, such teleological reductionism was only vaguely applied to most bodily acts, which were considered basically good or at least neutral. Eating's over-all services to health were enough to justify gourmandise short of outright drunkenness or Neronian regurgitation. But religious suspicion of sexuality led to far more rigorous application of the teleological test to each and every act of intercourse. For centuries Christian moralists forbade intercourse to sterile people and to all women after menopause, since the act could not then be ordered to procreation. By the time of Pius XI all such prohibitions had been softened, but only on the grounds that nonproductivity in these acts was outside man's control. As *Casti Connubii* put it: "Nor are those considered as acting against nature who in the married state use their right in the proper manner, although on account of natural reasons either of time or of certain defects new life cannot be brought forth." The "natural reasons of time" did not refer to planned use of infertile periods by the rhythm method, since that was not yet based on published knowledge. Indeed, the 1930 encyclical's main prohibitions still move in the realm of *intention* not to procreate. They ban *all* planned control of intercourse's consequences: *Cum autem actus conjugii suopte natura proli gen-*

erandae sit destinatus, qui, in eo exercendo, naturali hac eum vi atque virtute de industria destituunt, contra naturam agunt.
. . . "Since the marital act is of its very nature intended to beget offspring, those who *by design* deprive it of this natural quality and power, are acting at odds with nature. . . ." And he further offers this as the church's rule, that: *quemlibet matrimonii usum, in quo exercendo, actus, de industria hominum, naturali sua vitae procreandae vi destituatur, Dei et naturae legem infringere.* "Each and every marriage act in the exercise of which, *by human design,* the act is deprived of its natural power to beget life breaks the law of God and of nature."

As the use of "rhythm" grew up quietly in Catholic circles, in violation of the norms of *Casti Connubii,* Catholic moralists switched their line of defense—from the intention in intercourse to "the integrity of the act." This, too, had a long and embarrassing background over European centuries of sexual hysteria: Not only were oral and anal intercourse forbidden, but all varieties of stimulation or position were counted unnatural except the man-on-top performance. The act with a single goal was to have but a single mode of execution. In the Thirties and Forties, theologians returned to this unicity of the act, outlawing "artificial" contraceptives as a way of tampering with natural procedures. That left "normal" performance of the act during infertile periods in full accord with natural law.

This argument led to a subform of sexual apologetics, in praise of the machinery of sex. A Jesuit theologian wrote: "The woman who uses a diaphragm seals off physically the most intimate part of her body and thus, in symbol, closes the depths of her spirit to her husband." Since the act could only be performed one way, Rome found itself forced to condemn artificial insemination along with artificial contraceptives, even when that was the only way a husband's sperm could be united with his wife's ovum. Here the original ground for natural law arguments (procreation) had to yield to "integrity of the act." Once again the food parallel shows how absurd the sexual argument is—pushed with rigor, it would outlaw intravenous feeding as unnatural. The "integrity" argument was further played up when the pill came along, since anovulents do not directly interfere with the act of intercourse. In fact, it was this blatant manipulation of the arguments to serve a sexual bias that made many Catholics suspect the arguments were false. For, in the interval between *Casti Connubii* and the pill, Pius XII had finally (1951) authorized the rhythm system—on the grounds of its non-artificial means, even though he admitted that the intention could be to "avoid habitually the fecundity of the union." So long as the nature of the act was not altered, its "positive fulfillment may be omitted" for good reasons, even though this suspends temporarily "the positive and obligatory carrying out of the act" (Address to Midwives, 1951). To go back, after this, to the intention argument, in order to head off the threat of the pill, was to confess intellectual bankruptcy.

All these tortuous intellectual exercises have been at the service of one unvarying thing—the fear of sex; a sense that constantly thinking of babies is the only means for rescuing those who engage in sex from the charge of bestial concupiscence. The truly dismaying thing about *Humanae Vitae* was its revelation that Rome still held to these prejudices. The bias is omnipresent; it determines the way that questions are posed, the unspoken assumptions of argument, the moral ideals underlying papal exhortation. Example after example builds up the same picture:

1. The decision whether to have or avoid children is presented (and weighted) this way: "In relation to physical, economic, psychological and social conditions, responsible parenthood is exercised either by the deliberate and generous decision to raise a numerous family, or by the decision, made for grave motives and with due respect for the moral law, to avoid for the time being, or even for an undetermined period, a new birth" (10). The decision to have numerous offspring is presented as self-evidently "generous," without need for further justification; while the opposite decision is excused only for "grave motives." The encyclical does not present both sides

equally, either choice involving responsible reflection. The first alternative is not a choice at all, a thing that demands self-scrutiny and the balancing of alternatives. It is a simple un-hedging response to "generous" promptings.

2. The male user of contraceptives will undergo moral de-terioration, according to the Pope: "It is also to be feared that the man, growing used to the employment of contraceptive practices, may finally lose respect for the woman, and, no longer caring for her physical and psychological equilibrium, may come to the point of considering her as a mere instrument of selfish enjoyment, and no longer as his respected and be-loved companion." How will contraceptives bring this about? By making the possibility of intercourse more frequent. This will lower a man's respect for his wife. The physical sign and sacrament of married union must not be too often enacted, or it will cause disunion. The Pope might as well argue that frequent reception of the eucharist will cause disrespect for God.

Here, too, the Pope does not present both sides equally. It is only the male who is made degenerate by contraceptives. With women it is physical and psychological equilibrium that is endangered. Why is this? I remember well an evening spent with a Roman theologian, reputedly "liberal," who kept trying to tell an incredulous group of doctors that "rape in marriage" is a very common sin because only men really enjoy sex. Con-traceptives would allow a man to exact from his wife more frequent sacrifices to his pleasure, causing great wear and tear to her nerves and "equilibrium."

3. The Pope even says (17) that contraceptives will lead to conjugal infidelity. Why is that? By increasing the occasions of intercourse within marriage, contraceptives should make the husband (by the Pope's way of thinking, we need not worry about the wife) less likely to seek solace outside his marriage. But this is *not* the case if you presume that frequent inter-course is bestializing; that one needs abstinence from inter-course to build up that control of the passions which, apart from the problem of birth control, is presented as an ideal (10).

4. The Pope also says that contraceptives will lead to moral degeneration either (*sive*) in marriage or (*sive*) of a more general (*passim*) sort (17). Under this latter heading we are told: "Not much experience is needed in order to know human weakness, and to understand that men—especially the young, who are so vulnerable on this point—have need of encouragement to be faithful to the moral law, so that they must not be offered some easy means of eluding its observance." When he describes these *juvenes cupiditatibus tam obnoxios*, the Pope seems to have the fornication of adolescents in mind. Does he imagine that a boy who has no scruples about fornicating will be stopped in his tracks by a treatise against condoms? Surely one bent on what the church calls sin will not draw back because the church also calls the method sinful.

5. Distinguishing between the rhythm method and other contraceptive schemes, the encyclical says "only in the former case are they able to renounce the use of marriage in the fecund periods, when, for just motives, procreation is not desirable, while making use of it during infecund periods to manifest their affection and to safeguard their mutual fidelity. *By so doing, they give proof of a truly and integrally honest love.*" One "earns" the right to intermittent displays of affection—to a dose of sex sufficient to guard against infidelity without creating bestial appetites—by abstinence, which is presented as a good in itself, even apart from natural law arguments. Which prompts the question: if the act is intrinsically good, why must one earn it? The obvious answer is that the act is not felt to be intrinsically good by the Pope, though he will grudgingly allow it in small doses.

6. Indeed the Pope offers married abstinence from intercourse as a cure to all the world's great problems:

To dominate instinct by means of one's reason and free will undoubtedly requires ascetical practices, so that the affective manifestations of conjugal life may observe the correct order, in particular with regard to the observance of periodic continence. Yet this discipline which is proper to the purity of married couples, far from harming conjugal love, rather confers on it a higher human value. It demands continual effort, yet, thanks to its beneficent influence, husband and wife fully develop their personalities, being enriched with spiritual values. Such discipline bestows upon family life fruits of serenity and peace, and facilitates the solution of other problems: it favors attention for one's partner, helps both parties to drive out selfishness, the enemy of true love; and deepens their sense of responsibility. By its means, parents acquire the capacity of having a deeper and more efficacious influence in the education of their offspring; little children and youths grow up with a just appraisal of human values, and in the serene and harmonious development of their spiritual and sensitive faculties.

If these are the results, then everyone should start practicing the rhythm method immediately. After all, who does not want to develop his personality? (Those not practicing rhythm can only develop it partially.) Who does not seek to acquire serenity, solve problems, instill virtue in offspring? Indeed, if even partial abstinence can do this, wouldn't it be better for us all to strive for entire abstinence, with such high rewards promised us? And that is the point: the Pope is praising *celibate* standards within marriage, trying to make the wedded life approximate the standards of unmarried clergy. All his formal praise to the married state's separate dignity is mere formality. He considers marriage a second-class form of monasticism.

There are many reasons why priests are getting married in such numbers. But one aspect of this development should not be neglected: even a priest who feels called to celibacy must be reluctant to identify his own way of life with church authorities' views on sex; must feel his own witness cheapened and distorted by the imbalance and ignorance displayed at the very top rungs of the hierarchy; and must fear that he will end up resembling the obsessive old men who have risked all credibility, order, and good will within the church to uphold their animus against human intercourse. The bishops' intense concentration on this subject is simply the reverse of that one-dimensional hedonism they denounce; where playboys treat sex as the source of all enjoyment, cardinals treat it as the cause of all evil. Both sides are not only mistaken, but dreary;

and to the extent that Rome has identified itself with the one side, church teachers, theologians, and ministers cringe and hedge, trying to cover up their father's intellectual nakedness, growing more uncomfortable all the while; until, at last, they leave.

IV · DYING

---

a man stood on his nails

an ash like dew, a sweat
smelling of death and life.
Our evil Friday fell,
the blind face gently turned
another way, toward life

a man walks in his shroud

    —DANIEL BERRIGAN,
 They Call Us Dead Men

TEN

Living, and Partly Living

". . . Peace, but not the kiss of peace."
—*Murder in the Cathedral*

IT WAS A HARD DECISION IN SEVERAL WAYS—not to kiss Terence Cardinal Cooke, all dressed up and receptive, even wearing his silky episcopal bedslippers. The first four had done it, after all —newly ordained priests "concelebrating" Mass with the man who had just chrismed them with sacerdotal oils. Each of the four crossed the sacristy space before the altar and gave him the formal kiss of peace, their "Pax," both hands on his elbows, head ducked first one way, then the other (forget the sequence and you bang heads, knock his mitre off).

But the fifth man—lanky and Californianized with long hair after a year of graduate school at Stanford—ambled only a short way toward the Cardinal, then swerved and went to an open microphone used intermittently during the ceremony. "I am sorry," he told the Cardinal, indirectly through loudspeakers, "but I cannot give you the kiss of peace until you resign as vicar of the military forces of war. . . ." Father John Gallen, the liturgical Master of Ceremonies, by whose cues and whispers each part of the rite had proceeded, was expecting this, mentally jumping forward to decide what he could head off, adapt, curtail, or improvise when the confrontation came. He had been braced for it earlier, at the point where each applicant put his hands in the Cardinal's hands, to be asked if he would follow episcopal orders. When Tony Meyer (the young Jesuit back from Stanford) heard the question, there was an awkward pause, while Gallen tensed—then the cocky answer: "Yes, Terence." Obey, then, yes—hesitantly; but *not* do—what? Not kiss, as it turned out.

That *was* the next danger point, Gallen knew, the Pax— and now that it had come he busily gauged what effect this *défi* would have on the rest of the ceremony. He looked at the "old priests" in attendance, vested for concelebration, and saw their faces clouding—there went one part of the ceremony, the Pax between old priests and the new ones. It was clear that some fathers disapproved enough of Meyer's act to treat him in kind—no kiss for Terence, by God, no kiss for Tony! Gallen made a mental note: skip the new-old priests' kiss.

Meanwhile, other people were reacting. Father Robert Mitchell, superior of the fifteen Jesuits being brought before the Cardinal for ordination, had been seated in the sacristy when Meyer started speaking; but now he was up and moving, visibly angered, going for the mike—to rescue it, presumably, even if that meant wrestling Meyer for it. Father Mitchell had a right to feel betrayed. Fifteen minutes before the service began, Master of Ceremonies Gallen had come to him with a flyer passed out in front of the church. It had a photograph of Cardinal Cooke in an airplane cockpit, being catechized in the mazes of its instrument panel. Beside the picture ran the words of a satirical song, "Sky Pilot." A second sheet accused the Cardinal of war crimes as military vicar (head of the corps of chaplains) and as possessor of stock in war industries; and this page was signed by two of the men being ordained—Tony Meyer, of course, and also Joe O'Rourke. They had obviously printed the flyers and recruited the young people who were passing them out. Gallen feared for the ceremony: he had telephoned Meyer ahead of time, and asked if he meant to act decorously. Meyer, only a few years behind Gallen in the Jesuit training, said he did. The flyer indicated his con-

ception of decorum, and the ceremony was likely to be even
more instructive on that subject. Gallen asked Mitchell not to
present the two for ordination.

Father Mitchell had already been around this track, with
wearying persistence, over the last months—when, for instance,
Meyer asked to be ordained outside his own province, so he
would not be anointed by the Sky Pilot; or when O'Rourke,
long active in the peace movement, had been too busy organiz-
ing Phil Berrigan's defense to finish his required theology
courses. But O'Rourke, in the final speech at his trial for destroying Dow Chemical records, had made a moving declara-
tion of his aims in being a priest: "to be a celebrator of moments teeming with human possibility—birth, marriage, death."
The words were sincerely meant, so Mitchell had supported
him. But now, given another reason to reverse himself, just fifteen minutes before the Cardinal declared each man "a priest
forever," he had of course to weigh all the factors again, this
last hurried time. Ordination delayed, after all, is not ordination forever denied. The two men had chosen to risk this gesture, and had not let him in on it.

On the other hand, a last-minute hasty refusal to ordain
them might not go down with the other seminarians. Meyer
and O'Rourke were well-liked; their superiors had been careful
not to give the impression they were attacking the peace movement when disciplining any individual. Besides, Meyer's and
O'Rourke's parents were here, formal cards had been sent out,
first Masses arranged at their home parishes, friends and rela-
tives summoned in the customary way—it would be like calling
off a wedding halfway down the aisle. Worse, like having the
bride's father break up the service with a public announcement
that his daughter is a whore. He could not do that to Tony
and Joe. Both were firm in their desire for the priesthood—
who was he to reject men God had called? Life is hell on
religious superiors today.

It is no wonder, against this background, that Mitchell
was furious when Meyer insulted Cooke. He had gone out on a
limb for Tony, and Tony was sawing if off. No one knows

(perhaps Mitchell least of all) what he would have done had he reached Meyer—two ornate priest-dolls in costume, contending for a microphone around the altar. But the Cardinal is a diplomat, at home in ritual situations (which always have their cross-ups and crises, head-bumps to be absorbed, fallen mitres to be deftly and with poise retrieved). Now he glided up to Meyer, anticipating Father Mitchell's arrival, stretched his hand out in a friendly way and touched the arm of the young priest who refused to kiss him. "Brother," he began (and the mike was picking him up), "we look at things in a different way." Any nod, now, of agreement or acquiescence on Meyer's part might look like a grudging half-Pax, given after all despite the first refusal, Cooke melting even this intransigence (and therefore winning). So Meyer did an odd dance backward, from the Cardinal's hand, afraid of the Peace—and surrendered the mike (therefore losing). Then Cooke explained to the man, indirectly through loudspeakers, that his role as chief of chaplains is not meant to be political, but only to give spiritual solace to men dying or in danger of their death. The crowd's sympathy was entirely with Cooke, who was big enough to take an insult and not return it in kind. His action was so conciliatory in effect that it blunted Joe O'Rourke's resolve to follow Meyer's example. Instead, he mumbled that he, too, thought Cooke should resign, but would nonetheless wish him peace with the Pax. This merest shuffle of truculence did not have enough dignity to challenge the other Jesuits, now ordained and waiting in line for their Pax. They, too, had been won by Cooke's calm fatherly air, and they duck-ducked their successive kisses with special fervor, like stage Japanese in rites of demented politeness.

Gallen omitted not only the old priests' Pax, but the custom of sending the new priests out to mingle with the congregation they had just been ordained to serve—he saw the possibility of arguments out there, retaliatory comments or chill meetings, things getting out of hand. So he kept his troops in the sanctuary, subdued and near the altar, while he crafted together what could be saved of the liturgy. Downstairs, afterward, the priests (old and new) peeled off their vestments, layer on layer built up around them in successive rites of symbolic "investment"—for some, innovators of new liturgies, it might be the last time they would wear the whole panoply. One of them spoke to the whole room in a loud voice: "Tony and Joe, you chose to make your statement in public. I make mine here in private. You wrecked the day our parents have waited twelve years for." (This was one of the last classes to have gone—most of them anyway—through the old long Jesuit course of training.)

Later in that week, I heard others from the ordination class rip into O'Rourke: "You *used* us and our parents, made a captive audience out of people who had come to something they considered important, something which had nothing to do with your concerns."

"You can work for peace all you want, but not impose your views on others, or deny them the right to conduct a religious service in the manner they choose."

"How can you demonstrate for peace, yet refuse a fellow Christian—however mistaken or in error—the ancient kiss of peace?"

But O'Rourke was not without his arguments. The event had its importance because of the Cardinal's spiritual powers, and the social station they had given him. He uses that prominence to support a chaplain system in which priests wear military uniforms, take military pay, acquire the military mentality, and give implicit Christian blessing, by their uniformed and obedient presence, to military acts and to the war. A friend of Meyer's—the Puerto Rican Bishop, Antulio Parilla-Bonilla—had toured military stockades just the year before, and found that Catholic chaplains gave no support or sympathy to men imprisoned for protest against the war. Meyer, remember, had tried not to come back into Cooke's diocese. When ordered to return, he felt he had to point up the incongruity of roles in a Cardinal who ordains men as ministers of peace on earth, and yet presides over a chaplaincy that has become the instrument of war. Not to take this incongruity seriously is,

O'Rourke claims, a failure to take the Cardinal seriously—all that he stands for, all the obligation *he* has as a priest. It is a failure to take the gospel seriously. It would be indecorous.

The conflict between these two young priests and their fellow Jesuits is a good example of the dilemma faced by a church now going out into the political and secular world, yet retaining some instincts of religion as a "separate" thing—priesthood separate from politics, chaplaincy separate from war, ordination separate from preaching, preaching separate from demonstration, the pulpit at odds with the pamphlet. Most of Meyer's and O'Rourke's classmates would agree with them that this separation can no longer be upheld—yet when it *was* maintained in traditional terms, at their own ordination in 1971, the others would not follow Meyer's lead; they would not even support him.

Still, despite the disapproval of their fellows, Meyer and O'Rourke have made it clear that ordinations now join college commencements as chancy affairs, carried out under constant threat of "demonstration" or some disgraceful act. Superiors (and some subjects) shudder at what may lurk just offstage in the future—a pig's head served up to the Cardinal, or priests who view the liturgy as one type of "guerrilla theater." Their nightmare is that of Eliot's Canterbury chorus: "Corruption in the dish, incense in the latrine, the sewer in the incense."

Some have entertained this nightmare over several years—those who predicted trouble if the Jesuits moved their seminary out of Woodstock, Maryland, into New York, from an isolated semimonastery into apartments scattered through the upper West Side, its students living in groups of two-to-twenty-five in the buildings being reclaimed between 98th Street and 125th Street, young religious (average age just under thirty) out on the street without clerical attire, on West Side streets full of dogs and muggers, of rabbis and fashionable liberals, of divinity students from Union and braless Barnard girls. Incense into the sewer?—yes, but to sweeten the sewer.

What happened to Woodstock College is part of the general trend for Catholic seminaries. The isolation of the past has been rejected. Theology itself can no longer be studied (or "done" as the jargon has it) convincingly in a sectarian setting. All five of America's Jesuit schools of theology ("theologates") have moved into cities and established ecumenical relations with Protestant and Jewish houses of study. Woodstock, offered the chance of moving to New Haven as part of the Yale Divinity School, decided instead to go for what is in some ways the most desirable location of all, and the most dangerous —near the Union Theological and Jewish Theological seminaries, with all the facilities of Columbia at hand, plus NYU and the city's other schools, its general life of art and culture— indeed, all of New York's instructive variety, pace, and squalor.

This last quality was not the least of New York's charms— those million Puerto Ricans to be ministered to. Men chafing at a decade or so of studious rustication dreamed of taking on the Big Town and saving it despite itself. They had become numbed, many of them, in studies and their country seminary; they were counting on the city to galvanize them, give them back their youth, life, things to do, people to help, souls to save. And they did, from the first, get involved in a wide variety of tasks—one is at the UN office for religions; others teach or preach part-time in the area. One has worked with Richard Schechner in drama, another is a jazz impresario. Others do community relations work with local police and firemen, or help in drug clinics. One newly ordained priest supported himself by driving a cab for a year.

Most still find something to enjoy in the West Side environment, and think it as good a place as any for being reborn —it is, after all, undergoing its own rebirth as the intellectually most fashionable quarter of town, the neighborhood with a hint of old elegance restorable, new dangers survivable; where one can live in a mansion on a trashy street, combine funky luxury with social criticism, feel part of things without having to call in "rent-a-mugger." The place is middle-age bohemian, where old grads of the Village, adrift for years, find an afterlife; a colorful thin ridge of resolute survival be-

tween the stink of the Hudson River and the dense huddled
wounds of Harlem just over the cliff. Ideal.

When I went up, one afternoon, to the suite used as a
gathering place in one of the Jesuits' apartment buildings, I
found it filled with nice old ladies of both sexes, sedately
playing cards and sipping tea. It was the afternoon for the
house's geriatric apostolate. Those old people who sit in brittle
gossip on the median strip of Broadway or the concrete margins
of Riverside Drive, studying dogs in a state of perpetual evacu-
ation, had been invited up two days a week for some Jesuit
concern and hospitality.

The suite in which they meet is the most ambitious attempt
at a "common room" in the whole Woodstock complex. It has
a bar, with draft Budweiser served in cold tankards all night,
called "The Gang Plank"—a nautical motif carried out in its
planked floor, long tavern tables, and wooden benches. Models
of old ships, stiff and prickly with masts and spars and intricate
thread-rigging, hang from the ceiling and rest on the mantel-
piece. The dining nook (one meal is catered in, at night, by
Schrafft's) is furnished with round white tables and molded
white matching chairs, four to a table for intimacy. A young
Jesuit designed the scene, and has been criticized for his
clubby vision and posh tastes. The building is largely in-
habited by Jewish and Puerto Rican families able to pay a
hefty rent. When the marionette parade of neat molded white
chairs, one tucked head-down into another, filed on and on
(and up and out and out) of the small elevator serving this
wing, an awed tenant said, "Some rich outfit must be moving
in." A swarthy young fellow, doing the repetitive chair-shuffle
that tied up the elevator, muttered sourly, "You bet. The very
richest." He is Tony Perez, S.J., called by his fellow Jesuits the
only hard revolutionary in the Order. He refused to live in this
house on 98th Street because of its gentlemen's club atmosphere. But sixty others live, two or three men to an apartment,
around the building's various wings, and gather by night in its
white chairs or on its wooden benches.

Some find "98th Street," as the complex is called, the most

interesting spot not only in the whole Woodstock sprawl, or on the West Side, but in town. Catholic peace activity is largely centered here (with a correlative concentration of interest by the FBI). Some of the Jesuits' tenth-floor apartments (the Gang Plank is on the eighth floor) have become "crash pads" for transient peaceniks. Trendy rock is taped into the Gang Plank with politely high fidelity. One can add up an impressive list of arrests, or of years to be served (if appeals fail), at any late-night ideological rumble in the Gang Plank. There are friends and disciples, here, of Dorothy Day, Dan Berrigan, Cezar Chavez, Saul Alinsky, and "Bishop Parilla."

The place has a catchy pulse, as a kind of priestly hippie-pad—enough to excite the president of Columbia, Dr. William McGill, when he dropped by for a visit. And the academic president of Woodstock, Father Christopher Mooney, was reciprocally excited by McGill's enthusiasm. "The place really blew his mind," he confided to me enthusiastically. "He talked to young theologians in everything from beards and sandals to business suits and ties, working in places like the UN and police stations." There can be no doubt that McGill was impressed. When the General of the Jesuit order, Father Pedro Arrupe, came over from Rome in 1971 and was entertained at lunch by the Presidents of New York colleges, McGill offered him a toast that was all praise for Jesuit daring and risk: while others were calling the city dead or dying, some fleeing it, most cursing it for dangers or inconvenience, the Jesuits had moved in, unafraid, ready to cope with its seamier aspects and capitalize on its advantages. Father Arrupe accepted the compliment graciously, and did not let on that one reason for his visit was to decide whether the New York version of Woodstock College should be folded. It is, after all, a failure.

For that is the other way of viewing its move to New York —that the incense was just poured down the drain, became part of the general sewer odor, its distinct sweetness now irrecoverable. There is an aimlessness to the place. Despite "good works" done by individuals, the College has had no impact on the city. The million Puerto Ricans are still out there, their plight not appreciably changed by the Jesuits' advent. The seminarians' apostolic gestures are made on odd off-hours by young men in the city on a vague and transient basis, asking themselves if they made the big move to New York— or for that matter, studied so many years for the priesthood—in order to drive a cab or arrange card parties for old ladies, to fool with the theater or jazz. The source of the trouble is clear: The one thing all these men have in common, the very reason for their being together at all, is the College—and that can have little impact upon its surroundings, or grip upon their lives, because it is hardly a college at all. Most of the students are bored with theology at this point—indeed with all formal study (a reaction to long earlier training imposed on them, so much of which looks useless in light of the changes since Vatican II). Personal crises and uncertainty mix with ill-defined institutional goals—no one knows what Woodstock will be like several years from now, or whether it will exist. Even those still interested in a complete course of theology cannot plan it intelligently, since the very institution offering them courses may not last as long as their doctoral program. Most students are raising all over again the most basic problems of belief, and they find these better answered outside the classroom. They surely will not sit still for the old-style courses, which articulated all the most remote consequences of *assumed* belief.

I asked a number of students for an estimate of time spent on the study of theology—reading, lectures, seminars, or writing. The best guess seemed to be less than two hours a day, on the average. Jolted out of old ways, adapting painfully to new ones (some trade gossipy evaluations of their "shrinks"), these are very bright young men, dedicated and generous—but also very doubting ones, suspicious of authority, uncertain of their purpose. The two sets of qualities go together now, a fact older Jesuits have had to learn, painfully (and partially). The Woodstock student looks for a purpose that will get him out of bed every day, and it is clear that few find that purpose in theological speculation. The effect of this on the ecumenical reason for Woodstock's move is an ironic one. The more "open" the students become, the less they contribute to a dialogue with other faiths. Ecumenism at the academic level involves a study of each other's traditions, for mutual enrichment. Catholics are expected to contribute expertise on such things as Thomism, the Jesuit theologians (Bellarmine, Suarez, etc.), papal claims and ecclesial Romanism. But these are just what most Woodstock students have avoided, trying to escape the old seminary mold.

Some young men argue that if interest in "real" theology —in the gospel, in Christian tradition, in the spiritual life—has not been cultivated through all the earliers years of their training, it is hopeless to give eleventh-hour injections of it just before ordination. Others say that the active life of believers *is* theology, just as it is prayer. At any rate, they find it easier to get absorbed in things like drug rehabilitation and the peace movement than to worry all their old doubts for the thousandth time in class, or split the thousandth hair on the church's infallibility. They have lived so long with doubt, they want at least temporary surcease from it. They claim, moreover, they were sent here to join religious life with urban activism (all those Puerto Ricans); each man, therefore, should mix the two in the way that suits him best—or, perhaps, deny that the two are distinct or properly separable (how forget Cooke the Sky Pilot when being ordained by Cooke the Cardinal?).

The trouble with this is that it leads many to treat the city as therapy for themselves rather than a field for any co-ordinated apostolate. The sense of community is lost, along with the bond of common purpose. The strongest men carve out a life for themselves, and that carries them off from the others; the weak stay at home, or drift; enthusiasms like the peace movement become a surrogate vocation, supplying that sense of aim their religious training lacks. It was said that the Harrisburg indictments of Phil Berrigan and others revitalized part of the Woodstock community; it gave them, for a while, something to get passionate about again, a task to be done—just what New York was supposed to give them, but had not. Yes, the 98th Street "crash pad" has been vivifying; it supplies a bond of cohesion for men who would otherwise have none. But it is also an "anti-Order," a competing community nurtured in the larger one, drawing on its life, draining it away.

The results are foreseeable. Fewer courses are being required, and even those are neglected. The traditional four-year theology program has shrunk to three years; in some cases, two. Men can study in other fields and have it counted as "theology"—e.g., Tony Meyer's work at Stanford. Advisers for the Maryland and New York provinces (which Woodstock serves) have recommended that the situation be faced, that Woodstock be reduced to a one-year ministerial school of preparation for the priesthood, abandoning the traditional ideal of a theologate altogether. Others believe the only realistic thing to do, academically, is close Woodstock down. Thus President McGill's toast may have an unintended meaning: that the Jesuits rushed into the city just in time to get in on the dying —and they have gone about the task with suicidal efficiency.

Naturally, there is a good deal of criticism for those who risked the dispersal of Woodstock's unique resources in the city's incensy sewer. Others besides John Courtney Murray had opposed the move. But terrific pressures were at work on Father Felix Cardegna, the Rector of Woodstock College, and Father Edward Sponga, who had been Woodstock's Rector before he became Father Provincial to the Maryland Province. The Jesuits were experiencing the same drop-off in applications that all seminaries had. The spacious college, with its vast acres of farmland, had housed three hundred students around the end of the Vatican Council. It was down to one hundred and fifty by 1970. Official projections (now considered overgenerous) foresaw the enrollment by 1980 sinking to—fourteen men. (Only four people entered the New York novitiate in 1970—down from classes of fifty or sixty at the beginning of Vatican II.) The huge plant in Maryland could not be sustained for fourteen students. Furthermore there was competition with the other four theologates in America—each serving two provinces and each facing the same problem of a shrinking student body. A planning commission forecast, in 1970, that there would be about a hundred Jesuit theology students for the whole nation by 1980—and five large theologates for training them (plus another in English-speaking Canada). This is obviously wasteful, and the General of the Order visited each of the five places in turn during his 1971 visit, indicating the purpose of his journey. Some of the theologates obviously have to be closed, combined, or devoted to new purposes. Woodstock, if it stayed in Maryland—with only a community house, no neighboring university or ecumenical contacts—would not have survived. It was stay and die, or move and (perhaps) live.

The wisdom of the move is confirmed by the fact that later estimates indicate the number of Jesuit theology students in 1980 may be closer to seventy-five—or even to fifty—than to a hundred. (The original estimate did not allow for accelerated work by those already in the Order, or for drop-outs during the years of theology study.) Fathers Sponga and Cardegna felt New York would allow for the maximum adaptation of Woodstock to new purposes. As long as the library could be housed, the journal kept up, the better faculty allowed to teach some Union or Columbia students, Woodstock would have an identity and base, a reason for continued (if minimal) existence to weather future storms.

All these were realities difficult to face; they involved breaking old and strong ties. It was hard to get all the relevant discussions made; and hard to carry them out, once made. But Sponga and Cardegna, both of them energetic and widely admired, advocated the New York move, and won. Cardegna went up to the city with a pilot group of thirty or so in 1968, and found apartments for the whole body of students to occupy the following year. Some faculty members (including sub-superiors for each cluster of apartments) live with students; the rest were admitted to a new building reserved for Columbia faculty and their families at 125th Street. The academic offices of Woodstock were put in the Interchurch Building ("The God Box") on 120th Street. The library was given a

floor in the National Council of Churches Building on 125th
Street (just above the floor where Clergy and Laity Concerned About Vietnam and other "Movement" groups are
headquartered).

I interviewed the president of Woodstock, Father Christopher Mooney—an easy, acquiescent man in his first administrative post—at the God Box, where his office is. He seemed to look
only on the bright side of the New York move—both by temperament and on principle (his scholarly work has been devoted to Teilhard de Chardin): "This is where important
theology is being done. If we meant to do it, we had to come
here." I mentioned the students' own low estimate of the hours
spent on formal theology. "There is a question of different personal needs, and we are in a state of flux. The whole course
of training is being refashioned and these men are caught between the old ways and the new, not fully belonging to either.
But there are men spending time in the library and doing
serious work. A group living together at 102nd Street asked
Father Avery Dulles [a scholarly convert to Catholicism, the
son of John Foster Dulles] to move in with them and direct
their reading of eight major theologians this year. It has been
a great success. We arranged credit for them, and they have
made that their entire year's course, thinking and praying
together on the texts they read." But I thought the academic
and religious aspects of Woodstock had been separated? "Ad-
ministratively. They cannot be separated personally. What the
administrative separation does is give men freedom to adjust
and experiment. Each of the apartment complexes has a different style, draws a different type. The studious are (as a
group) at places like 102nd Street with Avery, or in Reed
House. The activists are at 98th Street. We want all these experiments to go on. Religious life is changing very rapidly.
We don't know, yet, what will work. But we have a better
chance to survive, the more options we keep open."

I mention the bad name Woodstock is supposed to have in
other Jesuit provinces: superiors do not want to send their
young men here because the life is too free in style, high in

cost, and full of dangers—danger that the men will like the city, and not come back; or dislike it, and leave the Order; or be unable to readjust to the conventional Jesuit residence again. "The conventional Jesuit residence is ceasing to exist. Even where it does exist, young men are not staying there—in our colleges, for instance—but going off-campus to rent apartments like non-clerical members of the faculty. Like our students here. After all, by the time our men reach theology they are nearly thirty years old. They can't be treated as children any more. That's why each student here has his own checking account; he gets monthly pay, a room, some services, a good library, a choice of courses from our own faculty or at Union—then he is on his own, to sink or swim. If he cannot take the new style of religious life, it is time we all found that out." The bank accounts are a great innovation for seminarians trained to old concepts of the vow of poverty. Back in Maryland, all money, even down to carfare, was handled by a single "Father Minister." The FBI recently looked into the whereabouts of Joe O'Rourke and his friends on the night when documents were stolen from the Bureau's office in Media, Pennsylvania. Catholic agents, once familiar with Jesuit ways at schools like Fordham and Georgetown, went to the Minister at 98th Street, Father Robert Curry, and asked where his subjects had been that night, whether they had left New York or had the funds for travel. When Father Curry answered, to all these questions, that he did not know, the agents looked puzzled and not entirely convinced.

Father Mooney realizes that Woodstock cannot remain a theologate of the sort it has been in the past—for one thing, academic theology of a solid sort is now being taught from the outset of a Jesuit's training, not all segregated off at the end. "Perhaps only graduate students who want to get their doctorate in theology will come to Woodstock in the future. We may become just a graduate school, or a research institute, or a theological school for laymen, or one for non-Jesuit priests as well as Jesuit—or a combination of several of these things. There are a number of ways we can go. We are keeping our options open." But what looks to Father Mooney like a maintenance of options looks to others like disintegration. "We had to become smaller in any event. This is forcing on us a return to the original concept of the Order; there has been a terrific revival of Ignation spirituality. Father Joe Whalen, who did his graduate work in England under E. L. Mascall, is a student of ascetical theology, with an emphasis on St. Ignatius [the Jesuits' founder]. He offered a course in prayer last year, and thought only a few people would sign up—more stuff on *prayer* after all these years in the Order? But nearly a third of the students registered, and stayed with it, and were very enthusiastic about the course. We are giving and taking St. Ignatius' *Spiritual Exercises* again in their original form— one man receiving them, under one director. Perhaps half the priests ordained this year decided to prepare for ordination by making the *Excercises*. Ignatius did not have in mind a large institutional Order, but a small mobile group of intense men."

In a very real sense these Jesuits are starting all over again—as are many religious, nuns as well as priests, but without the clear aims and uncluttered enthusiasm of those who founded Orders to meet specific needs. (As Ignazio Silone put it: "Founders are eagles; their followers are more often like hens.") For Woodstock students the problem of defining goals faces them the minute they get up in the morning, and takes the form of what is called "life style" in current searches for identity. What clothes, for instance, should the seminarian put on? For the Woodstock faculty, that problem has by and large been settled—an inconspicuous business suit. One sees them in their God Box offices, executives trying to live on office workers' salaries, ties too indistinguishable to be said to match or clash with muted suit colors, gray on gray. Rarely, if ever, a Roman collar—and the students follow them in this. One told me, "Put a collar on, around people who have not seen you wear it before, and the whole atmosphere changes. Something artificial enters in—deference, or condescension; arguments are inhibited, and one's entire relationship with others has to be renegotiated."

But what to wear when one does not wear the collar? Even a tie is out of place in the classrooms and movie houses of the area. So, then? Student guerrilla style? Che beard and boots? Flashy turtleneck and bell bottoms? Or ragged sneakers and moth-eaten sweater? Though the questions seem trivial at first, they tell a great deal about each man's concept of ministry. Is he to be one with those around him, or stand off from them, marked by specifically religious symbols? *Can* he be one of them without deeper pretense than the frank admission of difference? In particular, what does the concept of religious poverty mean in this situation? Does it mean cheap but clean attire? Actually sharing the want of New York's deprived? How can a man with a Jesuit's expensive education, and with all the Order's resources at his disposal, be truly poor with the poor? And if he does not feel comfortable "faking" indigence, is his standard to be that of the graduate student, or social worker, or street preacher?

Most of the men at Woodstock do not know the answer to such questions, and hedge their bets sartorially. In their own way, they adopt the faculty's working arrangement; they settle for unobtrusiveness. The result is a mishmash, not quite anything—Carlyle's tailor would read "confused vocation" in their very garb.

If style reflects these men's attitude toward priesthood, even in details of clothing, it is an even more sensitive indicator at their various liturgies. Woodstock has an institute for liturgical study, with a young dramatist-in-residence who likes to mix the techniques of stage, screen, and sensitivity group with old pageantries of worship. Some of his tamer ideas get tried out in the public chapel of the God Box, or in Columbia's chapel, or at first Masses of the "graduating" priests. But you get a better sense of their ongoing life of prayer at the private services held in Woodstock's apartment residences. The faculty building, and two other spots, have formal chapels; but most Masses are simple, brief, and take place in apartment living rooms. There are no robes, everyone sits, priests and students together; a reading from scripture is followed by comments, anyone who wants taking part. The bread is broken —chewy stuff, or cookies, not the flat wafers of old. Even back in Maryland, some students had found a crypt in their old stone building's basement, and abandoned its grandiose chapel, for such services.

There is an attempt at forging community in these quick preprandial get-togethers; but the comments are perfunctory, unprepared, some made to fill out the occasion, some verging toward the classroom, others toward the confessional. One young priest told me, "I'm proud to say there has never been a liturgy in this apartment" (which he shares with two other Jesuits). Why? "A liturgy should be a ministry to the people of God. We are not ministering to anyone, or speaking for them. We leave them and come back here to pray at each other, not with or for a people. The rites are kind of furtive, not connected with reality."

Obviously, "going out into the world"—the program implied in the whole move to New York—is not as easy as it looks. Some did not leave their Woodstock in Maryland, but brought it with them. Others resist all attempts to "sing the old songs" in exile, to circle back toward monasticism through the fiery furnace of "Sin City." Would the young men too urbane for the monastery be too monkish for the city? *Damned* if they would. There is a clear determination to be secular and "with it" in the rooms and decor of their apartments. They eschew religious symbols—no crosses on the wall, but posters of Woodstock (the New York rock "nation," not the Maryland site). The rooms are bachelor-disheveled, with a litter of political journals and *Playboys* (at the cheap clerical rate). Walls are garishly painted; one is filled with gloomy large glossies of the Living Theater cast, bodies all unwrapped, all "rapping" in upon themselves. The dining area in the Columbia faculty building is gaudily Mexican, afraid of being a "refectory," not sufficiently nervy to be a "supper club"—falling, once more, into indeterminacy.

Perhaps the most difficult furnishing job was encountered at 107th Street, the old Cathedral High School faculty building, purchased from Cardinal Cooke and the diocese. It would be the most "segregated" building, with no one but Jesuits in it—so men chose to live there because they wanted to maintain (or forge for the first time) a sense of religious community. What they found was a handsome Nineties-vintage town house, with grand stairs, beautiful carved wood, curving riverside façade. Yet this fine setting posed more problems of style than any other of the houses. Since 107th Street could best accommodate Jesuit passersby, its very stability made for a certain transiency. One resident there said, "We got all the old priests in town for a night or two, and those with breakdowns or health problems, looking for a place to rest. Community was hard because we had the highest median age most of the time." A Woodstock professor moved in to die with the College he had served. The one black maid who did not want to leave the College moved up from Maryland, and was bequeathed to this house. Instead of a new start, or a closer community, the students were given bits and remnants of the old establishment.

That partly explains the resentment of some who lived there when the parlor chandelier was shipped to them from Maryland. There was passionate opposition to hanging it—some claimed that sight of this fancy thing, the first object seen from an open front door, was a mockery of the poor life. But others said it would be silly to mar the old home's harmony with adventitious austerities—that a richness of accumulated care invests all houses that are loved over any period of time, even monasteries. The debate was heated; but the anti-chandelier forces prevailed. It was boxed again, sent back (at extra expense—in the name of poverty), to be hung, eventually, at the Jesuit Missions building in Baltimore. The students at 107th Street might have to take in the dying. But let the dead bury their dead, back where the cemetery—and Gabe Bennett—are all that is left of the Maryland Woodstock.

Father Mooney invited me, one night, to dinner at the

faculty building on 125th Street. The apartments there are commodious and modern, with large windows looking across the Hudson to the Palisades. A group of the inconspicuous teachers, priests in business suits, gathered in the chapel for 5:30 liturgy, then moved into the frilly Mexican lounge for cocktails. Joe Whalen, young and laughing, the man with a popular course on prayer, mixes Ignatius' *Spiritual Exercises* with Shakespeare's *Antony and Cleopatra* in discussing love; then he and Mooney compare Teilhard with Ignatius, a bit of Jesuit chauvinism creeping into the talk. (Whalen, by the doom that afflicts Woodstock, will be moved away shortly to advise the whole Province on spiritual training—there seems to be a *Saint* Peter's principle that haunts success at the lower rungs.)

The meal, catered in, is adequate. Discussion centers on Joe O'Rourke, who was in that day's *Times* as leader of the Harrisburg benefit party at Leonard Bernstein's apartment (a Catholic Chic party matching his Radical Chic night with Black Panthers). After dinner, Father Mooney offers to show me the library. That involves leaving the building, which has at nightfall been turned into a garrison. "During the day we can get to 125th Street through the garage; but there is only one way in or out of here at night"—heavily guarded. We are at the northernmost point (and then a bit some) of the fashionably shabby West Side; from here on things get plain shabby. The College's apartment building is itself a type of the self-aggravating problems to be faced in the city. How attract men with young wives and children to teach on the edge of Harlem?—well, offer them good housing, well-lit and guarded, with an enclosed playground and good security forces. Yet, if you do that, you have placed another provocative symbol of enclosed affluence between Columbia and its environs. It is a vicious circle—like the problems of the Jesuits. If things are coming apart, "seek options"—which means scatter and spread yourselves; which means coming apart. We go down the smooth elevators, past the guards and their phones, out the glass doors. The bright lit wheels of Palisades Amusement

Park—soon to be dismantled—are spinning garishly in the night.

It is a long route round the block—off Riverside via Tiemann Place, then duck under the El past taxis shooting the roller-coaster dip Broadway takes there—to the library, again a place locked and guarded. We ring, and a lay brother takes us around the physical treasure of Woodstock (it had a whole building to itself in Maryland)—rows on rows of rare Bellarmine in the shiny-horn old bindings. Will anyone ever read them again as John Courtney Murray read them, closely, wresting clever new distinctions from the thorniest old ones, countering text with text, authority with authority?

Back outside, it is beginning to rain. We stand under the El, across from a Puerto Rican shop full of religious gewgaws, talking of religion's changing style. "It is especially hard on the old," Mooney reflects; and has stories of older Jesuits now souring in their community dining halls while the young ones go out, flouting sacred customs, go out and do not come back. He is talking with regret and sympathy, without the cheery dentist's manner that does not do justice to the man: "The other day an old nun told me of her convent, 'This is not the Order I joined.' That's true and one feels sorry for her. But after all this is not the world we were born into." And there's the point: however sweet the nun, hers was a sweet presumptuousness, a naive unearthly arrogance not easily matched, the hope that by entering the convent she could stop time, step outside it, escape; that the Order would never change, once she joined, and the church she had found in childhood would always be the same. "This is not the Order I joined"—it was said, amazingly, in recrimination; what *right* had the Order to change? It is as if I should look at my ten-year-old son and attack him: "You are not the nine-pound infant I brought home from the hospital." For that matter, my wife is not the same girl I married (what *right* had she to change?), nor I the boy who married her (how unfair that *I* had to change, *if* I have).

The nun thought she could cheat time, because others

like her had done it in the past—but at a cost. Her Order, her church, idled and grew brittle, so fragile that a question, any question, could shake it to earth. There could be no motion, because no change; no life, because no death. It was in a state of suspended animation—"living, and partly living." One does not ease oneself into life, or into change (as facile celebrators of Vatican II thought their church could do). One lives, if at all, by parturition, the pangs and sundering; by successive resurrections, life out of death. Death to the past. The death involved in deciding, in moving, parting, breaking ties, breaking the mold. The Catholic church had not known death; and now, to know life, it has a lot of dying to catch up on. "We all owe God a death"?—no, many deaths; and the old nuns, priests, Orders—sweet and childlike, how we wanted them to be exempt from that law, be exceptions even if we could not be—have their own dying to do now.

The Society of Jesus is not, any more, the same Order that even its youngest Jesuits joined. Woodstock College is shaken, in anguish and exhilaration, by men discovering that fact at various stages of their lives (or part-lives, or dying lives), discovering it with despair or hope, feeling cheated, or feeling freed from the illusion's cheat. Not all the sounds are of disintegration, though all may seem to be. Some are sounds of trapped life crying to be let out—willing to pay dues, some life rising from much death; the "vocation" living through the institution's death, the individual living through the vocation's death, others strengthened as some fall (strengthened to stay by those who leave, strengthened to leave by those who stay). Woodstock is not only battered from the outside by history, but crumbling by the very throb of its own energies, as in Hart Crane's poem:

> The bells, I say, the bells break down their tower;
> And swing I know not where . . .

Standing under the El, talking in the rain with one who stayed, I asked about the two priests who, more than any others, performed the herculean labor of lifting the whole dead weight out of its slumber and flinging it into this sewery living city—but Sponga and Cardegna are, neither of them, Jesuits any more. Sponga left the Order while the move was still being made. Cardegna only after he had accomplished it. The most popular moral theologian on the faculty left just after Cardegna. Another man we had talked with at dinner in the building behind us was about to leave, and there are rumors of more going, as Mooney knows. There is still a lot of dying to be done.

· ELEVEN ·

Time's Eunuchs

Birds build—but not I build; no, but strain,
Time's eunuch, and not breed one work that wakes.

—GERARD MANLEY HOPKINS

ON THE NIGHT OF MARCH 21, 1969, a tall assured man came to the switchboard at Woodstock College in Maryland and asked the woman there to buzz seminarians Joe O'Rourke and Mike Dougherty.

"Who shall I say is calling?"

"They'll know."

Dougherty reached the phone first: "There is someone to see you."

"Who is it?"

"He won't say."

"Describe him."

"Tall, gray hair, blue eyes . . ."

"OK." He hung up.

The next day Joe O'Rourke and Mike Dougherty, along with seven others, were arrested while publicly destroying files taken from the Dow Chemical Company's offices in Washington. The woman at the switchboard, Barbara Meyer, of vague age and mixed girlish and maternal feelings toward "her boys" at Woodstock, was disturbed. "That man who came last night is the one who got them into trouble," she told her family. They asked if she knew who he was. "No, but I could pick him out of a crowd of thousands, with that height and those eyes."

During the trial of the D.C. Nine, Mrs. Meyer got to know "that man." He came to Woodstock often, and seemed just as concerned as she was over "the boys." He had not joined them in their act, she learned, because he was already convicted of one felony in Baltimore and was planning another one for Catonsville. Everyone called him Phil—except Mrs. Meyer, who made a stiffish point of addressing him as "Father Berrigan."

O'Rourke and Dougherty were the first Woodstock men to be caught in an illegal action, and Dougherty's New York superior decided to delay his ordination, at least till he had undergone his trial—perhaps, if it came to that, till he had served his prison term. The New York seminarians in Maryland resented this: a carload of them drove up to New York and exacted an agreement that their classmate would be made a priest. Although Dougherty knew of these efforts, and let them go forward, he also had other things in mind. One night, after a grueling session on the witness stand, he called Woodstock around midnight to summon friends back into Washington. A priest of their circle was about to marry him and a girl who had camped with the peaceniks at Woodstock. This dismayed some of Dougherty's supporters, not all of whom agreed with his politics; they had, after all, opposed their superior at some risk to their own priestly careers.

Not long ago, those who left the priesthood did it quietly under cover of night, not letting others know they had to leave. A tacit agreement had all along been assumed, that such men were lost to the community—an embarrassment to some, temptation for others—never to be welcomed back. Departure should remain, for others, unthinkable, an option neither considered nor imaginable. Even in the mid-Sixties, the poet and novelist John L'Heureux, studying for ordination at Woodstock, described a secret party for a departing semi-

narian as a daring unique act that "no one would believe"—
the violent wrench had been softened, friendships reaffirmed at
parting, in a way that old seminary rules were designed to forestall. Entry into the seminary was an abrupt and rending
thing, full of symbolic renunciation; similarly, one should
leave with a sharp break. Tabus were cultivated, inhibitions
to prop up the disciplines of poverty, celibacy, clerical apartness. The priest was safe inside this inviolable zone, the area
marked out by his stiff collar's magic circle. Being in or being
out was a matter of choice, clear-cut. Either-or. One could not
be both.

But all such walls of division have come down in recent
years, "the house" fraying out into "the world," students for
the priesthood coming and going casually, bringing their
friends in with them, even meeting their future wives at the
seminary. There had always been priests who married, but
new questions arose in this context: if priest-teachers were
now judged by professional academic norms, why should they
leave the institution in which their competence had been established? And so another tabu was shattered: priests who
married would no longer be pariahs at Catholic schools. Attempts to get rid of them were met with legal suits, appeals
to the American Association of University Professors, and
fights over the principle of tenure.

The problem arose for Woodstock soon after its move to
New York. The young moral theologian, Giles Milhaven, married and was asked by his students to stay on—not only as
professor, but as priest and Jesuit. Milhaven agreed with the
request in principle, though superiors begged him to spare
them the embarrassment. Milhaven saw the uneasiness that
would be caused by his staying, not only for old friends
on the faculty, but for his new wife—added strain placed on
the early trials of marriage. Besides, he was a qualified professor, and the college was uncertain of its academic future.
He accepted an offer from Brown University.

The students wished him well. But some thought he had
let them down by acquiescing, by perpetuating obsolete tabus.

That was the situation when Mike Dougherty (of the Dow Chemical trial) showed up again at Woodstock, along with his wife and their new baby. He was still appealing his conviction, along with Joe O'Rourke, and he wanted to keep active for peace. The Jesuits made room for his family in their apartments, on what seemed at first a temporary basis. When he expressed a desire to take his wife back to see her parents in California (where they had stayed for some time after their marriage), a collection was taken up throughout the community. Seminarians dug into exiguous salaries to finance the trip—some with pointed relief. Yet though the money disappeared, the Doughertys didn't. The plans for the trip faded along with the funds for it.

Sour comments were issuing from 98th Street. Diaper changing in the Gang Plank, baby crying in the TV lounge—what kind of gentleman's club *was* this anyway? At last a house meeting was called to thrash out the problem. The defenders of the family were clear in their position: Mike was doing work for which the house had prevailing sympathy, he should be supported. The opposition was ill-focused. Some objected that a baby around the house was an imposition; but undisturbed leisure and easy access to the TV are not very high grounds on which to vindicate the sacredness of cloister. How could the Jesuits kick out a Catholic folk hero—one of the D.C. Nine for God's sake—to preserve Colonel Blimp's favorite leather chair in the lounge? Others used an argument from religious poverty—Jesuit students live on the contributions of benefactors, who do not intend, when donating money, to house and feed non-Jesuits in a seminary. But that, too, was easily answered. The donations are given so that Jesuits may carry on their apostolate, and most of those at 98th Street would agree that peace work is part of that mission—more a part of it than work in laboratories or classrooms, on which donated funds are gladly expended. Besides, Joe O'Rourke is genially candid about use of his Order's funds: "We *should* be religious Robin Hoods, taking from the rich to feed the poor. Half the people who donate to us are making money from the war system or exploitative corporations, and hope they can buy their way into heaven with some Masses said for them."

It seemed to some that Dougherty came out of the meeting with stronger claims upon the resources of the house than many of those who were still Jesuits. What is given the Order, is given it for service; given to be given back, in the form of active ministry. The donations that make helping others possible also make it imperative; without this reason, nothing would be given in the first place. Thus most Jesuits were for Dougherty's staying. Given the poor quality of arguments against his staying, it is a wonder they did not all end up on his side. But the debate arose in the first place, one suspects, because of arguments no one voiced. These sophisticated young men were afraid to be "square" and bring up the question of celibacy, the traditional basis for cloister. If they are to remain celibate, it must be with eyes open, not as naive boys shut up monastically in cells. With all of New York around them, how can they exclude the regular contemplation of other men's sexual fulfillment? Indeed, sex takes far grosser forms than married life on almost any New York street. Families live just down the hall in the Woodstock students' apartment buildings. What does it matter, then, that one family lives in the next room?

So goes the argument—or so it would have gone if even one man had spelled out such obvious things. Yet, in practice, it does make a difference that the community, no matter how close it lives to the world and its cares, does not even try to create a celibate style of its own. If celibacy is not a mere accident and anomaly, but a thing chosen for its positive values, then that choice and those values should take external form, actual and symbolic. To strive for an "inner" celibacy that needs no outer expression is to dismiss the body and fall back on a simple-minded view of the soul as a detachable "ghost in the machine." The sophisticates turned out to be more naive than older guardians of the cloister walls.

It is also naive to think that the life of a religious order can continue if there is no difference between staying inside or going outside it. If there is nothing distinctive about this way of life, why belong to it? The crucial matter here is not whether priests will marry in the future, or religious orders find some new kind of communal discipline—I think both developments should take place, and will (with time). What matters is that liberated young religious men be honest with themselves, and realistic about what is at stake. Yet "liberals" are as subject to bad faith on the subject of sex as any targets of their criticism. That was true of the non-debate at 98th Street. It is true of many priests who leave to get married. There is continual nervous insistence that the priest had *other* objections to church discipline, not merely to celibacy—as if immaturity or shallowness must be assumed in any man who leaves "only" to marry. Friends would like to represent his act as one of all-inclusive protest against ecclesiastical backwardness. The *real* issue was authority, or reform, or social concerns —and then, well, yes, so long as the protest involved leaving the active exercise of priesthood, one might as well get married too.

There are some truths hidden in this line of argument, but they are distorted by the hiding process. The latent desire is to make marriage or non-marriage incidental to much larger issues—which is rather an insult to any woman who marries a priest. Not only was the man not "led astray" by her personally; their whole life together is reduced to an afterthought, made the vocational adjunct to more important decisions. The lucky woman is a beneficiary of her husband's dissatisfaction with the Roman Curia.

Why this denial that marriage can in itself be a worthy motive for vocational change? The argument is no doubt framed in response to Right-Wing prurience, which reduces all valid criticisms of the church to mere excuses for getting married. Faced with these sexual obsessions, church reformers insist that other reasons for dissatisfaction with the ministry do exist; that there are ways of repressing priests other than the sexual. But this response is too symmetrical, framed to meet the other side on common ground. The prude says priests leave just to get married—other objections are mere covers for concupiscence. His opponent answers that priests do *not* leave just to get married—there are many different reasons for dissent and departure. A tacit agreement has been reached that sex comes low in the scale of concerns—when priestly defectors are accused of submission to this inferior consideration, their defenders try to acquit them of it, forgetting in the process that sex is not something a man needs to be acquitted of.

Both sides, that is, treat sex as a separable part of life, something that can be placed over against "the issues." They do not recognize the way sex permeates all of life, the life of a man, of society, of a church. The priest who marries is often attacking sterile doctrine, sterile authority, sterile modes of expression, and experiencing a connection between these deprivations and the celibacy imposed by rule on Catholic ministers of the gospel. The priest who resents being set apart from life—political and intellectual life, as well as social—cannot tick off what is sexual in his desire to re-enter the human community and what is non-sexual. Those who believe in such neat divisions have retained some of the sterile habit of mind they are attacking.

It is not surprising that even critics of this attitude should continue (partially) to display it. Not only the Catholic church, but all Christian history—indeed, the whole Western religious tradition—is shot through with bad faith on the subject of sex. This shows itself in the customary defense made for a celibate clergy. Lack of a family is supposed to open a man to all people, make him more accessible, able to give himself wholly to others. If he had his own children, he would devote himself first to them, only secondarily to others. He would not have time to do all that priests do. What is given to his family would be taken from his flock.

Merely to state this argument is to reveal its absurdity. Priests are not more accessible than other men, but less—both at the literal level, and the symbolic one. Most Catholics have more frequent and easy access to their (married) doctor than to their (unmarried) pastor. I can more easily talk to my senator than to my bishop. Many things explain this remoteness, but the most obvious explanation took the form of a vicious circle: the priest (it was said) should remain celibate, to be less remote; and then a remote life style was built up around him, to keep him celibate. Grim rectory, forbidding chancery, sealed-off seminary, the "brand" of collar and black clothes—these were all meant to keep a man "safe" even when they destroyed the reason for wanting him to be safe.

This "practical" argument of accessibility was based on a psychological fallacy, the quantification of love—as if one had a fixed *amount* of love to give, and what goes to the family is lost to all others. It is everyone's experience that the more one loves, the more one can love; that love is denied not by intensity of love directed elsewhere, but by general lovelessness and desiccation of spirit. (It is interesting that Catholic authorities abandoned the quantum theory of love when they moved over from the question of clerical celibacy to that of birth control; none of them argued that the big family reduces love, that what one gives to a third or fourth child is necessarily "subtracted" from the first or second.)

Even if the quantum approach were valid, it would not serve as a defense of institutional celibacy, since most priests have not exemplified it, any more than they lived by the norm of greater accessibility. If they did, they would seek to develop wider forms of love, social forms of giving and total ministry —yet the kinds of men most adamant on retaining celibacy are also most opposed to social activism; they try to *restrict* the range of services to be rendered by a priest. These men are the victims of their training, so much of it focused on repression of sexual love in all its stimulants, concomitants, and consequences. This amounts to systematic undermining of all kinds of love, which are all, in their own way, sexual, since they all have to do with one's sense of self, and therefore with sexual identity.

The fact that sex itself, as well as marriage, was denied

in clerical training is symbolized by nuns' old habits, which made breasts and hips not only invisible, but very nearly unimaginable—explaining that *frisson* of illogical guilt felt by little boys in Elizabeth Cullinan's story when they glimpse a nun without her headdress. Her short hair in a napkin is enough to suggest all the body's shame of nakedness. Not only breasts and thighs were to be hidden, but calves and hair. The face could not be entirely veiled, if nuns were to do practical work in the schools; but it was framed, cosmeticless and with very little mobility, in a stiff coif-apparatus, cut off from the rest of the body as if floating above it—a picture hung on a wall, or a waif-face of indeterminate age and sex glimpsed though the grating of a cell.

This deliberate effacement of all womanly attributes was meant to affect others as well as to guard the woman inside. She was not to be available as an object of "concupiscence." Because of this laundering of possible responses to her, she experienced a diminishing reality. She was a neuter, felt and treated as such; and she had, for reasons of self-preservation, to shrink into this assigned state, learn to be content with it, not venturing out of it, not trying any but the most tested gestures of human affection or need.

Even when nuns were "humanized" in jokes and funny stories, there were unspoken rules to be observed. They could display little foibles and vanities, so long as they were not feminine vanities—Ingrid Bergman up at bat during recess, Celeste Holme playing tennis in her habit; or a long-unsuspected, then dramatically revealed, wizardry at playing marbles. A nun could even touch you, so long as it was a teammate's pat on the back. She could be something other than a neuter, so long as that something was a little boy.

Yet nuns often survived their training better than priests —remained more human, more spontaneous and loving. They were saved by another Catholic prejudice—the view that women are basically emotional, not capable of much logic. The priest, by contrast, had a specific duty and ability to "rise above" the emotional life—he was (or should be) more a creature of intellect, and he had more occasions of danger. The nun could stay in her convent, but the priest had to go out into the world—to deathbeds, for the last sacraments; to banks, for the parish mortgage. Yet even this degree of mobility was felt as a dangerous traffic with the secular; so the ideal of fulfillment in the priest's line of work was the man who could labor his way toward isolation—up hierarchic rungs to that large office where a bishop can be all alone with his ledgers.

The priest's own instincts fit in with those of many Catholic laymen, who rejoiced in the fact that priests were aloof and different. "We would not respect priests so much if they were just like us." That judgment was betrayed by its selective character. A priest could be "just like us" in enjoying food, or sports, or pets. Despite the fact that Irish Catholics have suffered a good deal for their all-too-human love of the bottle, Catholics have not expected the priest to set an example of abstinence in this regard. He can be just like others in most of their weaknesses—in all of them, actually, except one. If he resembles them by "indulging in" sex, he loses their respect.

Why should Catholics respect doctors and lawyers, Presidents and Senators, Protestant ministers and Jewish rabbis, without demanding this sexual apartness? Where priests are concerned, we were told that having no family would make a man more open and caring; if that were true, then we should require celibacy in our Presidents, who tend the nuclear-destruct button, and need all the humanitarian inhibitions we can place upon them. But of course it is not true. The reason Catholics admired celibacy in their priests was simple—they still believed, despite formal professions to the contrary, that sex, though not quite evil, is somehow sullying, makes a person subtly contaminated or second-rate. The married person is allowed sex—a minimum amount, anyway; enough to beget children and blunt concupiscence—as an indulgence to weakness. The "better way" is that of priests, who are "above all that"—an attitude expressed whenever women said they could not go to confession to a married priest (one not neuter, above-all-that, a non-man).

Thus Catholics were sorted out into first-class citizens (priests and nuns), and second-class ones (the married laity), with an unrecognized group of resident aliens (the unmarried laity). It was unfortunate that the debate on "states of life" began at all, and doubly unfortunate that it drew on Aristotelian ideas of perfection as "self-sufficiency." The religious life of the three vows became "the state of perfection" (martyrs, since they were considered perfect, became first-class citizens *honoris causa*, even if they had been married). Other celibates, those without the formal profession of vows, were lower down in the scale of things—priests outside the religious orders; or pious widows, too old to take the vows, leading a single life of dedication to God (widows also were "above all that"). But widows fell back into the second-rate category if they remarried. This second stratum was a whole different world so far as "merit" was concerned: the great class distinction was given a spurious biblical sanction by dividing Christ's commands from his "counsels." Hard sayings like "turn the other cheek," or "become a stranger to father and mother," or "go and sell all" were held to be additions to the minimal course man could steer to salvation. The "ordinary" Christian strove for salvation—to scrape through, as it were. The more generous strove to live up to the full gospel by *adding things onto* the preaching that made for salvation, obeying not only what Christ commanded but what he merely counseled.

The result was a professionalization of virtue: if one really did seek perfection, he would hardly do it in the second-rate context. To get married was to admit you were not in the big race, not even in the running for the Perfection Stakes. Perfection came as a package deal—true poverty, chastity, and obedience were all to be found together, in the religious life. Note the quiet assumption that "chastity" (sexual virtue) was synonymous with "celibacy." Terrible misconceptions were bred by this set of norms: saintly Christian laymen feeling they could never practice the full gospel—indeed, had no right to do so; lax religious priests and nuns feeling superior "by virtue of their state"; the reversal of all the gospel's reversals

—the "first" making themselves first; the idea of competitive virtue reintroduced after Christ had mocked it in his own roles of slave and clown and criminal, had said "the kingdom" is saved as a whole, not splintered into individuals.

Perhaps the worst injustice, in this systematized round of wrongs done to others and oneself in the name of the gospel, was embodied in this fact: the religion that gave such honor to celibacy was cruel to the unmarried laity. This, too, came from professionalizing the virtues: if a person were seeking perfection, he would enter the State of Perfection. If people were equally holy outside that State, what would happen to that State's claims, to all the prerogatives of professionals? Bachelors and old maids did not belong to the union. They had not chosen, but only been rejected—nobody wanted them. A nun was the pride of an old-fashioned Catholic family; an old maid was its shame.

It should be clear, by now, that all the arguments for institutionalized celibacy are dodges and deceits. The church's problem lay in its double heritage, a Hebrew tradition firmly rooted in the goodness of the Creator and his gifts ("It is not good for man to be alone"), and a classical tradition insistent on the body-soul dualism, treating the body as enemy and encumbrance. Some young Catholics have rediscovered the bias against sex in early Christian fathers, and treated it with a judgment as ahistorical as the blanket approval of all patristic texts by their elders. We get endless replays, now, of the idea that St. Augustine laid down repressive rules for the church out of his own guilt-ridden past and half-shed Manicheism. But anything he said against sex can be topped by even the most casual reading in late classical authors or early Christian heretics. Augustine's importance, in this context, lies not where he echoed the culture, but where he opposed it—opposed the Platonizers by saying this life is properly imperfect, even in its Christian sectors; opposed the Manicheans by saying marriage is a good in itself (though not the highest one); opposed those who, like Tertullian, said men should not bring children into this imperfect state of trial;

opposed the prejudice against bastards by lavishing praise and love on his son (defiantly named "God's Gift"); and opposed those who were critical of his "confessions" as too frank about sex.

Over against his background and environment, Augustine was on the side of life—and that is the point: there is cultural struggle, all the way, in man's attitude toward sex. The ahistorical mind cannot take this in. It strives for *one* rule, a perduring thing, one discerned from earliest to latest times, dimly or clearly grasped but always there. Such a predisposition toward changelessness is destructive wherever we find it, but nowhere more so than in dealing with sex—where, as Chesterton says, we are all a little mad, and those maddest who think they are most rational. There is always clash and tension in the charged area of sex. Those who deny this by saying it is all a blessing are as idiotic as those who think of it only as a curse. The Catholic church, in trying to deny such contradictions, has been forced in an eminent way to embody them: all its formulae say sex is good, the Creator's gift, while all its instincts and many of its actions say just the opposite.

The whole church teaching went astray over two virginities misinterpreted—that of Jesus, and that of his mother. The ancient Hebrew world was as harsh on unmarried people as any Catholic community of the past—a common prejudice in tribes seeking perpetuity of lineage. Why, then, are Mary and Jesus presented as virgins in the Gospels? Bible scholars argue that the virgin birth can be interpreted only in conjunction with the schematic genealogy of Jesus, as a balance of continuity against discontinuity. Jesus was the heir of David, fulfiller of the kingly dreams; yet not in the line of expected hopes. He fulfills unexpectedly (his kingdom not being of this world), and represents a new departure, a beginning; a birth as unindebted to the past as Adam's own. He is both the heir of David, and the canceler of David's line, of all earthly hopes for power; the heir of Adam, and his own Adam —"second Adam," man returning to God, as the first Adam had come from him. So, as the Spirit moved through an inchoate universe to call Adam up in abrupt creative act, the Spirit once more moves over "virgin territory" to begin anew with another Adam. Mary is not virgin because she is "above all that"—though her statues in the modern age have been as vague about breasts and hips as those of a habited nun. She was "virginal" as the dust from which Adam came—innocent, as yet, of history; for history was about to be reversed.

Then what of the virgin Jesus? He did not "fall through woman," it is true—though Genesis itself does not have this misogynist and anti-sexual note, as do patristic interpretations of Adam's fall. Adam fell out of his self-sufficient isolation into human need—into complex possibilities created by the existence of another person. He fell to his "own flesh," the rib that yearned outward and turned back wearing a different face; and he fell because it is not good for man to be alone. The fall was an escape from Aristotelian self-sufficiency into history and mutual need. Adam is the sacrament of the beginning, mere promise; he could not be more. Jesus is a sign of the End, of the gospel's disturbance of ordinary life, and of Christianity's union with Jesus in that "last time" he lives.

That is the gospel message, one very far from Catholics' feeling that an ideal mother (i.e., Mary) would not actually —well, spread her legs; do *that;* take that thing into her, even for the noble purpose of producing *me.* (Sure, Mom's all right, she couldn't help it—it's the price of original sin, there's no other way any more. But if only Adam hadn't fallen, then she could have been a mother and still have been as pure as Mary.) And the gospel message is very far from the claim that anyone who wants to follow Jesus must be a virgin like Jesus. One can no more *be* Jesus (shouldering expensive tombstones down, all over Catholic cemeteries, on the third day after burial) than one can *be* Adam and draw a woman from one's ribs. The sign is, in both cases, a *sign,* a teaching—something pointing outward to fact, not contained in itself for itself.

Only once, in the four Gospels, does Jesus seem to call men to celibacy (Matt. 19.12) as "eunuchs for the kingdom of heaven's sake"—and that passage has probably been as badly misinterpreted as the Onan story in the Old Testament. A number of modern scholars have returned to Clement of Alexandria's understanding of the verse, which involves no reference to celibacy at all (see Q. Quesnell, *Catholic Biblical Quarterly*, 1968). Otherwise, scripture contains only Paul's commendation of virginity to the Corinthians (I Cor. 7)— and even there he makes it clear that "I have no mandate from the Lord" (v. 25). He writes in the very shadow of the final crisis (the "impending calamity" of v. 26, in which "our time is a contracted one," v. 29). Out of the urgency of his own preaching activities before the end of the world, he recommends that no one bother to change his state in life—not slaves (21), not the married (10–11), *nor* the unmarried (8–9). "Let everyone abide in the condition he has been called to already" (20). Why set up household in a crumbling world? Paul writes on the run, calling others to come with him if they can—there is so much to be done before the end.

When the expectation of an immediate end to the world disappeared, Paul's norms had to undergo a change. Men thought in terms of greater permanency, while adapting the idea of "the last time" to new uses. Is there a place for celibacy in a last time so reinterpreted? Some think so—including Daniel Berrigan. He has seen nuns and priests risk jail with easier minds than some who will be leaving spouses and children behind. Indeed, so harsh has he been on the modern family—as a "sitting duck for the State"—that some think he is trying to limit the full gospel once more, set up another clerical monopoly on it. I think this is a misunderstanding of his position. As Berrigan puts it, the family is weak insofar as it meshes with other institutions that make up the suicide-machine of our System: "The middle class breeds kids to become social engineers, the poor breeds kids to kill—and their progeny stay in conflict with each other and support the state." The answer, clearly, is not for everyone to go off to seminaries—for the institutional church is also engaged with the System; and it uses celibacy, not to invite risk, but to minimize it. The gospel can be received by those in any state of life, as St. Paul emphasized—and certain things (including the comatose family) can only be changed from within. But it is probably true that no change will occur without those who take special risks, wage a special kind of war upon the world. In Berrigan's words: "With regard to most of our fellows in Church and State, both my brother and I are really dead men. It makes no sense not to start with that fact. We have no stake in Church or State, as currently in evidence; their aims, their values, their mutual transfusions of comfort. We have said no to all that."

This kind of lonely no said to the System has nothing to do with mass-produced eunuch-servants to the church bureaucracy. It is a way of going, individually, out to an edge of hyperawareness and risk, signifying in one's own "breakaway" the most radical rejection of this order's living death. It is a highly personal way of becoming "dead men" in order to bring life back into the world, thinking in terms of ultimates, of an Ending to our whole scheme of things. Religious celibacy, to be justified at all, must be a radical, exceptional, exceedingly private choice related to crisis. To make of it a taming institutional device simply mocks the spirit of freedom for which it should stand. Most priests, like the rest of us, have not gone far enough into danger to say, with Daniel Berrigan: "We have jail records, we have been turbulent, uncharitable, we have failed in love for the brethren, have yielded to fear and despair and pride, often in our lives. Forgive us. We are no more, when the truth is told, than ignorant beset men, jockeying against all chance, at the hour of death, for a place at the right hand of the Dying One."

TWELVE

Church Against State

Make use of power? What a pernicious illusion.
It's power that makes use of us.

—SILONE'S "ST. CELESTINE"

IT HAD BEEN A FLAMBOYANT MASS, that drear ghetto night, in
the brightly lit church—the choir attacked old spirituals with
the zest of a Fred Waring group suddenly given "soul." But a
hush, as is customary, came over the church while bread and
wine were consecrated, to the words of the Last Supper. Father
Philip Linden—young, black, tall (six-feet-five), his resisting
hair frizzed up into a natural, his vestment a dashiki—picked
up communion bread and recited: "On the night he was betrayed, he took bread, broke it, and gave it to his friends, saying 'This is my body . . . This is my blood . . . It shall be shed
for many . . . Do this in memory of me.'"

On the night he was betrayed. The sermon had just called
to mind "our brother Martin," for whom this Mass was offered. It was Dr. King's birthday; the mule train and Coretta
were back in town. Father Linden and his choir had come over
from Baltimore to celebrate and pray where fires had burned
all that long night after King's death, the night he was betrayed. Not betrayed, admittedly, by any one Judas of his circle. Still, all his last years King had been spied on, slandered,

his every act pried into, rights of privacy denied him—treated like an outlaw, someone to be trapped. No wonder anger broke out in fire across the nation, anger at all King's opponents, minimizers of his work, enemies of his mission, those would who would not hear, who said, "Do not listen," called him liar. They resembled the men who had ridiculed Isaiah, those who

> . . . say to the seers, "You shall not see,"
> and to the visionaries, "You shall have no true vision;
> give us smooth words. . . ."
> —Isaiah 30.10

Enemies of the word are betrayers of its bearer—so this was done in memory of him, our brother Martin.

And, the priest added after communion, in memory of "our sisters and brothers of the Conspiracy." Father Linden, you see, was a member of the East Coast Conspiracy to Save Lives, some of whose members had just then been accused of planning to bomb and kidnap.

Recent history must seem like a nightmare confirmation of every redneck's fears. First, a Baptist minister (of all people) started a revolution, one of those safe black oversolemn preacher types out of *Green Pastures,* with a bible full of submissiveness—yet suddenly that book caught fire in his hand; the pulpit had become a force again, source of militant strength for blacks, menace for whites. Churches, long the most innocuous parts of our landscape, were becoming dangerous —as they had been when Patrick Henry spoke from a pew in St. John's of Richmond. No wonder Southerners felt betrayed by "their" blacks and "their" religion. This preacher was actually *preaching,* and his words were not smooth.

Then new fears came to the Bible Belt as Catholic priests were charged with political conspiracy—memories of the Al Smith candidacy and "How many troops does the Pope have?" It was the kind of fear that had been laughed at for a long time, pooh-poohed in the Kennedy campaign, considered by the knowing a mere joke in questionable taste. Catholics themselves had spent cautious years dispelling any notion that a priest would meddle in American politics. And they had done their work well. By the early Sixties there was nothing less dangerous than a Catholic priest.

But no longer. Some priests now carry danger with them—as friends of Philip and Daniel Berrigan have found out. A Pennsylvania grand jury indictment treated visits with one of these jailed priests as "overt acts" of conspiracy. When two other priests, as a result of that indictment, were arrested in Baltimore, their Cardinal, Lawrence Shehan, went instantly to visit them. Was that to be considered an "overt act" of conspiracy? Probably not; though another of the "overt acts"—a nun's move to Washington—was performed in response to her superior's command. It seems only fair that this superior, responsible for the overt act, should have been indicted, too. And even if Baltimore's Cardinal escaped the law, he is treated by some as a guilty man. After his visit to the jail, Catholics picketed Masses at his Cathedral, bearing signs that said DOWN WITH RED PRIESTS—and if Catholics say that, what are the rednecks saying? A man in clerical dress and Roman collar went into a Baltimore hardware store to buy a length of lead pipe—a transaction that caught the eye of a crapulous gentleman just over from a nearby tavern. He wanted to know what the unpatriotic priest would blow up *next?* The first response given was a measured one: that the purchaser was neither American nor a Roman Catholic, but an Anglican visitor to this country. His critic, badly deflated, making one last try, asked then just what the pipe *was* for—and the answer, this time, was gratifyingly obscene.

And what of the many Catholic FBI men who pursue or spy on priests and nuns, tap their wires, attend new liturgies, send informers into parish circles? When Sister Sue Cordes, working for the Berrigan defense committee, went to her sister's wedding, her mother warned the Sister not to talk much about peace work—the bridegroom was an agent. Father Redmond McGoldrick, a Jesuit priest who has been arrested many times at political protests, is on polite but guarded terms with *his* FBI brother-in-law. When agents finally ran down a Protestant minister who yielded his pulpit to Dan Berrigan, while he was loose and being hunted, they spent fifteen minutes talking about the priest's whereabouts, and forty minutes explaining why they, as Catholics, felt justified in stalking priests. The "conspiracy" and the FBI have drawn heavily on the same Catholic subculture.

Why this odd Kafkan pursuit of Catholics by Catholics? It is not mysterious. Catholics had in recent decades nurtured a harsh theological animus against Communism, and that attitude dovetailed neatly with old immigrant desires to prove their loyalty to America. The structure of their church, moreover, elicited from Catholics deep respect for authority, and made them familiar with doctrinal ways of testing that respect. Catholics therefore drifted naturally toward investigative agencies in the fiercest Cold War time. This was as natural as the drift of other young men to the discipline and authority of the priesthood. The process was a mere updating of the classic choice offered in Italian (or other ethnic) ghettos: while an older brother—Dominic, say, played by Victor Mature—joined the police force, his younger brother Salvatore (played by Sal Mineo) went off to study for the priesthood. And Dom and Sal were equally good boys.

By the Fifties, of course, Dom had moved up—from cop on the beat to college graduate, eagerly recruited now by the FBI, by federal and military investigative agencies. As the overworked joke put it, Fordham graduates were hired to check on Harvard graduates. If I may cast the situation in personal terms, one of my best friends from Catholic high school days is still in the CIA. Both brothers of the girl I dated back then were in a seminary—until one of the brothers left and joined the FBI. This was a common progression. A scripture scholar at the seminary where three of the Harrisburg defendants were trained says hardly a year went by, in the late Fifties and early Sixties, without his receiving an FBI clearance sheet on one of his former students, become by then an applicant to the Bureau. Hoover's force was attractive to the ex-seminarian at several levels of conscious and unconscious motivation. It gave young men a corps to join, a fellowship, with an outsider's role as scrutinizer of men's failings and as guardian of order. Boys who might have been uneasy at too abrupt re-entry into secular life could stand partly off from it, still, in distrust—spying on it. God's spies upon the world.

And if, by the Fifties, Dom had moved up from cop on the beat to regional director of the FBI, Sal too had gone to college, risen socially, taken on new responsibilities. A good example is the "worker priest," John Cronin, who found Communists easing into union jobs during World War II, and worked with the FBI to expose them. He was thus in an excellent position, after the war, to draw on the FBI's secret files, which he used to draft the American bishops' hard statement against Communism. His contacts—with labor, Congress, church hierarchy, and the FBI—put him at the very center of postwar anti-communist patriotism, a situation symbolized by the fact that he (along with Monsignor Fulton Sheen) served as philosophical mentor to freshman congressman Richard Nixon in 1947. Father Cronin even acted as Nixon's intermediary for reports smuggled out of the FBI (through Catholic agent Ed Hummer) when the Truman administration was trying to halt inquiry into the case of Alger Hiss. Later, when Nixon became Vice-President, Father Cronin became his *very* ghostly ghost-writer. Dom and Sal, once marginal Americans, were now a (largely secret) team at the top of things, quiet well-intentioned saviors of their country. No wonder a myth began to shape itself in terms of Communist menace and Catholic solution—Monsignor Sheen guiding Louis Budenz out of his Marxist darkness into light, Whittaker Chambers joining Clare Luce and Bill Buckley on crusade, an Irish Catholic midwestern Senator taking on smug Ivy League Dean Achesons and Averell Harrimans. Rome, once suspect, now seemed the firmest bastion of Washington. No wonder Catholic patriots rejoiced—theirs were the country's shrivers and godly protectors and policemen.

Imagine, then, the harsh cheating of expectation when Catholic loyalists were sent out to trap—their grade-school teachers, "the good nuns." The awkwardness of it showed up when churches had to be searched; raids were actually made on sacristies, where agents had robed themselves when they were altar boys. The FBI men probed in a gingerly way and asked "Are you there, Father Dan?"—always the polite "Father" appended, giving the whole thing an air of the child's game, "Come out, come out, wherever you are." Could it really be a Father who was hiding from the law? Or, alternatively, if he was doing all this, could he still be called a Father?

Little in the agents' personal experience equipped them to answer such hard questions. They were brought up to consider all Authority as one, in church and state, and to think of priests as especially allied with American values against all "outside" forces (for outside, read: Communist). How, then, cope with a force not only inside the country and its citizenry, but deep inside the Catholic structure of holy things? It would be easy enough to handle a merely selfish or crooked Catholic gone astray. If Dom and Sal had become, respectively, cop and priest, another route of escape from the ghetto was taken by their third brother, Rocco (played by Richard Conte after Edward G. Robinson grew too old for the part). Rocco was always the slick one, who finally outsmarted himself, went too far too fast; yet he would stagger back at the end, to die in the flicker of candles down the side aisle of his neighborhood church. Dom had hunted him down, but Sal would find and absolve him—"Are you there, Rocco?"

These new outlaws, however, are of a different order altogether. Rocco, when caught, obligingly repented. The real problem with men like the Berrigans is not that they are priests, but that they refuse to recognize their crimes *as* crime, to give in to the good guys in the only way that matters—giving in to their standards and values. No, these men cling to their defiance, make of it what used to be called "an outward sign of an inward reality"—a *sacramental* criminality. As Bureau agents probed deeper into this enigma—"Are you *there*, Father Dan?"—did they remember dark confessionals from their youth (is Father there, can he hear?), remember peering through the screen until a panel shuffled back and one hastily mumbled, "Bless me, Father, for I have sinned. . . ."?

Catholic boys were brought up, once, on stories of heroic priests who kept "the seal of confession"—the pledge not to reveal things said to them by penitents—when government investigators tried to learn what was said inside that box. *Government* investigators. It is striking how many Catholic saints defied "Caesar," the eternal Caesar of state power—and how little impact that fact has had on Catholics in America. It took the most fundamentalist kind of church in America—the Southern Baptist one—to remind them that all Christians have a heritage of resistance from catacomb days. But by 1965, some had been reminded. That year a young man named David Miller became the first American prosecuted for burning his draft card. He was a disciple of Dorothy Day and the Catholic Worker movement. When the judge sentenced him, he turned toward prison with a touch of the ancient defiance, told his judge, "Caesar will never have me." That should have been the warning sign that fools were on the loose again. It was almost as bad as living in the early days of Christianity, when St. Paul's moves through Asia Minor were charted fearfully— at his arrival men complained to local authorities, "The world's troublemakers are now here" (Acts of the Apostles 17.6).

Few brothers could be more different than the Berrigan brothers. Philip is a large and incendiary Irishman born something of a brawler, like his father. (They lived in a shower of sparks, as flint rubbed flint—with Dan conciliatory, patience wearing pugnacity down at the end.) Phil was a good man to have with you in a war; but more and more at war with the warrior in himself, as well as in the world; going from battlefield promotion in the Second World War to service in the only Order founded to help blacks in America. He practically dragged his brother into the Catonsville raid (or drank him into it, through a long night of passionate fraternal arguing). Daniel is slight and dark, and more aloof. Where Phil inspires, Dan disturbs; in his quiet way, probes deeper; the lines in his

young-old face are the map of some country unexplored. A
shrewd woman, the first time she met him, said he should wear
warning bells on the curved-back toes of leprechaun boots.
The world's troublemakers—not a bad description of these
two. First came Phil, daring authorities over and over again to
jail him—until, at last, they did. He was the first priest to go to
jail in America as a political prisoner. Yet Phil inside was not
nearly the embarrassment that Dan was to prove outside. For
four maddening months in 1970, the FBI pursued him while he
preached, wrote, broadcast, was photographed, was interviewed, moved with pedagogic elusiveness, made his very absence felt as an omnipresence. During this whole time, did
any agent recollect tales of priests being hunted—of Topcliffe
promising Queen Elizabeth I to find all the Jesuits in her
realm; of the principled ascetic who, having let Graham
Greene's "whisky priest" slip through his hands, had to vindicate the purity of his new regime by finding and exterminating
this remnant of the shabby past; or of the SS troops—some
probably Catholic—who arrested Father Albert Delp for resistance to Hitler; the men who ran Padré Miguel Pro to earth
in Mexico?

It is an interesting coincidence that, just one month before
the FBI's Director claimed Catholics had plotted to kidnap a
government agent, fourteen thousand British Catholics gathered in Rome to celebrate the canonization of forty Welsh and
English martyrs from the sixteenth and seventeenth centuries.
These had all, in different ways, defied the English government
—indeed, their canonization had been held up for years because of their proximity to anti-Tudor and Hispanophile
politics. These martyrs lived, perforce, underground, among
enemies of government—Catholics of the more defiant sort,
rebellious nobles, the criminals always used by or against such
undergrounds, desperate men, many of them with blighted
hopes or bitter pasts.

Two such men, both priests, were caught planning to kidnap King James in 1603—they were so wild-eyed that their

own co-religionists tipped off the authorities. And once this "Bye Plot" (by-plot) was discovered, investigation linked it with an even skimpier "Main Plot," interesting to authorities because Walter Ralegh seemed to be involved in it. Ralegh, greatly feared by the government, was indicted with a pack of Catholic sympathizers (only one odd man in the lot, dour Puritan Lord Grey). The "overt act" of conspiracy cited against Ralegh was a conversation in which he was told the King of Spain would pay well for his services. Ralegh answered that such a "crime," a mere discussion of possibilities, would put subjects at the mercy of anyone speaking objectionable things in their presence. The priests were executed, but Ralegh lived—in the Tower, his death postponed (though he was effectively put out of action).

It was a Jesuit, Henry Garnett, who informed on the would-be kidnapers of King James; but he got little credit for the act. It was ascribed to Jesuit hatred for all priests not of their Order. Elizabeth's and James's ministers were brilliant at setting one part of the Catholic world against another, a policy the King himself called "using tame ducks to catch wild ones." When Father Garnett was himself captured, and denied any knowledge of Guy Fawkes's Gunpowder Plot—he knew of it, but only under the seal of confession—his prison guard was suborned to feign conversion by Garnett, arrange a meeting with another priest, and then listen in while Garnett made his confession. It was a world where no one was completely safe, nor proof against government bribes and pressures, spies and provocateurs.

Yet some men moved through that compromised time of plot and counterplot with almost ablutionary innocence. The forty canonized in Rome represent a mere tenth of the Catholics, mainly priests, who were killed on England's gallows. Equivocal men and those who dabbled in politics were excluded from consideration—not only the two priest-kidnapers, but men like Garnett, tangentially involved with Guy Fawkes. Those left for canonization, after this winnowing, were men like Robert Southwell, the Jesuit poet, a kind of minor Blake nodding in on England a century ahead of time:

> The same you saw in heavenly seate,
> Is he that now sucks Maries teate.

Southwell returned to England, after ordination as a priest in Rome, bringing the sacraments (Mass, confession, communion) to his fellow believers. The very simplicity of his aim seemed to give his work a charmed immunity. Clothed like a swashbuckler, he lived next door to one of Elizabeth's own London houses, just across from the Earl of Leicester, at a time when other priests avoided London as too dangerous (they were scattered about the country, in Catholic mansions equipped with "priest holes" to hide them). Southwell was pure Elizabethan in all but his religion; he boasted of his love for the Virgin Queen, a lady who (like him) "hath for her self made Choise of a single life." In time Southwell made his way to Her Majesty's gallows—betrayed, like most of his fellow victims, by a need to keep in touch with the Catholic underground in all its aspects, both careful and careless. Loneliness and despair were the enemies, and community the main psychic need of these men, no matter how risky its purchase. Southwell bribed his way into prisons to assure condemned priests they were not alone in their ordeal.

But Southwell had no illusions about certain of the Catholics he met. In an appeal he wrote to the Queen, he did not try to excuse all men of his faith; only asked her to remember, "It were a hard Course to reprove all Prophetts for one Saul." He also knew that the strongest have their weaknesses. As he wrote of St. Peter,

> Muse not to see some mud in cleerest brooke,
> They once were brittle mould, that now are Saintes.

When Catholic hotheads let themselves be drawn into the so-called Babington Plot by government provocateurs, Southwell compared them to "simple Isaac," who carried the fire and fuel to his own execution. But he also mocked the government for its exaggerated reaction, its attempt to whip up fear over this plot—"hues and Cries raised, frights bruted in the peoples eares, and all mens eyes filled with such a smoake, as though the whole Realme had bene on fire, whereas in truth it was but the hissinge of a few greene twigges of their owne kindling, which they might without any such up-rores have quenched with a handfull of water, but that it made not so much for their purpose as these buggish and terrible shewes . . . (and) generall demonstrations of a need-les feare."

Daniel Berrigan is very conscious of his Jesuit forebears. He has written poems and essays on Jesuits in the French resistance and worker-priest movement; on Père Sebastian Rasles, S.J., who ministered to American Indians; on John Urey, a priest who helped Bahamian slaves escape through the American colonies, who was executed under British law—like the Elizabethan Jesuits—by being "hanged, drawn, and quartered." He comforts himself with the thought that Philip in the Lewisburg prison "hole" had at last brought the priest hole to America. He reread Southwell while underground, and recalled the martyred French Jesuits of Canada and upper New York State. One way Daniel Berrigan contrasts himself with Philip is in terms of their two Orders: "Philip doesn't have as strong or passionate sense of belonging to his Order as I do. . . . His congregation's traditions are by no means as old or as exciting or as imaginative; his Order hasn't under-gone the test of so many centuries. . . ." When psychiatrist Robert Coles interviewed Daniel, he was told what the Jesuit Order means in his life:

The Jesuits of the sixteenth or seventeenth century lived underground in England to vindicate the unity of the church. They were willing to do so rather than sit back and take no action to signify their sense of horror at the breakaway of England, an event which was to them a life and death question. And Jesuits have died to vindicate the truth of the Eucharist in other European countries.

These were, of course, religious questions posed in a religious context. Protestants can speak in the same way about their martyrs. The difference now is, a man like Bonhoeffer illustrated for us, that the questions are being posed across the board in a way that says: Shall man survive?

In his belief that the Spirit has different missions in different ages, Berrigan refers to Deitrich Bonhoeffer, the evangelical pastor who moved from absolute pacifism to violent resistance against Hitler. Eberhard Bethge has described Bonhoeffer's own sense that Christians have a constantly varying witness to bear against the world:

Like Kierkegaard, Bonhoeffer had always believed that "Luther would say now the opposite of what he said then," whereby he would really be saying the same thing, the vital thing. Once, faith had meant leaving the cloister; faith might come to mean a reopening of the cloister; and faith might also mean taking part in politics.

Berrigan spelled out the continuity-in-difference this way:

I can't conceive of myself as a Jesuit priest dying on behalf of the Eucharist, trying to vindicate the truth of the Eucharist, except in a very new way—except as the Eucharist would imply the fact that man is of value. . . . Today, in other words, the important questions have an extraordinarily secularized kind of context. So I find myself at the side of the prophets or the martyrs, in however absurd and inferior a way, and I find no break with their tradition in what I am trying to stand for. . . . I cannot pose in such a time as ours these questions as sacred questions involving what I conceive to be a kind of Platonic dogma—even though I hope I believe as firmly in the reality of the Eucharist as seventeenth-century Jesuits did; and that belief is still very much at the center of my understanding of my life. For me to be underground because of my position and deeds with respect to the Vietnam war—well, I find in that predicament a continuity of spirit with what other Jesuits stood for.

The sense of a large moral heritage, of belonging in the great line of Christian witnesses against the world, gives to the Berrigans and their followers an insouciance that often looks like arrogance. They do not care about the things that interest so many others, the here-and-now little issues, even of their own church. They call debate about things like papal infallibility, or birth control, or priestly celibacy, Mickey Mouse issues that have nothing to do with Christianity. One of the nuns working on the Harrisburg defense committee explained the solidarity on large personal issues felt throughout the Catholic underground. "I always wanted to work against the war, but I was afraid. I worried that I wouldn't be able to stand it if I went to jail. Phil gave us a sense that we could support each other, we would never be alone, we could stand together." At the Lewisburg prison, Philip Berrigan ended up in the hole (or isolation ward) for leaving his assigned prison sector—one of the Catonsville prisoners was being threatened with homosexual rape, and Phil took him away from danger.

This determination to "keep in touch," to provide each other mutual comfort, involves some risk—sympathetic hearing even to desperate people, assurance to those jailed that resistance will continue, dangerous communication with fugitives and those in prison. It is said that union boss James Hoffa's mail service in and out of Lewisburg prison was offered Philip; but he preferred to trust committed Movement types—and was betrayed by a bogus Movement type.

Still, despite the dangers, those whose priorities are so radically different seem to move through our diminished times with strange jauntiness, a refusal to be cowed by the institutions of menace. Daniel, during his four months of exposed risky preaching and witty escape, displayed some of Southwell's own panache. He stayed invisible by sheer audacity— as when he spoke to an audience full of FBI agents at Cornell, then escaped in a twelve-foot-tall papier-mâché costume of an apostle, left over from a mime group's act. The agents had been waiting for the talk to end, so they could arrest him unobtrusively, but he slipped away in a symbol far too obvious for them to see, twirling blind yet untouched through danger, safe in the guiding hands of his friends. The lawmen had come to arrest a small priest, and they let a large apostle go. The incident sums up all J. Edgar Hoover's attempts to bring down these new kinds of hero—each act just increases their stature.

When the Berrigans and seven others were convicted of

destroying draft files, Dan said, "We agree that this is the greatest day of our lives," and politely asked the judge if they could offer a prayer. The poor robed man, aware of judiciary action to keep prayer out of classrooms, did not know what to do with his own courtroom. There is nothing these people do that is not dangerous in some way. At last the judge submitted to his ordeal by liturgy, as the convicts linked hands and recited their "Pater noster." Some of the Elizabethan priests, when sentenced to death, had sung in the courtroom a "Te Deum," the traditional hymn for celebrating victories. Mutual comfort at the scaffold became a task that Catholics imposed upon themselves, treating the gallows as an altar, gathering there for prayer. One man, brought out late, saw a number of his fellow priests lined up for execution, shouted, "Here's a jolly company," and ran up the stairs. Another, when the sun came out—and caused a shiver in the superstitious crowd—laughed off the supposedly favorable sign by saying, "Soon I shall be above yon fellow." When Edmund Campion was told to stop praying in Latin, just before his death, he said, "I pray God in a language we both well understand." What can you do with people who are so irresponsible, who will not be had by Caesar? Even while he ran, Dan Berrigan reminded his pursuers: "We have chosen our fate; we have not been condemned to it."

When "Father Dan" was captured at last, he was whisked past newsmen, his handcuffs lifted in crippled wave of the V-sign—a baffled hawk, his wings pinned back, but the eyes still bright and mocking. Reporters asked what he would do now, and he grinned back, "Resist." When priests and laymen made a "pentecostal fire" of Chicago draft files, police found that a twenty-year-old among them had just recently left jail, after serving time for a similar offense. When Dorothy Day, that veteran resister, leader of the Catholic Worker movement, was asked what Catholics could do about the war, she said, "Pack the jails with our young men. *Pack* the jails."

Dan Berrigan has in large part inherited the constituency of Dorothy Day, who kept alive an ardent Catholicism of the outcast through our country's militaristic Forties and apathetic Fifties. She looked, for a while, old-fashioned in the "cool" liberal Sixties of Jack Kennedy, when a new image was being given the church by Pope John and Vatican II. Invited over to the Council, she went with her customary way of obliging church superiors. But there was always something unbought under her deference. How could she be bought off? She deals in a coinage no Pope can mint in his palace; in young lives—poor lives, desperate lives. She was jailed, in the apathetic time, for sitting on a park bench when sirens wailed the least complacent people of the world, sour jaded New Yorkers, into bomb shelters. When all the rest were fooled, she wasn't. She wrote what turned out to be the first pages of a growing prison literature on the Catholic Left.

It was Dorothy's young people—men like David Miller and Jim Forest—who were restive, even under Kennedy; who moved from civil rights toward peace activism; who knew the war at once for what it was, and said, "No incense to Mars, not even a pinch." They burned draft cards—one, in crazy ardor, even burnt himself; and Dan Berrigan, preaching at his funeral, realized he must take these young people into dangers less ultimate and futile; into danger, nonetheless; they had shown their mettle for that. New Catholic radicalisms were coming to birth elsewhere—*Ramparts* began as a slick kind of *Commonweal* West, then alternated futility with opportunism. Products of Catholic schools were now writing the Port Huron Statement and running the Free Speech Movement.

The change in tone between Dorothy Day's time and Dan Berrigan's can be seen in the reaction of officials to the two. They moved from chagrined permissiveness to hysterical repression. Though Dorothy was arrested for defying the air-raid drills of the Fifties, she had often been on picket lines where New York's finest managed to ignore her and her people, though arresting others. Even more important, Dorothy was never in trouble with church authorities. Cardinal Spellman let her carry on her work in his diocese—without encouragement or endorsement, true; but also without major hindrance. Partly, I suppose, he did not think a mere woman could be all that dangerous; and Dorothy, for her part, was reassuringly "churchy"—orthodox on purely doctrinal matters, content with the Latin rite and silences of liturgical *Romanitá*. But Dan was a priest, and he experimented with new Mass-forms, and he would have no trouble getting into jail—he must be taken care of. Spellman pressured Berrigan's Jesuit superiors to ship him off for Mexico. But then something new happened, something Spellman had not counted on, had spent a whole career not counting on, though only now did he realize it: Catholics throughout the country rallied behind Dan (who had gone off obediently to Cuernavaca). The resulting furor backed Spellman up against his cathedral wall. Berrigan was brought back in honor, and a new age of resistance was born, to state authority *and church officials*.

This was something that could not be coped with in the old way—Spellman's way, or Cardinal McIntyre's way, or J. Edgar Hoover's way. Now, instead of Dom and Sal working together, cop-priest with priest-cop, Tom (named for St. Thomas Aquinas) Foran was prosecuting Tom (named for St. Thomas More) Hayden. Rocco had become Mario Savio. Catholic judges were listening to Thomistic arguments on higher law and conscience and the limits put on Caesar, then reluctantly sentencing the priests who used all that seminary learning in court to a harsher penal monasticism. Tame ducks were brought in to catch wild ducks—four Irish Catholic prosecutors were lined up for the Harrisburg trial. Monasteries and convents were hiding draft resisters, nuns raiding draft boards, and an underground railway grew up to support fugitives. This underground, despite wild things done by and in it, has been surprisingly successful. Dan, of course, got caught; but only in time, and while courting maximum publicity, and after being given high FBI priority, a heavy assignment of agents. But people forget that at least eleven other convicted Catholics remained loose in the underground, including one of the Catonsville Nine, Mary Moylan.

Those Catholics who go underground would not be so offensive to "normal" Catholics if it meant going *out*—leaving the church, the priesthood, the Christian fellowship, once for all. Timorous episcopal "fishers of men" would gladly shake these fish out of their nets; but the unwanted catch just laughs and hangs in there. Philip writes to Daniel, "We'll muckle through for old Mother Church." Daniel says that the institutional church nibbled away at Christ—yet Christ was there to be nibbled at. Philip answers, "Yes, she is a whore, but she's our mother." Part a whore, and part a queen, and these sons admire her even when she embarrasses them (in a time of world danger, the Vatican newspaper gets most worked up about the subject of miniskirts). Mother may be a wacky dame at best, but these disturbing sons—Phil raucous, Dan ironic—pay her the compliment of finding her "serious" (Phil's word—the statement released when his Baltimore Four burned draft files was signed, "Seriously yours") and "interesting" (Dan's cooler accolade).

No wonder agents of law—all those submissive agents of Americanism who wear collars and mitres as well as badges—fear such men and women, yet fear to move against them. They *must* be enemies—Good Lord, they think the church is *disreputable*. These agents have never thought her that, or found her dangerous. The church's enemies, they feel, are men who call her Mother Church while remaining unrepentant, those clerical black sheep. And if such criminals persevere, the agents will, following their consciences, hunt them down, arrest and imprison them, remain good Catholics even when the good nuns accuse them of being good Germans. The Berrigans, it seems clear to these men, have hurt the church even more than they have hurt their country: Bless me, Father, but *you* have sinned—and the night you eluded us, our gentlemanly agreement and forbearance at Cornell, was the night *we* were betrayed. And so the "bird watcher" on Block Island who captured Dan prayed audibly over his deed, *Ad majorem Dei gloriam* (To God's great glory). It is the motto of Dan Berrigan's religious Order—his captor was saying that *he* was the true Jesuit, distinguisher of duties, maintaining allegiance to the great J. Edgar in the sky.

One can understand the agent's prayer, his claim to be acting for his church as well as the state. The Berrigans have turned against their fellow Catholics in certain ways, destroyed that good safe name built up by years of protesting that the church has nothing to tell politicians. They have brought down the precarious public dignity of priests, exposed sacred things to new Maria Monk ridicule—so that a White House dignitary can make jokes about sex-starved nuns, something even Paul Blanshard would not have dared back in the Fifties. But in fact it was not Kissinger who "cheapened" the nuns' life so much as braless "sisters" in bell-bottoms showing up at protests where four-letter words fill the air and naked kids splash in nearby fountains. Were all Sister Ingrid Bergman's movie vows taken in vain?

It was a delicate balance Catholics had achieved in this country, which the Berrigans were destroying—on the one hand, Catholics grew up "safe," trusted as fully American; yet they had their own little enclave of comforting familiar things, some borrowed, some adapted, some preserved, all forming a distinctive texture, a weave of memories. The child was nurtured in the closed jewel box of a Catholic education— open the lid, little girls in white turned around and around to Latin music-box tunes. Catholics "belonged" in America, yet had special ways of belonging to each other, traditional means of recognizing each other anywhere (the telltale vocabulary, fish on Friday, girls' hats on Sunday). The recurrent things were instantly recognizable—painless unsunned faces of the nuns, each looking like the one who used to teach you; the undertipping otherworldly priest in ill-fitting clothes; porcine monsignori puffing on cigars. The cigar-box style of art—garish mantillaed Madonnas, baby saints, Jesus as Latin Lover without the hair oil. All these things held "the people of God" together without pitting them against the people of America—of whom, indeed, the people of God were a part, and the most accommodating part.

All these symbols had a binding effect on those inside the church, and impressed those outside with the institution's weight and presence, made the church a pillar of society, a source of stability in the Free World (as John Kennedy liked to call it). That was "the Catholic contribution" to America, one long labored at, finally achieved, celebrated, recognized—and, at the moment of victory, betrayed. Betrayed from within, by those who should have proved most loyal. By priests who changed the parish liturgy and then deserted the parish. Betrayed by nuns, who no longer taught the girls in white dresses a catechism music they could dance to, in time with the machinery of Truth. No wonder the young were bewildered, ready to follow false prophets.

And not only the young. Even Dom, the good cop, is confused. When a defense lawyer asked an FBI man outside the courtroom in Harrisburg if he thought priests would advocate or indulge in violent politics, the agent said, "Why not? Look at the Crusades." In that sentence, abysses open, to swallow poor Dom. The Crusades—a holy war, waged by kings and led by priests, church and state one authority, all its parts self-confirming, none self-doubting. But the Harrisburg defendants were *opposed* to war, the warrior-kings and chaplain-priests. Where does that put the agent, along with his God and J. Edgar? *They* are the crusaders, men of political force and holy war. By "staying out of politics," the church has tacitly endorsed and been endorsed by our warfare state, and finds itself at bay, along with the warmakers.

One part of Catholicism is a captive of the state; and the other part is trying to free it. This latter part of the church not only looks free itself, but has a greater sense of identity, of continuity with the past. By contrast, the official church looks lost, out of contact with its own principles—the timorous parish prays in a mishmash of styles, all forced and unfelt, while Daniel Berrigan speaks confidently out of what he calls "the ennobling common partrimony." It has been the Catholic lot, in America, to "live in a kind of moral slum, across the tracks from our past . . . The minds [of Catholics] wear the costumes of their ancestors, a clothing that was once befitting, literally, but is now simply a folklore. . . ."

Berrigan is interested in the substance of that past, what it means to carry forward its spirit, not its clothes and trappings, priestly rags, dimmed jewels. Christianity's *basic* documents and ideals are what he preaches from. Asked what he did while on the run, he answered an interviewer: "Every day, at some point, I read some New Testament and meditate upon it; it's a strict Jesuit tradition to us, Scripture as a point of departure for prayer, and I love the whole penumbra of those words in history." More and more he sees his task in terms of the difficulty of being a man of tradition. "A man can claim to be going somewhere only if he has come from somewhere," for "we are what we have been"—those who reject their past lose the main thing given to one by that past, oneself. Yet, correlatively, "a man can claim to have come from somewhere only if he is going somewhere"—we *are* what we must *become*. Jeremiah, says Berrigan, was "a man profoundly in touch with his tradition, a man profoundly at odds with his tradition." Less and less does the merely recent, the fashionably liberal, sound in Dan Berrigan's prose. Once, for instance, he praised the cosmic optimism of Teilhard de Chardin. Yet as he moves toward a gospel conservatism, he has come to recognize the demonic in our cult of progress, our "obscene olympianism based on technology." He contrasts the reaction of Sartre to the Hiroshima bomb, the rending awareness of tragedy, with Teilhard's rosy encomium to that mushroom, a bomb cloud whose drift proves that all things that rise do *not*, necessarily, converge. Berrigan's eyes look down, to the evil fruit dropped from that mushroom—charred bodies, and a scarred earth, and the city of man undone in an instant.

He found in the moon shot a symbol of our culture's "moral weightlessness," and he sought chains. The prisoner and the astronaut, seared bodies and the cloud, the children and the mushroom—those are the choices we move among, and Dan Berrigan has made his choice. He stands for roots instead of rockets, tradition over progress, tragedy over arrogance, weakness over power, gospel over Caesar. Nor is this unique in him. Much serious religion tends, today, to be politically radical and theologically conservative. This is true not only of Catholics like Dorothy Day and the Berrigans and Cesar Chavez, but of Protestants like Martin King, A. J. Mustie, William Stringfellow, and William Coffin, and of Jewish radicals like Arthur Waskow and Everett Gendler. Despite all verbal play, often tendentious, over the fact that radical can mean rooted, it does seem now that what goes *downward* is what converges. Men meet each other returning to their sources. That is why, apparently, each of the faiths has turned new attention back on its own and one another's prophets—and, behind them, to those great figures of the past from whom the very word is derived. If St. Paul was called a troublemaker, Ahab had earlier called Elijah "the troubler of Israel" (I Kings 18.17). Prophets were men rebuking kings, calling power back to God. No wonder the bearers of such warning were not welcomed—not Elijah in Samaria, not Amos in Bethel; neither Isaiah in Jerusalem nor Jonah in Nineveh. Certainly not the Baptist, facing Herod—any more than Jesus, facing Pilate. All the seers have been told they must not see, all visionaries have been ordered to give up their visions.

This is not because they are innovators. Professor Delbert Hillers has demonstrated that prophets called kings back to an older tradition of the Lord's covenant; and R. B. Y. Scott writes that "They were social revolutionaries because they were religious conservatives." Prophecy looks simultaneously backward and forward, assigns men fresh tasks with an urgency born of ancient obligation. In this way prophets summon men *into* history, down to where the deep streams run, fed by oldest springs. Even Jesus, who looked forward when he said, "Do this in memory of me," also looked backward to the prophets (to Isaiah 53.12, to blood shed "for many, for forgiveness of sins") on the night he was betrayed.

V · HOPING

Charity means pardoning what is unpardonable,
or it is no virtue at all. Hope means hoping
when things are hopeless, or it is no virtue
at all. . . . As long as matters are really hopeful,
hope is a mere flattery or platitude; it is only
when everything is hopeless that hope begins to
be a strength.

—GILBERT CHESTERTON

· **T H I R T E E N** ·

Church Against Church

*The church was not in any special crisis when the Second
Vatican Council was convened in 1962. On the contrary, it
was in a particularly flourishing state, institutionally,
intellectually, and religiously. As John Lukacs pointed out
in 1959 (in his introduction to Alexis de Tocqueville's*
The European Revolution), *"for the first time since the
Counter-Reformation, conversions have been flowing almost
unilaterally toward Catholicism." But today, after the
Council, the entire trend has been reversed: institutionally,
intellectually, religiously, the Church is under attack, is
falling back, is in crisis.*

—WILL HERBERG

So WHAT WENT WRONG? How did the anchor tear loose? Things
did not look so bad before the Council; and during it they
looked very good indeed—*bound* to get better. But they didn't.
They went rapidly from good, to better, to worst. And now
men look about for someone or something to blame.

Was the trouble bad leadership? Pope Paul unable to
steer Peter's bark? Many think so. Those on the Left say he
lost all hope of influence when he staked his position on the

birth control and celibacy issues. A church cannot live if it is at war with its own ministers, generals shelling the position of their own élite officer corps—and that is what the Pope did when he told the clergy to preach what they considered counter to reason, and to live in conditions felt as inimical to life. The enemy was not outside the church, nor was conflict inevitable. It did not even—so runs this argument—have to rise *within* the church. Paul stirred it up himself.

The Right has been just as dissatisfied with the Pope. Even *National Review,* which has kept a careful distance from the extremist journal *Triumph,* ran a 1969 attack on Pope Paul for not being tough enough, for abolishing his ties with the Roman nobility, and for "constant flattery of the common people":

> When he praises the motives of high-ranking prelates who openly attack his authority he resembles President Perkins of Cornell smiling gamely through a confrontation with SDS and the black militants.

The Pope should not have encouraged the trends he was trying to counter. Why appoint a birth control commission, and encourage talk of change, if he meant all along not to change? Although the burden of the attack is on the Pope's ability (he shows "a congenital incapacity to govern"), the writer thinks at times that he intended chaos. This is clearest in the indictment of Paul's attitude on priestly celibacy.

> If he intended to retain it, why does he allow it to be discussed endlessly as an open question in the official Catholic press? He personally made the decision to relax the ancient discipline and make it very easy for priests to marry [on condition of their leaving the ministry]. By so doing he has substantially devalued the vow of celibacy. By that and by tolerating the endless discussion of celibacy he has unsettled and confused large numbers of the younger priests and seminarians.

> If priestly celibacy is not only defensible, but noble and praiseworthy, why should the Pope prevent discussion of it? All other matters of church discipline are regularly canvassed in the Catholic press. Also, if the Pope lets priests marry when they ask to *leave* the active ministry, how does that contribute

to a married (yet still active) priesthood? The same author later reproaches Paul for letting critics stay inside the church—just after saying that he should not let priests out in order to get married! And, again, why should discussion confuse the clergy, supposedly the experts on this subject; or be denied "young priests and seminarians" at the very stage when they are supposed to be making a conscious and reasoned choice, with full knowledge of its consequences? Apparently the author thinks only sheltered ignorance can protect young theologians from predatory priest groupies, for he continues—

Moreover, by making clerical marriage both easy and respectable he has served notice that the clergy are fair game for husband hunters. Recently released statistics indicate that the number of applications for release from celibacy have increased over 1,000 per cent since the election of Paul VI, and that the rate is increasing steadily. *It is hard to believe he neither foresaw nor intended the consequences of his decision* [my italics], though he may not have foreseen that it would spread to bishops and to his own entourage.

If the Pope really intended all these consequences, why did he not take the easier path to their achievement—just approve optional marriage for the clergy? Apparently because he is trying to circumvent the Curia. The Hamlet has become a Machiavelli.

Critical thunder from both poles of opinion shows how unsatisfactory has been Paul's stewardship. But if his actual course of governing has disappointed, so would any other course. If he had changed the official line on birth control, not only would the Curial side have been stunned and rebellious, the "liberals" would not have been placated. Would they have been less critical of authority in general and on other questions? Wouldn't this decision just give them ammunition for demonstrating how often authority has erred? Paul did try to outlaw popular discussion of contraception, and his order was ignored—just as his encyclical has been ignored in the practice of most Catholics. How could he cut off debate on clerical marriages? Many men were marrying without his permission;

how could he make the rest stop talking about that development?

It is true that Paul has made things worse than they had to be. Still, the basic problem has not been what he did or did not do. The trouble is not administrative, a thing to be solved by ruling tactics. The question is no longer to be asked at the level of the Pope's decisiveness, but of his relevance. Does he *matter* at all? If he restricts himself to problems like those of birth control, I think history has already given its answer. His authority has been futile in opposing contraception; he would have rendered it empty, in conventional terms, had he approved it. The Christian life has simply moved away from concerns of that sort, especially when they are subordinated to the Pope's own prerogatives. That kind of argument is a luxury most feel they cannot afford when questions of belief, gospel, and ministry are posed at such a basic level. The Pope is not so much right or wrong in this context, as unimportant.

What made him so? If he is the victim of events, how did they get shaped this way? Perhaps, some suggest, he was victimized by the Second Vatican Council. Given that, and the forces it loosed, how could he any longer silence Christians with a fiat? If one man did not bring down the church as a stable institution, maybe the assemblage of bishops did it. It was once an article of faith with liberals that Vatican II was a blessing. But even those who held that view look back somewhat skeptically now, and remember that Pope John was vigorously opposed when he planned to summon the conclave, and that one thing must be said for his opponents: their predictions were the most accurate ones voiced at that time. They said changes in the liturgy would not make the sacraments more popular and available, but would scatter the faithful and unsettle belief—and it turns out they were right. They said restive priests would marry once discipline had been relaxed—right again. They said pastoral change would lead to doctrinal challenge. Right.

There is no way to write the history of hypotheses. If

"aggiornamento" had not occurred, would the church have gone on its course essentially unchanged? There is no way to know. The only question that can be answered, by those involved, is this: would one *want* a church that stayed successful at that cost? It is a cost the churches are used to paying. Their prosperity has often been secured by a quiet agreement not to disturb society around them. That is the situation portrayed in Rolf Hochhuth's play, *The Deputy*—which argues that Pope Pius XII should have denounced the murder of thousands of Jews by a people nominally Christian (and in large measure Catholic). The Pope of the play answers that he might waste, by such action, a moral credit better used in other ways:

> Do you not see
> that disaster looms for Christian Europe
> unless God makes Us, the Holy See,
> the mediator?

But what kind of moral credit can be credible, when secured by moral obtuseness during the Holocaust? What distant or hypothetical uses can justify such non-use?

Defenders of Pius argue that his heart was in the right place—but so was that of many Christians, to whom mankind did not look for guidance; that he helped Jews privately—so did others, at greater personal risk than the Pope ever ran; that he might have caused extra burdens, for Jews as well as Catholics—but who said preaching the gospel would make life easier; that he had to balance, one against another, reasons of state—but so did statesmen ruling conventional powers: is he no more than they, to be judged by no higher standards, just another ruler with separate interests to maintain? His office is given him so he may voice the corporate Christian witness, going beyond mere weight of individuals' concern. If he uses it to take *less* courageous stands than we expect of unofficial Christian laymen, is it any wonder that the papacy becomes a moral irrelevancy? Hochhuth marks the irony that a cardinal's scarlet robes signify a readiness to witness unto death. Yet the hierarchy's transformation into ecclesiastical politicians has made its members weight every question in favor of "prudence" and against courage, trying to make of the faith a safe bet.

By this refusal to live for others, spend and risk for others, the church had dammed up all its energies in one effort, that of self-sustenance—to the point where, if that task was suspended, churchmen did not know what to do with themselves. The faithful, for their part, had come to believe in the church rather than the gospel, the messenger apart from his message. Many Catholics' operative faith was in the Pope, not Christ: confuse their picture of the first, and the second altogether disappears. Accepting that situation, *National Review* reduces the moral question to an administrative one. The only thing that can go wrong with the church is failure of the machinery, or of the will to use its levers:

One of the major causes of the success of the Reformation was the administrative chaos in the Church. It has often been said that the smoothly functioning, highly centralized system of the past century would make it impossible for anything remotely resembling the Reformation to occur now. But no system can help if the man on top is unable or unwilling to put it in motion. . . . Every Pope's task is to rule, teach, and sanctify the Universal Church, in that order. . . . The one service rendered by authority, that is peculiar to it and one of its specific functions, is to settle things.

Prosperity in the preconciliar church was the pinguidity of a thing that knew how to take care of itself—success in that purely custodial role was guaranteed by severe reduction of all tasks to this one. To step outside this function was tantamount, for many, to leaving the church. As Vice-President Agnew put it in 1971, "A lot of people resent the insertion of too much contemporary politics in sermons." The church should speak only to "churchy" things if it would satisfy the American ideal, which Karl Shapiro summed up as a basic religiosity combined with basic contempt for religion. Mr. Agnew granted that clergymen must pray for the contemporary needs of their faithful, but only after the faithful have defined those needs: "Maybe the [religious] leaders ought to realize

that their total function is not only to enlighten their con-
gregations, but to live with their parishioners and serve them
and be aware of the values that are inherent in the community
they enter—instead of entering that community convinced of
the need to instill a new set of values before they've even found
out about the ones that exist."

The gospel is to follow the supermarket flag, propping up
the values of a middle-class society, not making any demands
upon it. But what of this democratic approach in ghetto parishes, where parishioners are not disturbed by "liberal" talk
from the pulpit, like typical suburbanites, but by the irrele-
vance of religion to a degrading life imposed by prejudice?
Should clergymen in this situation adopt values "inherent in
the community"? No, our White House theologian's norms
change rapidly in such a case: Mr. Agnew laments that clergymen in ghetto assignments "become hostile toward the existing establishment," and start blaming society, rather than helping individuals to achieve a pious resignation. Religion is a
private matter—a thing, as Pope Pius might have said, of the
heart and not the voice—whenever that voice might indict existing power.

It is clear, then, what matters to the Establishment—not,
as Agnew claims, an acceptance of the congregation's values,
but acceptance of the Establishment. This obsequious role now
forced upon religion can be disguised in suburbs, where accepting community values is the same as accepting the ruling
System. But when something must give, it is the clergy's rap-
port with his community—never his submission to middle-class
values. Clergymen can minister to the private needs of ghetto
dwellers; they must never ask after men's accountability for
those ghettos' existence.

Agnew's emphasis on the private vs. the social is a way of
stating the American division of religion from politics. Yet
religion plays a very political role here. By acquiescing in the
standards of our rulers, the churches give them tacit endorsement. That is what religion is for—why we had the mild prism-
range of preachers at Mr. Nixon's inauguration, why the Rev-

erend Graham equates support for the Establishment with patriotism, and patriotism with religion. Our preachers must not criticize society—and so we have "official" chaplains who pray over cities, and watch them crumble; who minister to prisoners and see, without protest, how they are wronged; who pray at club meetings, blinking codes of racial exclusion; who pray over the country's Senate while it forfeits the power to end war; pray, finally, with and to a President for the favor of East Wing services on Sunday. The chaplain—despite America's pieties about division of church and state—has been wearing the government's uniform, has been on the government's payroll, and has shared the government's disasters, all through this century.

We have, therefore, a very one-sided arrangement, based on mutual aggrandizement—the state will leave the church alone, so long as church never criticizes state. Such criticism would be "politics," in which churches should not meddle. But agreeing with the state—to congratulate and celebrate it— is not "politics." Thus is religion trapped, frozen, in its perpetual de facto accommodation of power. It becomes a social ornament and buttress, not changing men's lives, only blessing them; not telling men to do this or omit that, just congratulating them for whatever they do or do not do. Religion is invited in on sufferance, to praise our country, our rulers, our past and present, our goals and pretensions, under the polite fiction of praying for them all. The divine is subordinated to the human —God serves Caesar. This is what Americans quaintly call "freedom of religion," and what the bible calls idolatry.

Thus did the preconciliar church prosper and grow fat; it was successful. Bringing that thing down—if the Council really accomplished this—was not a work of confusion, but a holy task, the destroying of idols.

Yet, even if the Council *had* to come, as an act of self-realization and purgation, to reveal the church's servility and mere survivalmanship—could it not have put this chance to better use, once it occurred? A good deal of recrimination after the Council resembles post-coup talk of a "revolution betrayed." Was the Council betrayed by impatient men (so Father Greeley would suggest in his criticism of the Berrigans) or by frivolous advocates of change not steeled to the hard work of reform? This latter view is argued in James Hitchcock's *The Decline of and Fall of Radical Catholicism:*

Radical reformers succeeded merely in destroying all community, the good with the bad, the general with the fraudulent. The death of this community has meant for a large number of people the death of their religious faith as well. For an even larger number, perhaps for almost everyone [in the church], it has meant a weakening of belief—a loss of certitude, a diminution of joy and serenity, an unaccustomed cynicism and vague spiritual malaise, an embarrassment about expressing beliefs.

Who were these powerful radicals, guilty of "destroying all community"? Hitchcock is a bit evasive on this point, but the men he attacks and cites most consistently are part-time journalists like Daniel Callahan. Defecting priests and audacious theologians are sometimes referred to; but even they seem to receive their impetus or public (or both) through the Callahans writing in *Commonweal* and the *National Catholic Reporter*. (Between them, these two journals make up almost the whole of Hitchcock's sources.) Now a church that can be brought down by Dan Callahan articles is even more friable than one done in by Paul VI's blunders. Does Hitchcock really think that two or three young American journalists spread doubt through the world-wide church? If so, it is the wildest compliment to their power. And whence such willful power? Hitchcock describes his villains as peripheral and dilettantish, neither scholarly nor charitable, not even minimally honest with themselves or others. If the church is prey to such cynical passersby, then it moves through crueler straits than anyone realized.

So we have the Council's promise blighted—all its hopes betrayed—by Callahan: "For a rigid, closed system like the preconciliar Church the most creative and fruitful moment of its development is likely to be the precise instant at which it opens itself, which in recent times has been the immediate postconciliar years when reformers enjoyed the benefits of both tradition and innovation." But not for long. The reformers squandered their chance. One keeps wondering, however, *how* they effected this. Grant that foolhardy journalists were unwilling or unable to use the Council's suggested freedoms in a responsible way—why should that prevent the mass of bishops, nuns, priests, theologians, and laity from doing so? Were they all spellbound by offending marauders, held in thrall by *Commonweal*, on which religion's destiny depended? Was church leadership entirely surrendered to people who cared nothing for the church, who were barely (if at all) Christians? And, if so, whose fault was that?

The story of the church's demise is not one of heretical betrayers, but of fatal insufficiencies in its very fabric; and this tale runs parallel to revelations of weakness in our society at large. In Pope John and President John, liberals at last got the kind of leaders they thought would suffice; and found that this was not enough. The System, even given bright leadership, did not work. We are witnessing a basic failure in authoritative standards; they no longer convince, because they barely can stand. All the mortising begins to give; and it makes no sense for Hitchcock to shout that some boys threw pebbles at the castle walls and made them collapse. No, the emptied parts of men's lives leaned on the hollowed-out walls of institutions that had propped them up; and everywhere now one can hear such brittle things, not very noisily, crashing down. Escape leads beneath this honeycombing of ruins, into catacombs.

Any challenge to "the System" means—for Catholics, as for other Christians—renewed critique of the very idea of "church," as something tending always toward enmity with the gospel truths committed to its care. Of this the Catholic church is supreme example: reform within it is always heavy labor, since it fronts the world's oldest and trickiest, best-guarded bureaucracy. And therefore another law has its largest statement here—that the life of church machinery is death to any church's spirit. So Rome is always dying (partially) from head down, while being (in part) resurrected from feet up. New forms of life have come from unexpected places—from Athanasius at local councils, Benedict in the monasteries, Albertus and Thomas in the universities, Francis of Assisi in the lanes and roads, Ignatius alone with a penitent making *The Spiritual Exercises*, Xavier and Ricci out at the rim of the world, Acton and Newman in pamphlets and journals.

These stirrings of life are not normally inspired, or even approved, by officials. Their leaders were held suspect, their teachings suppressed. Reformers could count themselves lucky if they were only silenced (like Abelard and Newman), condemned (like Erasmus and Wyclif), exiled by church authorities (like Athanasius and Chrysostom), or jailed by them (like St. John of the Cross and St. Ignatius of Loyola)—after all, St. Joan and Savonarola and John Hus were tortured and killed by them. But it has always been the task of the prophetic church, despite officials opposed to its opposition, to redeem the kingly church. Peter needs Paul—as Pope Innocent needed St. Francis, Pope Urban needed St. Catherine, or Pope Paul III needed Ignatius. As Paul VI needs Dan Berrigan. The Christian message is not authenticated from a throne.

The redemption of the governing church by its friendly enemy happens in many ways—as when a Cardinal visits prison because two of his priests have been arrested. It is no mean achievement to make a Cardinal act like a Christian. But church rulers fight off their own correction, their recall to credibility and risk. They want their redeemers to go away. One side in this struggle issues, or hints at, Anathema. The other "hangs in there" and "muckles through." The conflict is embodied in the Pope Celestine V of Ignazio Silone's play *The Story of a Humble Christian*. St. Celestine is the Christian needed by deadlocked ruling families (the Orsinis and the Colonnas); but he will not play their power game—he resigns the papacy, becomes the prisoner of his successor, the jailed Christian on whom his jailers depend; the scandal, the saint, hidden in cellars of church power; Peter in prison, at once justifying and accusing any man who holds a throne in his name.

The scene where Celestine tells his successor why he must resign the papacy (since it endangers his Christianity) is apt pendant to the scene where Hochhuth's Pius XII argues that he must guard all his prerogatives (despite what his soul cries for). The ruler has less Christian freedom, less of the new law's "parrhesia," than do the ruled—unless, of course, the ruled act only at their ruler's promptings, hold a freedom doubly diminished, the king's lesser faith diluted out among his followers, wine turned back to water. Thus, if Paul VI is a Pope in chains, so was John XXIII. So are all the "Peters" trying to fish for men from the incongruous perch of a *sedia gestatoria*. They can resign their power (like St. Celestine or Gregory XII); or they can live off the moral credit of those who serve without subservience, the troublemakers who make the institution work (intermittently) for the people, instead of the reverse. Those are the choices, and they make the history of the church read like a single repetitive tale with new plot turns—the *Prisoner of Zenda* replayed as religious comedy; double tale, of a pretender who ascends the throne, for the sake of the man who rejects it; of empty splendor above, and hidden worth below; the false king on the throne, and his brother-image, the true king, in jail. Two kinds of men—even two *sides* of a man—fraternally contend within the church and for the church: the man who is climbing to power, and the man who runs away from it.

The most fascinating aspect of this tale is not the mere conflict, but reciprocal need as well, experienced by such disparate types. Anathematizers try to deny this bond: they want to expunge the dark part of the story, define the church as solely that which separates itself from "heretics," reformers, troublemakers (though some of that number will later be sneaked "upstairs," once safely dead—Joan of Arc may be canonized after she has been incinerated). The vulnerability of the preconciliar church in America lay not in the fact that it denied the need for troublers of church peace—officialdom has always done that. No, its greatest failure lay in an ignorance that such troublers occur and recur throughout history. *Triumph* magazine spoke of such Catholics as something brand new, a thing unheard of heretofore: "We are to have, it seems, something entirely unprecedented in the history of Christendom; we may call it the Renegade Church. . . . Indeed, the most remarkable feature of the rebels' stance throughout the world is that it seems to have occurred to almost none of them—to get out. Remarkable, we say, because the watchword of most of them has been 'honesty,' and it is hard to imagine anything more dishonest than to pretend to be something (in this case a Catholic) that you are not." American "conservatives," who praise history and the past, know very little about it. *Triumph's* editors, for instance, do not know how hard it has been for men down through the ages—from Alexander and Athanasius, to Abelard and Erasmus, to Montalembert and Von Hügel—to remain with the body of the faithful, over efforts of authority to force them out. John Hus was so willing to justify himself in terms of orthodoxy that he went voluntarily to the Council that burnt him at the stake. And even when such men have not themselves been posthumously honored, much of their hard teaching gets swallowed, as church medicine, once they are gone. The institution has drawn life from such men's death. It is an old, old story; for every Luther who left the church, there has been an Erasmus who stayed. For every Döllinger, an Acton; for each Lamennais, a Lacordaire; for a Loisy, a Bremond; and, for Tyrrell, Newman. Those who stayed were often more denounced than those who left, called traitors from within. It is true that they were, at times, undermining the papal throne; but only to lay bare the prison cell of Peter underneath.

─────────────

FOURTEEN

Church Against World

─────────────

*To attain truth, man must pass forty-nine gates, each
opening onto a new question. Only to arrive finally
before the last gate, the last question, beyond which
he could not live without faith.*

—HASIDIC SAYING

WHY, THE ANGERED *Triumph* EDITORS COMPLAIN, will troublemakers not agreeably *leave?*

Because this is, for them, a question of love, and of
honor; of solidarity with their own. So long as they stay, men
cannot believe that the church is just a clerical branch of the
Establishment. How could parts of the Establishment be se-
questered in so many prisons? As Daniel Berrigan wrote of
Dietrich Bonhoeffer, who returned from America to his own
captive and monstrous nation:

> A man belongs with his people, when his people
> are ill and power is awry and only a lively tongue and mind
> and that courage which is more crucial than intelligence
> and (if required)
> imprisonment and death
> can bring access to health.

The critic-redeemer of authority does not simply deny its scope
and depart, seeking some private salvation in rejection of the

People (along with Pharaoh and his ways). "A man belongs with his people"—that is the burden of William Stringfellow's meditations on baptism into Christian fellowship. It is an incorporation into mutual responsibility, and sinfulness, and a common hope:

Daniel Berrigan and Philip Berrigan did not just personally conclude that the illegitimacy of the Vietnamese war is symptomatic of a more profound illegitimacy affecting both the officers and the institution of the State, but their witness—as in any use of conscience for a Christian—is as participants in the whole body of the Church, under the ecumenical discipline of baptism which makes them, as it does all Christians, responsible in a primary sense to all human beings.

It is this responsibility to a people that certifies the prophet. Some try to use "prophet" (or poet, or seer) to mark a man off as eccentric, having private urges that take him away from the rest of us. Nothing could be farther from biblical standards, by which the prophet exists for his message, and the message exists for delivery, for those it addresses. God sends the prophet to his people; rejection of the message is denial of its Source.

The note of responsibility to a people is what separates the Christianity of Stringfellow or Berrigan from faddist and romantic "Jesus talk" such as young people have adopted out of mere disillusionment with the System. This was a religious variant of Charles Reich's facile optimism, perpetrated in *The Greening of America.* (What could be farther from underground risk than Reich's ethos of didactic relaxation?) Jesus came to the drug culture as both a Superstar and the safest kind of "high"—as an experience, not a demand; an escape, not a task. He was an hallucinogen approved for private use by the Food and Drug Administration. But revolutionaries have no use for such a drug, especially not for Jesus as an anodyne to doubt.

Doubt. That is the enemy most feared, isolated, and for that very reason made palpable, in the meetings of "Jesus people"—which take place in an atmosphere of indiscriminate assent. Everything is to be accepted—tongues, healing, miracles —unhesitatingly, without question. Mutter what you will—

rapid Latin obscenities or gibberish— your neighbor will mutter back "Praise the Lord." No doubts need apply. And not only do these people accept, themselves; they have various forms of gentle coercion to make outsiders just as uncritical. You *must* join in; only curmudgeons can keep up resistance to their smiling siege of repeated soft nudges and signals. You join, or you leave; it is wrong merely to observe or question.

This manic assent leads to a cultivated joy—people having to tell themselves repeatedly how happy they are now. That is the message of their rocking closed-eyed smiles, rhythmic sighs that build mild parodies of orgasm, continual nods of palsied readiness to be agreeable, overhearty laughs, hurried forgiveness for gaffes not yet committed. The Jesus they experience is said to have wept over cities, rebuked and been angry, felt grieved at ingratitude, been betrayed and "sorrowful unto death." Judging from those signs, Jesus himself was not a Jesus freak. He was not happy enough. Gilbert Chesterton described Eastern mysticism as symbolized by the Buddha, whose legs and arms circle in, seal the body off in contentment, close up the path to eyes and heart and genitals, forming one curl of self-containment, the human flower shrunk back into its bud. The Christian icon, by contrast, shows a man spread-eagled by a torture instrument, in an openness to all things, even to doubt—"Why hast thou forsaken me?" If to be Christian is to be so uncritically slaphappy as these Jesus kids, then even so devout a skeptic as Dr. Johnson would be excluded from the definition. Though he would as lief pray with mad Kit Smart as with anyone else, he refused to be *happy* with him—for that would mean being blind. Truly seeing is a painful thing—and the mysterious point of the gospel is that such pain is worth experiencing, even for God.

Doubt is the test. Faith is rooted in it, as life in death. Faith, unless it is mere credulity, which does not deserve the name, is a series of encounters with doubt, perpetual little resurrections; cynicisms met and transcended, never evaded —so that, as Melanchthon said, doubters become the best preachers. John Henry Newman had the most deeply believing mind of his time and place because it was the most skeptical mind—Swinburne himself said he put the atheists' arguments better than atheists had: "I never could have imagined any intelligent creature existing in such a state of utter unbelief."

The great enemy of believing is pretending to believe; and the Jesus people have not found a short cut to belief—only a method for forgetting they pretend. There are no short cuts. The only way is the long way, through indirection, doubt, and a faith that survives its own death daily. The marks of such faith, rooted in doubt and not in drugs, are observable in radical religions of our time, which are quite distinct from the trendy "Jesus movement" that gives us Billy Graham in hippie attire. Daniel Berrigan, for instance, more closely resembles a radical Jew like Arthur Waskow than a Jesus celebrant like Arthur Blessett. The charge leveled against a man like Waskow is that his theology is just the "baptizing" (or circumcising) of his politics—as when he calls Talmud the seminar notes from a free university, or Shabbat man's first general strike. The test of such things must always be in practice—do they deepen religious insight, or opportunistically feed on it? It would be difficult for readers of Waskow's *The Bush Is Burning* to consider it an exploitation of Judaism rather than the expression of stunned new reverence for it. The radical politics was always there in Waskow; what has been added gives new richness to the politics, but also extends beyond it. The life to which Waskow is drawn, to which he calls others, has a biblical prefigurative quality. Man foreshadows the Great Shabbat, brings it into being, by living forward into it, proleptically.

This is the deepest source for Waskow's ethic of nonviolence, the renunciation of mere countertactics used against Pharaoh: "The only means we may use are those that partake of the ends themselves, and to reject illegitimate means is not to postpone the revolution but to bring it nearer." It is the same religious motive one finds in Berrigan: "Jesus refused again and again to confront the sword with his own sword. No, he drew back from that method—that mirror game—in

a gesture of ineffaceable dignity." William Stringfellow contrasts the revolution of Jesus with that of Barabbas—saying
of the latter: "Authorities, in any particular time or place,
can accommodate, where they cannot destroy, the factions
and ideas that would overthrow them because those revolutionary forces have essentially the same identity and character as do the established powers."

The religious critique cannot simply be made *against* the
state, on its same level. That is why church authority, even
erring, is potentially redeemable. It stands to a different
accusation, having such higher claims, professing an action
beyond mere politics. Even when the Pope is guilty, his conviction takes place in a larger sphere—which explains why
there is greater dramatic intensity in Hochhuth's play about
Pius XII than in his anti-Churchill drama. The relationship
of these two plays to each other underlines an aspect of
prophecy: the most searching criticism of the church is not
mounted in the world's name, but as part of a larger indictment of that world. If the church has failed, it has been by
surrender to power and the Caesars. The crime of Pius is, in
the station of Christ's deputy, to approximate the thinking of
a Churchill, the voice of sheer power, of saturation bombing
and unconditional surrender. This is that regimen of death to
which Dan Berrigan says the church must die: "Suppose . . .
the poor benignly neglected, and the rich seated unassailably
in places of power; and religion, in the midst of this game,
ambiguous in its own voice; and the spiritual goods of the
people diminished beyond recognition. Supposing all this to
be true, what is the tactic of the believer, of a man? Quite
simply, I think, reading the New Testament, one says NO."

Reading the New Testament . . . Seen in this light, the
gospel is of itself subversive of the world. Which leads one
to ask: if religion is dead, how do such "men alive" find strength
in it? How does it judge other living things with its so large
NO? The religious critics of the church are those who feel
most acutely the need for a biblical people in which to live
one's NO to death. As I have said, this can be seen in rad-

icals of Jewish thought as well as in Christians, in Protestants as well as Catholics. Arthur Waskow's book is the tale of a tradition revived *and* of personal rebirth. Waskow lives himself back into the critical vocation of Moses, just as Moses lived himself forward into the life of his people. Moses prefigured exodus by his personal "going out" when he killed the Egyptian; he anticipated the covenant on Sinai when he heard God's Name from the bush. Waskow reflects that this going out is a continuing human imperative, for the Name is given, the Law proclaimed, only on the Way. Zion is formulated as a goal by those who have already gone out and now travel toward it (since Zion is not simply equatable with the Israeli nation—though there is a growing Zion in Israel, as in the Diaspora).

Waskow's account of this human crisis recalls exodus patterns in the Christian tale: Jesus calls *away*—from the nets, and tax offices, and Temple; he goes *out*—to pray in hiding, teach on a mount, feed in a wilderness (new Manna); to suffer heavy demands, and agreement to those demands, alone in a garden (new Sinai) while his followers lapse into old habits (the new Calf); and to die while still on the Way. Christianity did not leave the Temple once for all; it must go out constantly from new temples, sacred and secular, fulfilling the exodus Jesus pre-enacted. For Jesus is to Caesar as Moses to Pharaoh; and the real war of Belief is with idols, not with other believers. Waskow emphasizes the teaching that Judah is itself Messiah, in process of coming—as Stringfellow repeats the Christian doctrine of baptism's "passage" into a body of the faithful that is itself Jesus, all its living stones being built into that unseen Zion to which man is called; or as Berrigan stresses that the solidarity of mankind is a dying into life, a reaching down to the springs of resurrection—

(Jesus) went underground; and some days later, when it was expedient for others, he surfaced again and with great pains identified himself as the One of the Friday we call Good.

The people of the One become Messiah by looking outward to the One—and it is a people with two faces, as it were, each unable to see itself or its God except by looking at the other, as in a mirror's kindly reversals. That is the true meaning of resemblances between the spokesmen of radical religion. A Jew like Waskow, a Protestant like Stringfellow, a Catholic like Berrigan—such men grow closer to each other the more profoundly they reflect on *and reflect* Exodus, and Immersion, and Resurrection. The path to one's buried self runs through the unearthing of one's corporate past, however that has (like all our private pasts) been betrayed, its vision lost, its call unheeded. The best things in the church, as in a nation, or in individuals, are hidden and partially disowned, the vital impulse buried under all our cowardly misuses of it—as the life of a nation lies under and is oppressed by its crude governing machinery; as the self lies far below the various roles imposed on or adopted by it; as covenant and gospel run, subterranean, beneath temple and cathedral. Life's streams lie far down, for us, below the surface of our lives—where we must look for them. It is time to join the underground.